D1527709

VALENTIN
GORODNOV

Soweto
Life and Struggles of a South African Township

PROGRESS
PUBLISHERS
MOSCOW

Translated from the Russian by *David Skvirsky*
Designed by *Alexander Smirnov*

Валентин Городнов
Черные жители „белого" города:
Жизнь и борьба африканского гетто

На английском языке

English translation of the revised Russian text
© Progress Publishers 1988

Printed in the Union of Soviet Socialist Republics

Г $\frac{0803000000 - 361}{014\,(01) - 88}$ 66—88

ISBN 5—01—000491—7

Contents

FOREWORD

This book *Soweto: Life and Struggles of South African Township* by the Soviet social scientist, Dr. Valentin P. Gorodnov, should be read and studied by all freedom-loving people and revolutionaries, not only in our country and Africa, but throughout the world. After reading the book, one gets a better insight into the racial conflicts that have now plagued the apartheid republic and the subcontinent for decades.

What makes the book particularly interesting and valuable is the fact that it is written by an author situated thousands and thousands of kilometres from the scene of the developments. Added to this problem of distance is the question of the permanent news blackout imposed by the racist rulers of South Africa on the actual activities and processes going on inside the country. According to the calculations of ruling circles, the citizens of the country itself and the outside world must not know the real magnitude of the repressions, persecutions, and barbarities perpetrated by the apartheid rulers, on the one hand, and the acts of mass heroism and revolutionary upsurge among the oppressed and exploited people, on the other. Yet, despite these big handicaps, the book by Dr. V. P. Gorodnov is well-researched, packed with statistical evidence, and well presented for the reader to grasp the essence of the forces at play, the direction of the social, economic and political developments, and the inevitable outcome of that strife.

The choice of the title and the area of study are quite appropriate on that they immediately introduce one to the crux of the problem — the eversharpening contradictions between the white minority ruling class and the black oppressed majority. In other words, the contrast is reflected sharply in the heading and elaborated upon in the body of the book supported with factual details.

The subject of study is the "white" city of Johannesburg and its satellite black ghettos, popularly known as Soweto. Perhaps one could ask — why choose Johannesburg? Well, it could have been any other city in South Africa because the book really does not deal with Johannesburg as such. But rather, it deals with South Africa as a whole. Johannesburg and Soweto are but an example of the apartheid system in practice. Yet one should remember that Johannesburg is the heart or centre of capitalist industrial development in South Africa. In that sense it becomes a natural choice.

Johannesburg, like all the big centres of industrial growth in the country, produces the biggest concentrations of the contradictions between the oppressor and the oppressed. It is here that the oppressed masses come face to face, on a daily basis, with the capitalist exploiter, with the racist ruler and bureaucrat, with the repressive state machinery — the uniformed police, the secret police, and army. Again it is here that the stiffest battles between the racists and the black masses are fought. In this book, Dr. Gorodnov traces and exposes the roots of this revolt against the system by the blacks not only in Soweto but finally throughout the country. After all, South Africa is full of "Sowetos" today.

It is therefore against this background that the 1976 Soweto uprisings should be taken. Outside South Africa today the word "Soweto" symbolises national resistance to oppression and exploitation. The fact of the matter is that the Soweto events marked a new and higher stage in the long drawn-out struggle of our people for national and social emancipation. That momentum is gaining and escalating by the day.

Finally I would like to reiterate that reading this book gives one a deeper and broader understanding of what apartheid is, not only in theory, but more importantly, in its actual application.

Sipo Simon Makana
Member of the NEC
of the ANC

March 10, 1988

We, the People of South
Africa,
declare for all our country
and the world to know:
that South Africa
belongs to all
who live in it,
black and white.

*(Opening lines of the
Freedom Charter, the
general programme of
the liberation movement)*

INTRODUCTION

South Africa is called, with good reason, the last citadel of racism and colonialism. The relations between the peoples inhabiting it and their way of life may be characterised with one word--apartheid. In Afrikaans it means "separation", but a literal translation rather obscures than reveals its true meaning. Formally, it is a theory postulating the separate development of races, but in fact this is a racist theory vindicating domination of the country's black majority by a white minority.[1] Apartheid does not merely separate races. It institutionalises their unequal status, thereby enabling one race to rule another. It spells out racial discrimination against and oppression and brutal exploitation of the black majority by the white minority. Little wonder that from the rostrum of the UN General Assembly world community has called apartheid a crime against humanity.

Defining all aspects of life in South Africa, apartheid has its roots deep in the past of that country where, as the Programme of the South African Communist Party characterises it, colonialism of a special kind took shape. "A new type of colonialism," this Programme says, "was developed, in which the oppressing white nation occupied the same territory as the oppressed people themselves and lived side by side with them."[2] This new type of colonialism has the hallmarks of modern developed capitalist production and of a colony.

The present regime in South Africa is a menace to the surrounding world as well. Aggressive, terrorist actions against neighbouring nations now follow one after another. There have been repeated armed incursions into Mozambique, Lesotho, and Botswana. The regime of Pretoria is out to destabilise the independent nations of southern Africa politically and economically and stop the liberation process. There is no other way to qualify the occupation of Namibia by South African troops, the acts of aggression against free Angola, and the support for the bandit operations of the UNITA in Angola and of the MNR in Mozambique. The South African racists have close ties with international imperialism and its most reactionary elements and they are becoming an increasingly serious threat to world peace.

In South Africa itself resistance from the oppressed and the exploited is mounting steadily. The struggle for freedom and democracy, for the abolition of the racist regime is led by the African National Congress and the South African Communist Party. These constitute the vanguard of the resistance and the liberation movement, which is involving over larger numbers of working people, chiefly African workers.

This book is, in the first place, about Soweto[3] and its inhabitants, the Sowetans, as they call themselves.

Since June 16, 1976, when oppressed and disinherited people rose in revolt in Soweto, the name of this huge black ghetto on the outskirts of Johannesburg has entered the modern political language and become known worldwide. Although it was crushed in cold blood, this revolt marked the beginning of a new stage of the ongoing struggle in South Africa.

I have tried to describe Soweto and its population of one and a half million and show the place that has been prepared for it by the proponents of apartheid and the place that it actually holds in the history of South Africa.

Soweto epitomises South African reality, practically the same conditions prevailing for another four million blacks[4] living in the townships around "white" cities[5] such as Pretoria, Cape Town, Durban, and Port Elizabeth. And yet Soweto is unique in South Africa; it is a phenomenon in its own right. What I mean is that it is not merely a large suburb inhabited by blacks serving a city of whites. It is a huge cluster of townships that have fused and formed their own, "black" city. It is the product of urbanisation perniciously influenced by apartheid and racial discrimination.

7

More so, this black ghetto has been created in keeping with the apartheid system set up to perpetuate white racist domination. Soweto was seen as a testing ground, and it was so used by the racist regime to try out its system of control over the social processes taking place among the black urban population in order to keep it in obedience and submission. In spite of everything, the inhabitants of the black ghetto rose against their oppressors. Soweto took a stand against apartheid.

One can find the reasons for this by reviewing the history of Soweto and learning how its inhabitants live and what their concerns and aspirations are. To shed light on the factors motivating the resistance to the apartheid regime, particularly the Soweto revolt, one has to analyse the socio-economic condition of black inhabitants in the townships and identify the socio-psychological processes taking place in their midst.

The history and destiny of Soweto and its inhabitants encapsulate the most acute, critical problems confronting blacks in South Africa. One of the processes to be observed as the Sowetans become settled and permanent city dwellers is that urbanisation is changing their way of life, way of thinking, and values. And all this despite the Damocles sword of apartheid, despite the racial discrimination and brutal constraints imposed by a misanthropic government.

The Sowetans are an inalienable part of white Johannesburg. They work at the factories run by whites and are servants in white households. The white city pays for their labour—the pay is in no instance commensurate with the expended labour—and "graciously" permits them to live in the ghetto laid out for them. Ruthlessly exploited and oppressed, the black workers are challenging this tyranny by the white who exploit minority personified by the apartheid system. The revolt of 1976 was only one of the explosive developments of the liberation struggle—from the anti-colonial risings of the past to the present mass resistance to the apartheid regime.

The relations between black Soweto and white Johannesburg and between the black majority and the white minority in the whole of South Africa are described in the book. These relations are determined, on the one hand, by the development of the capitalist economy, which unites them, and, on the other, by apartheid, which divides them. This underlies the deep antagonism and the bitter struggle.

Soweto attracts special attention not only because in the latter half of the 1970s, it became the epicentre of the resistance to apartheid. It is the largest urban unit in South Africa, but it may only be called a city with the greatest of reservations because it is bereft of many essential functional indicators of a modern city. It would be more correct to call it a satellite-town set up for the labour force serving Johannesburg.

Soweto is in the centre of South Africa's main industrial region embracing Johannesburg with its outlying territory of the Witwatersrand, the capital Pretoria with its many industries, and the large industrial city of Vereeniging south of Johannesburg. In the cities and townships of this region, which is in Transvaal Province, the black population numbered 2,272 million in 1980 and 3 million in 1985 (see *Addenda*, Table No. 9). This number constitutes more than half of the black urban population of South Africa (5,070,000). Roughly half of the black urban population of this industrial region, i.e., one-fourth of the country's entire black urban population, lives in Soweto.

The majority of urban blacks are industrial workers, and also workers employed in the services industry and the trade network. Subjected to capitalist exploitation, the workers of Johannesburg and the entire industrial region have long been involved in the working class and trade union movement fighting for their class interests. It was here, on the basis of the trade unions existing at the time, that the ramified South African Congress of Trade Unions, representing the advanced contingent of the South African working class, was founded in 1955. The South African Communists (the South African Communist Party was founded in 1921) are active in Johannesburg, working with dedication underground, championing the interests of the South African working people despite harassment by the racist regime.

Johannesburg and Soweto are more than a theatre of incessant class conflicts and battles. They are an arena of the struggle against racial discrimination and apartheid, for the national liberation of the black population. In the course of this struggle there have been massive actions such as the Defiance Campaign against the unjust laws passed in 1952; countless demonstrations against passes, which enable the police to keep the blacks in "white" cities under surveillance; the campaigns for the release of persons sentenced after the long "treason" trial that began in 1956; the many general political strikes, including the May 1961 strike staged to protest the proclamation of the racist "republic"; and, lastly, the cardinal outcome of the liberation struggle of the 1950s and 1960s—the Congress of People which adopted the Freedom Charter in 1955.

The Congress of People was held in Kliptown, now incorporated in Soweto. The Freedom Charter is regarded as the programme of the South African national liberation movement. Its basic provisions—"South Africa belongs to all who live in it, black and white" and "no government can justly claim authority unless it is based on the will of all the people"[6] —are valid to this day and define the overall orientation of the struggle of the South African people.

The majority of the inhabitants of Soweto and the other townships of Johannesburg are workers, of whom a large segment are skilled industrial workers; but there also are many newcomers looking for jobs. A considerable section of the workers have settled permanently with their families. They can no longer see themselves outside urban life. However, apart from these urbanised workers there is a fairly large group of migrant workers, who have temporary jobs and live in the township without their families.

The middle, or intermediate, strata play a prominent part in Soweto's life. These are the urban petty bourgeoisie, intellectuals, junior officials and clerks, shopkeepers, and artisans. In terms of the revolutionary potential it is of paramount significance that there are intellectuals in this social conglomerate.

However, the urban petty bourgeoisie likewise cannot keep aloof from the liberation struggle. It holds a dual status on account of its link to private property and its direct participation in the labour process. Under the apartheid regime, which continues to restrict the development of the black bourgeoisie's proprietorship tendencies, the urban petty bourgeoisie is visibly drawing closer to the working masses. The fairly substantial social, political, and psychological links of the urban petty bourgeoisie and the other intermediate strata with the working class prompt them to join in the revolutionary class struggle.

In Soweto there is also a bourgeoisie with relatively big capital and inclined to collaborate with the apartheid regime. But while allowing the bourgeoisie to develop in the homelands, the regime blocks its growth in urban regions with, just as in the sphere of labour, a "colour bar" to protect the interests of the capitalist class of the white minority.

Furthermore, Soweto is indicative in that the urbanisation rate has been the highest in it. Blacks began to settle on the outskirts of Johannesburg as early as at the turn of the century. Townships such as Pimville, Orlando (both of which have merged with Soweto), Sophiatown (levelled by the authorities in the 1950s), and some others were in existence for several decades. The long process of community development resulted in Soweto's conversion into a social organism, whose evolution continues with the further urbanisation of the black population.

Urbanisation is a complex and many-sided process in which, alongside the demographic aspect, there is a social aspect, i.e., the transition to the urban way of life. The latter aspect of urbanisation is given a close look in this study. The social aspect includes the cultural and psychological adaptation of those who become permanent urban residents to what for them are new living conditions.

Modern society develops through the growth of cities, through urbanisation, which is both the impetus and factor of humanity's social, economic and cultural development. In this context it would be proper to recall Lenin's words that the migration of the rural population to the towns "is a *progressive phenomenon*". It "tears the population out of the neglected, backward, history-forgotten remote spots and draws them into the whirlpool of modern social life. ... increases literacy among the population, heightens their understanding, and gives them civilised habits and requirements."[7]

The classics of Marxism-Leninism noted the progressive role played by cities as centres of society's economic, social, and cultural advancement. Also indicative of this advancement is that "urbanisation gives a powerful impetus to

11

the break-up of traditional social structures and readjustment of the way of life and of the forms of social organisation to harmonise with modern requirements".[8]

At the same time, as it studies the development of the capitalist city, Marixst-Leninist science takes note also of the negative aspects of urbanisation. Frederick Engels wrote: "In the huge towns civilisation has bequeathed us a heritage which it will take much time and trouble to get rid of. But it must and will be got rid of, however, protracted a process it may be."[9] These words in no way negate the leading role of big cities. The modern city is not an isolated social phenomenon but an essential form of society's life, "in some sense a model of that society, mirroring and crystallising the basic laws of its development".[10] Consequently, it is a question not of a "crisis of inner-cities" generally, as some bourgeois sociologists assert, but of capitalist society as a whole. One has to agree with the view that in the capitalist city, in that concentration of bourgeois society's social contradictions, the positive social effect of urbanisation is diminished, held back, and sometimes turned into it opposite.[11]

The urban population's place and role in the liberation struggle are determined chiefly by its economic condition and also by its political status. Moreover, a large role is played by the socio-psychological and ethno-psychological factors motivating the behaviour of town-dwellers in this or that, particularly critical, situation. The replacement of one value orientation (the traditional, in which elements of tribalism are predominant) by another (intrinsic to capitalist society with its present-day culture) in the process of the urbanisation of South Africa' population enhances the significance of psychological factors.

The blacks who come to the South African city and take up permanent residence there—despite everything that the racist authorities do to deny them rights and the possibility of living in that city--come into contact with what for them is an uncustomary way of life, an uncustomary culture, in other words, with the present-day bourgeois society. This conflict situation arose (and continues to arise for newcomers to the city) because in South Africa colonialism acquired the above-mentioned special form.

As well as oppression and capitalist exploitation the

colonialists brought European civilisation to South Africa: technical expertise and an alien culture. In an article entitled "The Future Results of British Rule in India", Marx wrote that "The British were the first conquerors superior, and therefore, inaccessible to Hindoo civilisation," adding: "England has to fulfill a double mission in India: one destructive, the other regenerating—the annihilation of old Asiatic society, and the laying the material foundations of Western society in Asia."[12] This may also be said of the role of the European, including British, colonialists in South Africa.

The black proletariat, whose labour is essential to the existence of the South African colonialist-capitalist system, is becoming urbanised and together with the already urbanised middle classes bringing two cultures into contact: the traditional African and the modern European culture. That Africans had begun to assimilate European culture was noted at the turn of the century by the South African writer Olive Schreiner. She wrote that "the dark man is with us to stay... not only does he refuse to die out in contact with our civilisation ... and rather tries to grasp and make it his own".[13]

Under the distinctive South African colonial regime, a regime under which Africans come into contact with European colonialists resident in the same geographical region and in the same urban areas, assimilation of the new culture proceeds more rapidly than under conventional colonialism where the colonial power and the colony exist separately. As the South African scholar F. R. Tomlinson pointed out, "alterations in their way of life have taken place in a revolutionary and not in an evolutionary manner".[14]

The cultural-psychological urbanisation of the blacks is most striking in the Johannesburg industrial area, notably in Soweto. There they are becoming town-dwellers, mostly workers, persons with a new worldview whose development depends to a large extent on the relationship between traditional and modern culture. "It is here that the greatest cultural clash and the resulting marked cultural changes are taking place ... it is here that what has so often been called the 'new Africa' is taking shape. The urban areas are the African political melting-pots ... and the type of personality emerging from this cultural cauldron is of political and economic interest, as well as being of psychological and sociological significance."[15]

The formation of black urban culture and of the corresponding mentality, i.e., the sum-total of views and emotions determining people's behaviour in this or that situation, is far from consummation. For the time being one can only speak of a phase of cultural transition (from traditional to modern). Nevertheless, even at this stage of cultural-psychological urbanisation one can identify clear-cut tendencies crucial to the crystallisation of the socio-psychological foundation of black socio-political movements in South Africa, chiefly of the national liberation movement and the movement of resistance to the racist regime.

The synthesis of elements of traditional and modern cultures is considered in this book in family relations, religion, and society. Of course, here the paramount role is played by economic factors stemming from the essence of South Africa's capitalist system, which, despite its particulars and distinctions (specific type of colonialism, apartheid), sustains a class structure with, above all, its inherent class contradictions and class struggles. However, this is mainly a study not of these basic economic factors (which is not to say that they are underestimated) but of their derivatives, i.e., these superstructural factors that also participate in shaping the socio-political face of the black town-dweller and which I feel have been researched least of all.

In specifying the conceptual terminology relative to the conditions in South Africa, we should stop to consider the term "cultural-psychological urbanisation". It may be defined as the sum-total of the processes of cultural and psychological adaptation of the black population to life in a modern capitalist city. This adaptation proceeds as blacks take up residence in the city.

The cultural-psychological urbanisation of the black population in South Africa has features in common with the same process in the rest of Africa and also distinctions implicit in South Africa. These distinctions are due to concrete historical conditions, namely, the existence of a racist regime with its doctrine and policy of apartheid. Detribalisation, i.e., the shedding of traditional, principally tribalist, values and of tribal survivals and customs, and the obliteration of tribal and ethnic divisions, may be regarded as a feature common to cultural-psychological urbanisation in South Africa and analogous processes in other African countries. Cultural-psychological urbanisation comes into collision with the counter-process of a return to some traditional norms and customs and the restoration of some elements of tribalism. The latter process is a reaction to the difficulties and problems encountered by blacks as they adapt to city life, and it is to be observed not only in South African cities.

The restoration of some traditional values in South African cities is accompanied by the spread of a new form of retribalisation that is being injected forcibly from without into the process of cultural-psychological urbanisation. Precisely this is a distinctive feature of such urbanisation in South Africa. Forcible retribalisation is an element of the South African government's policy of restoring and preserving archaic forms of South African reality in order to bolster apartheid. This is inhibiting and warping cultural-psychological urbanisation. On account of imperialist practices, the deformation of social processes has gone to extremes in South Africa.

This is aggravating the social problems facing people in the capitalist city and is reflected in their way of thinking. In the situation prevailing in South Africa this may result in an exacerbation of racial contradictions and in a slide by individual elements of the national liberation movement into narrow nationalism and black racism.

From the methodological viewpoint I have found the use of the terms "detribalisation", "tribalism", and "retribalisation" expedient in this study of socio-political problems. The apartheid regime's policy of retribalisation is an objective reality that has to be taken into account. Although the economic foundation of the tribal system—communal, tribal land ownership—and, correspondingly, the tribal structure and tribal organisation have been destroyed, the apartheid regime is conserving remnants of the tribal system. This conservation and, in many cases, restoration of elements of tribalism spell out nothing less than retribalisation. It must be noted that while the tribe as such has, for all intents and purposes, disappeared in South Africa, the terms "tribalism", "detribalisation", and "retribalisation" are used to designate bigger ethnic entities than the tribe, namely, the Zulu, Xhosa, Swazi, Sotho, and others.

The terms "tribe" and "tribal" are used widely in studies of South Africa by South African and Western researchers. I believe this is unjustified because they usually designate nations or ethnic groups, not tribes. However, I use these terms when I quote Western authors.

Some bourgeois sociologists specialising in African studies, for example, J. G. Mitchell and M. J. Herskovits, have objected to the use of the term "detribalisation" on the grounds that the social aspect of urbanisation includes the process of detribalisation[16] and that, consequently, the need for it does not arise. In researching South African problems this attitude seems unjustified because it blurs a major element of apartheid, namely retribalisation.

The 1976 revolt in Soweto and the many subsequent Sowetan actions and demonstrations against apartheid indicate that the socio-political and cultural-psychological processes in Soweto are bearing fruit. The upward spiral of the struggle against apartheid, particularly the revolt in Soweto, has shown the extent individual strata of the Soweto community take part in this struggle and also their place and role in the resistance movement.

One can hardly claim to give an exhaustive description of the different phenomena and events or make a categorical and definitive judgment of the development of the social processes in South Africa, especially as many of the processes dealt with in this book are still far from completion and it is, consequently, early to assess their final outcome. But I feel it is possible to define the direction of developments and identify basic trends.

Conditionally, for methodological purposes, the history of Soweto may be divided into two periods. The first period was characterised by spontaneous urbanisation, when townships or locations sprang up and grew on the outskirts of Johannesburg. The most vigorous phase of this period was in the 1940s and 1950s, although the first townships, including those where Soweto now stands, appeared early in this century. The second period commenced in the mid-1950s, and since then the racist regime has been seeking to control the urbanisation processes and harness them to the interests of apartheid. This is being done in order to sustain white minority domination over the black population of South Africa.

* * *

Very little information filters out about what is actually happening in South Africa. A stringent censorship prevents the publication of anything even remotely contradicting the racist dogmas of apartheid, let alone criticism. For example, by June 1969 as many as 1,300 publications had been banned.[17] The censor did not spare even the *Oxford History of South Africa*. A whole chapter headed "African Nationalism", written by the sociologist Leo Kuper, was deleted because it speaks of the African National Congress. In a bid to embellish and vindicate apartheid in the eyes of the world, official quarters often present a doctored picture of the situation in South Africa, especially where the life of the black population is concerned.

While South Africa is closed to people from the Soviet Union, who thus have no opportunity to see that country for themselves, Soweto is out of bounds even for many South Africans.

The government keeps Soweto and similar townships as real ghettos for blacks and is therefore averse to letting the world know of what is taking place in these townships. The curtain of silence was steadily drawn tighter around Soweto. Only bits of information leaked out. Such was the case until June 16, 1976.

The Soweto revolt virtually tore this curtain down. It shed vivid light in the true sense of the word—from the flames of innumerable fires—on the miseries of Sowetans that had been concealed from outsiders. The events in Soweto in those days made banner headlines and were given front-page coverage by many newspapers throughout the world. Scores of articles were printed in journals of all political orientations, and then books appeared.

But in the newspaper accounts of the violent clashes between the oppressed black majority and the racist government little was said, of course, about the underlying sociopolitical processes that led to this explosion. Where was one to get the information that could serve as the basis for an analysis of what was taking place among the urban black population? The sources of such information are scarce, but they are to be found.

To begin with, there are official documents, legislative acts, and published statistics. Of particular interests among the latter are the data produced by the censuses of 1960 and 1970.

The local periodical press, notably the daily newspapers, are usually a very substantial source of information for a study of the situation in this or that country. This applies fully also to South Africa.

Books written by those who lived in the ghetto-townships and personally experienced all the hardships of that life may rightly be regarded as prime sources. The most significant of these are books by Nelson Mandela (*No Easy Walk to Freedom*), Ezekiel Mphahlele (*Down Second Avenue*), and Joyce Sikakane (*A Window on Soweto*).

Much information is to be gleaned from books by Brian Bunting (*The Rise of the South African Reich, Moses Kotane—South African Revolutionary*), Trevor Huddleston (*Naught for Your Comfort*), Hilda Bernstein (*The World That Was Ours*), J. C. de Ridder (*The Personality of the Urban African in South Africa*), Laura Longmore (*The Dispossessed. A Study of the Sexlife of Women in Urban Areas In and Around Johannesburg*), Leo Kuper (*An African Bourgeoisie. Race, Class and Politics in South Africa*), M. Wilson and Archie Mafeje (*Langa: A Study of Social Groups in an African Township*), John Gunther (*Inside Africa*), Francis Wilson (*Migrant Labour*), and Peter Becker (*Tribe to Township*).

Very little was written about Soweto prior to the 1976 revolt. The South African sociologist Ellen Hellmann published a booklet with general information about Soweto itself, its inhabitations, and its system of administration in 1971. Ellen Hellmann used data, put together by the relevant departments of the Johannesburg City Council, chiefly on the condition of families and young people in Soweto, drawing attention to the abnormal life of both categories.

Soweto, she writes, "is a strange satellite-type of city in a symbiotic relationship with Johannesburg," which depends upon the inhabitants of Soweto for the labour to operate its factories and shops, while the Sowetans themselves depend upon Johannesburg for the wherewithal of life. "Administratively and technically it is within Johannesburg, but it is not of Johannesburg... It is a city within a city."[18]

Ellen Hellmann's approach in describing the relationship between Soweto and Johannesburg is largely stereotyped, for she takes no account of the character of this relationship, namely the fact that one rules the other. Soweto is not simply a "strange" city within another city, but a ghetto in the real sense, in which labour is kept instead of living a normal life.

Ellen Hellmann highlights a problem that is directly related to the revolt in Soweto. It is the condition of young people. She must be given her due for not only having seen the roots of this calamitous condition (no access whatever to education, unemployment, an abnormal environment for family life, a high crime rate) but also identifying the specific that makes the "youth problem" intensely acute. This specific is the code of discriminative laws which decree certain actions a criminal offense for some and unpunishable for others. Ellen Hellmann brings her reader round to the conclusion that the racist regime with its policy of apartheid is the primary cause of all the anguish in South Africa.

A Window on Soweto, by the South African journalist Joyce Sikakane, is a contrast to the calm, academic language of the Hellmann study. This is not an impartial look of a passerby, not information obtained at second hand, but a narration of the misery life in Soweto written by a person who lives there. In some ways it is autobiographical.

Joyce Sikakane relates how people live in Soweto, what they eat, how they raise their children, how they work, and how they spend their leisure time. Midnight raids by the police breaking into houses to check the notorious "passes", searches, detentions, humiliation of human dignity, manhandling, and killing are part and parcel of the daily run in Soweto, and they are recounted by the author. Indeed, Joyce Sikakane opens a window on Soweto to let the reader see what life is like in the township. "Poverty is the overriding aspect of economic life in Soweto... Soweto lives on credit—its future wages are pledged in meeting debts, paying rent and buying food."[19]

Although *A Window on Soweto* was published in 1977, it was written prior to the Soweto revolt. In reading it one comes round to the realisation that this explosion was inevitable. The fuse that ignited it was the introduction of new forms of school instruction that were unacceptable to the black population. In Joyce Sikakane's book we find an assessment of the discriminative system of education for the Bantus introduced by the racist government. This system, the authoress justifiably writes, was blue-printed to make schools train people to be reconciled to their subordinate station in South African society, to accept the status of inferior citizens. But the actual cause was the smoldering discontent of the Soweto inhabitants with their economic, social, and political status—and this, too, is shown in the book.

After 1976 books about Soweto, to say nothing of articles in academic and popular journals, began appearing one after another. A book entitled *Soweto: Black Revolt, White Reaction*, which in the next three years ran to another four printings, was published in Johannesburg in 1978. The author, the South African journalist John Kane-Berman, gives a detailed account of what took place in Soweto and other townships during those turbulent days of June 1976. He analyses the economic and socio-political conditions of the life of blacks and the policy of the government towards the black inhabitants of "white" towns. He presents a factual picture of the revolt while the evidence was still fresh, basing himself on what he saw with his own eyes, heard from other eye-witnesses, and read in the local press.

The closing chapters give a good idea of the reaction of the business world and political circles to the revolt of black citizens. Kane-Berman offers interesting judgments about the problems and prospects of apartheid, namely, the credibility of the countless, persevering assertions that there would be changes, a relaxation of the apartheid regime and of racial discrimination, and "concessions" to the blacks. He writes: "Talk of change has indeed become a political tactic in itself, designed on the one hand to keep blacks quiescent and on the other to stave off foreign pressures against apartheid."[20]

There are two more noteworthy books among the literature about the revolt in Soweto: *Year of Fire, Year of Ash. The Soweto Revolt: Roots of Revolution?* by Baruch Hirson and *Whirlwind Before the Storm* by Alan Brooks and Jeremy Brickhill. Both are about the revolt and present an examination of its causes and motive forces. The authors are persons who are supporting the liberation struggle of the South African people.

The revolt, started by schoolchildren and other young people, is seen by Baruch Hirson as the logical outcome of the entire preceding struggle against the apartheid regime and the supremacy of the white minority. He believes that the strike movement of the black proletariat that peaked in 1973-1975 was of special significance for the development of the liberation movement, writing that "these strikes must be seen as constituting the beginning of the Revolt, and as having affected a far wider section of the population".[21] He devotes whole chapters to the Soweto revolt, substantively describing the relationship between various youth organisations and political parties involving large sections of the black population. He writes at length about the tactics of the revolt, about how legal and illegal forms of struggle were combined.

Baruch Hirson's acknowledgement of the considerable influence exercised by the African National Congress on young people and his assessment of the role played by the ANC during the Soweto revolt are highly indicative. He rightly notes: "The ANC has the initiative in its hands now, in being the only movement with the capability of mounting some armed incursion."[22] His concluding remarks are that the events in Soweto fostered the growth of the political awareness of young people in South Africa.

A book entitled *Whirlwind Before the Storm*, published in 1980, attracted considerable attention. The epigraph are words spoken by B. John Vorster, South Africa's Prime Minister at the time: "The storm has not struck yet. We are only experiencing the whirlwinds that go before it." The authors end their book with the statement that the storm will unquestionably strike.[23]

In showing the underlying causes of the Soweto revolt, which they describe as an explicit and vivid expression of the black population's general discontent with the racist regime and its apartheid policies, Alan Brooks and Jeremy Brickhill draw attention to the urbanisation of this population. The rapid growth of the black urban population, fostered by the country's industrial development, posed the Pretoria government with a problem that apartheid cannot

21

resolve: blacks are denied permanent residency in "white" cities, but the cities themselves (and the national economy) cannot manage without black labour. In an effort to solve this problem, the South African government is obstructing the urbanisation of blacks, turning city-dwellers into migrants. Brooks and Brickhill write that this policy requires systematic and brutal control over urban blacks and a limitation of their rights; "this is precisely what the government has been doing in the 1970s, and what led to the situation which exploded in three of the four main urban concentrations... The 1976 explosion was inevitable."[24]

Brooks and Brickhill describe the various social forces involved in the revolt to one extent or another, their organisation, forms of participation, and the relationship between them. All this is given against the background of an illuminating picture of the political situation prevailing in Soweto itself and the country at large.

In particular, attention is attested by the accounts of the general political strikes staged in August 1976. These undeniably marked the peak in the development of the Soweto revolt. In the course of six weeks the black proletariat had recourse to this weapon three times with each strike being more successful than the previous one, spreading from Soweto to the whole of the Witwatersrand and the Capetown area. These strikes, as well as the demonstrations, the street clashes with the police, the setting of fires, and other acts, showed how much discontent and anger had accumulated, and how strong and far-flung these sentiments were.[25]

It is highly important and vital to bring to light the role of the working class in the revolt of 1976 because some researchers are accentuating the youth factor of this stage of the revolutionary struggle in South Africa. The circumstance that the revolt was initiated by students and that these young people proved to be in the forefront of the struggle is used in an attempt to mute the role of the working class and identify discord between the young revolutionaries and the "non-class-conscious" adult workers. Brooks and Brickhill agree with Baruch Hirson that this would be a misinterpretation of the events.

An even more explicit and definitive reply to these

questions is given in Z. Nkosi's article "Lessons of Soweto" printed in *The African Communist*, journal of the South African Communist Party: "The disturbances at Soweto and elsewhere throughout South Africa have not only shown the growth of black determination and capacity to fight. They have also revealed the class content of national resistance. The initiative was taken by the youth, but became a formidable force when allied with the power of the urban African working class which rallied to its call."[26] The same journal published a Political Report delivered at the South African Communist Party's plenary meeting in April 1977. The comprehensive, in-depth analysis of the Soweto revolt in this report says, in part, that "it is clear that what started as a protest by school students against the government's educational policies, soon extended to broader sections of the people and advanced wider demands. Although it remained essentially a youth revolt, it would be wrong to see it in purely generational terms, as if youth constitute an independent social force separate from the basic line-up of national and class forces".[27] The conclusion offered in the report is: "Soweto confirmed that the black working class is the most decisive revolutionary force. This class once again revealed its collective strength and underlined the close relationship between national and class struggle in our conditions."[28]

This book is an attempt to show the character of the socio-psychological processes accompanying the urbanisation of blacks in South Africa. Here the accent is placed on the relationship between traditional and present-day factors influencing the way of life, psychology, and worldview of the inhabitants of Soweto, which may be called the black capital of South Africa. These processes and factors play a role of no little importance in the formation of the social base of the movement of resistance to the apartheid regime, as was demonstrated very strikingly during the revolt in Soweto and subsequent developments.

The author expresses his gratitude to direct participants in the liberation movement in South Africa, with whom he had occasion to meet and who helped him considerably in his work on this book.

The photographs are from the Information Service for South Africa of the International Defence and Aid Fund.

Lucky Cyril Mabasa of Soweto contributed to preparing this book for the translation into the English language. His helpful comments and corrections were accepted gratefully by the author.

[1] The term "black" is used widely in official South African documents and the mass media to designate "African". In recent years it has acquired one more meaning. Many organisations of the liberation movement, including the South African Communist Party and the African National Congress, use the terms "black majority", "black population", "black working class", and so on in their publications as designating the entire non-white population of South Africa (blacks, coloureds/persons of mixed race/, and Asians /Indians/). In this work the term "black" is used to designate "African".

[2] South African Communists Speak. Documents from the History of the South African Communist Party. 1915-1980, Inkululeko Publications, London, 1981, p. 299.

[3] The name Soweto derives from the words South Western Townships.

[4] In 1985 the population of South Africa numbered 33.6 million. This figure is broken up as follows: Africans — 24.9 million (74.1 per cent); Indians — 878,000 million (2,6 per cent); coloureds — 2.9 million (8.6 per cent) and whites — 4.9 million (14.7 per cent). (Weekly Mail, Johannesburg, November 5, 1987).

[5] As envisaged by the apartheid theory, the territory of South Africa is subdivided into Bantustans (homelands) for blacks, "white" rural areas and "white" urban regions, each of which consists of a "white" city and "black" suburban townships.

[6] ANC Speaks. Documents and Statements of the African National Congress. 1955-1976, 1977, p. 12.

[7] V. I. Lenin, Collected Works, Vol. 3, Progress Publishers, Moscow, 1977, p. 576.

[8] O. N. Yanitsky, Urbanisation and Capitalism's Contradictions, Moscow, 1975, p. 6 (in Russian).

[9] Engels, Anti-Dühring, Progress Publishers, Moscow, 1975, p. 341.

[10] A. M. Rumyantsev, "Urbanisation and Society", Urbanisation, the Scientific and Technological Revolution, and the Working Class, Moscow, 1972, p. 14 (in Russian).

[11] O. N. Yanitsky, op. cit., p. 5.

[12] Karl Marx, Frederick Engels, Collected Works, Vol. 12, Progress Publishers, Moscow, 1979, pp. 217-218.

[13] Olive Schreiner, Closer Union, Constitutional Reform Association, Wynberg (Cape), pp. 24-25.

[14] South Africa (Union) Commission for the Socio-Economic Development of the Bantu Areas within the Union of South Africa. Summary Report, Government Printer, Pretoria, 1955, p. 10.

[15] J. C. de Ridder, *The Personality of the Urban African in South Africa. A Thematic Apperception Test Study*, Routledge & Paul, London, 1961, p. 170.

[16] See *The African Town (A Critique of Foreign Conceptions)*, Moscow, 1979, pp. 13-14 (in Russian).

[17] *Apartheid: Its Effect on Education, Science, Culture and Information*, UNESCO, 1972, p. 240.

[18] Ellen Hellmann, *Soweto, Johannesburg's African City*, South African Institute of Race Relations, Johannesburg, 1971, p. 1.

[19] Joyce Sikakane, *A Window on Soweto*, International Defence and Aid Fund, London, 1977, pp. 30, 32.

[20] John Kane-Berman, *Soweto: Black Revolt, White Reaction*, Ravan Press, Johannesburg, 1981, p. 230.

[21] Baruch Hirson, *Year of Fire, Year of Ash. The Soweto Revolt: Roots of Revolution?*, Zed Press, London, 1979, p. 156.

[22] Ibid., p. 328.

[23] Alan Brooks, Jeremy Brickhill, *Whirlwind Before the Storm*, IDAF, London, 1980, p. 306.

[24] Ibid., p. 169.

[25] Ibid., p. 3.

[26] *The African Communist*, London, No. 68, 1977, pp. 32-33.

[27] Ibid., No. 70, 1977, pp. 34-35.

[28] Ibid., p. 47.

Chapter One

TOWNSHIPS AROUND JOHANNESBURG

Johannesburg and the Blacks

Often and not without good reason Johannesburg is called a "golden city"—*Igoli* (in Zulu) or *Ganteng* (in Sotho), as the Africans say, perverting the word "golden". The city owes its rise to the goldfields discovered in the Transvaal at the close of the nineteenth century. The Witwatersrand extending around Johannesburg is still South Africa's biggest producer of gold. Three goldmines are still in operation in the city itself.

As well as the gold bars that earned Johannesburg its world-wide repute, there is a gold mirage—the brilliance of a huge modern city that blinds and mesmerises thousands of people, making them eager to go to this *Igoli*. But once they get there most find backbreaking labour, destitution, and brutality instead of wealth. Indeed, Johannesburg is not a "golden city" but a city of the "demon of gold", for gold is the source and cause of much of the distress afflicting its inhabitants. Life in *Igoli* is particularly oppressive for those who create its wealth, for the blacks.

In Johannesburg the appalling ulcers of a capitalist city are glaringly in evidence. The reason for this is not merely that capital rules the city but that it rules in racist garb. The workers are not merely exploited brutally. They are robbed of their human dignity. They are harassed and oppressed on account of the colour of their skin. Class oppression is compounded by racial discrimination, by the unhuman practices of apartheid. All this makes the life of the black unbearable in the "golden city".

> *Jo'burg City, I salute you;*
> *When I run out, or roar in a bus to you,*
> *I leave behind me, my love.*
> *My comic houses and people, my dongas and my*
> *ever whirling dust,*

My death,
That's so related to me as a wink to the eye.
Jo'burg City
I travel on your black and white and roboted roads,
Through your thick iron breath that you inhale,
At six in the morning and exhale from five noon.
Jo'burg City
That is the time when I come to you.
When your neon flowers flaunt from your electrical
wind.

That is the time when I leave you,
When your neon flowers flaunt their way
Through the falling darkness
On your cement trees.

These lines were written by the black South African poet Wally Mongane Serote.[1]

Johannesburg has much in common with New York, and not only externally. As New York, it has its Harlem. But in Johannesburg this is not an inner-city district, not a part of it, but a string of townships encompassing the inner centre on almost all sides. Conspicuous in this ring is its south-western section—Soweto.

Johannesburg's black population is growing much faster than its white population. Back in 1936 the city had more whites than blacks (see *Addenda*, Table No. 11). But the situation began to change as early as in 1951, when it was found that there were 126,000 more blacks than whites. In 1970 there were 501,000 whites and 810,000 blacks, but this figure is only the number of registered Africans, i.e., those permitted to reside in the city. In addition, there were 125,000 coloureds (people of mixed race) and Indians. Thus, there were only about half as many white as non-white residents in Johannesburg. The actual number of black inhabitants is much higher than the above-mentioned fugure, which is from the 1970 census statistics—it is considerrably in excess of one million. In the opinion of Ellen Hellmann, a South African sociologist, 17 per cent of Soweto's inhabitants were not covered by the census, because many of them had no permission to be in the city and avoided the census-takers in the fear that they would be expelled to homelands.

The trend towards a change in the correlation of inhabitants continues in favour of the blacks. True, in recent years the growth rate of Johannesburg's black population has been declining, and is now only 3.1 per cent higher than the increment of the white population. This is due to a tightening of the control over the influx of blacks into the city and to the mass evictions to reserves in rural areas. But in preceding years, as the 1936, 1946, and 1960 censuses show, the difference in the growth rates exceeded 40 per cent.

Life had always been a grind in Johannesburg. The rapid growth of the gold industry and, since the 1940s, of the manufacturing, retailing, and services industries, in short, of all the branches of the modern economy, demanded more and more labour. The steadily increasing influx of blacks to the city generated new social problems and exacerbated those that Johannesburg already had. With the assumption of power by the manifestly racist National Party in 1948 these problems were further inflamed and aggravated.

As conceived by its architects apartheid was to ensure the separate development of the races inhabiting South Africa and thereby preclude conflict between them. In the 40 years that the policy based on this doctrine has been in operation it has not proved possible to enforce absolute separation, i.e., total apartheid. Although South Africa's rulers succeeded in separating races socially, they changed nothing in the economy. Nor had they ever wanted a change—blacks, of course, constitute the bulk of the workforce. Because black labour is cheap there is a steadily growing demand for it. Consequently, the economy's dependence on black labour is likewise growing. The pattern for political separation is highly peculiar: the blacks have been divested of their last political rights, while the white minority hold all political power in their hands. The South African government's assertions that the creation of the homelands signified the granting of political rights and even independence to blacks do not hold water and cannot be taken seriously. The separation of races into those politically deprived and those in possession of all political rights has only intensified existing contradictions and problems.

Under the apartheid regime tensions in Johannesburg have risen steadily during the past few decades, bringing the threat of acute conflicts and explosions. This is manifested most strikingly in Johannesburg's relationship with the belt of "black" townships around it. The people living in these townships are needed by the city, for it cannot exist without them. And, at the same time, they are seen as a danger to Johannesburg, much as the slave is dangerous to the master. The principal means of controlling blacks in "white" inner-city neighbourhoods was the system of passes, which the Africans themselves justifiably call a "brand of slavery". When a black was within the inner-city boundaries he was obligated to have on his person a pass in which was noted everything that he was permitted to do. The least violation, the absence of any authorisation or the passbook itself brought immediate detention and eviction from the city.

For the time being the "white" city is in command of the situation despite the fact that in numerical terms its population is smaller than that of the belt of "black" townships. It destroys townships, then brings others into existence, regulating all aspects of the life of their inhabitants, punishing or pardoning them (with the latter outcome being very rare indeed). But the city cannot afford to do without the satellite townships altogether. The complex relationship between them is coming under a growing strain and is steadily deteriorating. This to all intents and purposes is what is visible to the eye. But at the roots is an uncompromising, violent struggle between the forces of liberation and the forces of enslavement, between labour and capital, a struggle against racism and apartheid.

Industrialisation attracted thousands of blacks to cities. They went to the rapidly expanding industrial areas, among which the Johannesburg area was conspicuous.

The first townships[2] appeared in the latter area at the beginning of the century. One of these, Pimville, sprang up in 1904 on a Klipspruit River farm 15 miles southwest of the centre of Johannesburg. In Pimville a small plot of land for a tiny hut could be rented for 80 cents a month. True, what building material people could get was usually what they managed to gather on scrap heaps—crates, tin cans, and so on. Wretched and squalid as these were, the first Africans (about a thousand) to settle in Pimville had to rest content with them.

But as time passed the township's population grew. People came from rural localities to find jobs and earnings in Johannesburg, which was expanding swiftly. Many rented rooms or even corners in the shacks that were already standing, while others "rented" bits of land from the first-comers and built their own shacks. Pimville had 24,000[3] inhabitants by the beginning of the 1950s, and 35,000 by the year 1960.

Another location, Orlando, began to grow rapidly near Pimville, closer to Johannesburg, in 1932-1933. Within three years this location had about 3,000 shanties accommodating more than 18,000 people. At first the township was situated exclusively east of the railway running from Johannesburg to Potchefstroom and occupied an area of roughly 1,000 hectares. Between 25,000-30,000 people lived in 5,000 tiny shacks. Orlando soon expanded beyond the railway and the narrow Klipspruit river. This gave rise to Orlando-West, while the old location was called Orlando-East.

The South African author Ezekiel Mphahlele, who settled in Orlando-East in September 1945 and worked as a teacher at the time, gives the following description of the hovel in which his family lived: "There were only two rooms with an old sunken floor and a sooty hessian ceiling. The school had the floor dug up and new concrete flooring put in. The ceiling was repainted white. We paid 17s. 4d. a month for rent. We carried water from a communal tap in the street."[4] The cooling unit of the thermal power station supplying electricity to half of Johannesburg towered over Orlando-East. In the township itself there were only a few street lights, and the houses were usually lit with candles. This neighbourhood—the power station and the township—symbolised the way of life of urban blacks: living next door to the latest achievements of science and technology and, more, helping to build and operate them, they were denied access to the benefits of this technology, of this civilisation.

Towards the beginning of the 1950s, Orlando had a population of 97,000. This huge location was regarded as the best compared with the others. It was not fenced: most likely it was thought that it would be too difficult to fence such a congregation of shanties sprawling on the hills on either side of the railway running to Johannesburg. It had one clinic, one cinema and even—one public telephone;

nothing more for nearly 100,000 inhabitants. Most of the houses were on unnamed streets and were unnumbered. The American author John Gunther, who visited Orlando at the time, wrote: "...it is an example of the deliberate, calculated effort by the authorities to make it as difficult as possible for Africans to communicate with each other. Any attempt at native organization will, it is hoped, be severely handicapped by difficulties in communication... If a person should, for some reason, want to round up half a dozen Africans in a hurry, the difficulties merely in the realm of communications would be almost insuperable."[5]

Other locations—Mlamlankunzi, Jabavu, Moroka—appeared in this area after the Second World War.

Mlamlankunzi is a small location situated by the railway; this was the site of a railway station of the same name—it was the closest to Johannesburg on this line. The Moroka location first rose in 1939 as a temporary camp formed as an emergency project by the Johannesburg City Council. The territory of the camp was divided into 11,000 plots of six square metres each for the shacks and hovels built by homeless people by their own labour and on whatever means they could put together. By 1947 the location had 60,000 inhabitants—an entire decade had passed and it was only then that this temporary emergency camp became the present township of Moroka in Soweto. The authorities tried to put some limit on the disorderly occupation of plots of land on which the blacks built their shanties. These efforts yielded little. Their only effect was that yet another location appeared with even more horrible conditions that in the given case were justified with the pretext that all this was temporary.

The locations of the 1930s-1950s were in fact those very same bidonvilles. They could not accommodate the human tide flooding the city. They spilled out of their designated limits, giving rise to more shanty-towns. This growth was particularly marked in the latter half of the 1940s, although by 1940, according to official statistics, about one-third of the black urban population was already living outside the limits of the officially recognised locations. Hilda Bernstein, who was a member of the Johannesburg City Council in those years, writes: "The war had brought a halt to building, and industrialisation brought a flood of people to the city. The locations filled beyond capacity. In a phrase they themselves used, the African people 'overflowed' and set up squatters camps, shacks of cardboards and hessian, on the edges of the locations."[6]

In the 1940s this spontaneous occupation of vacant land and the willful building of hovels on this land became a mass phenomenon in South African cities and their environs. A particularly big impression was made by the "way out" taken by homeless people in Orlando-East, an action which began on March 25, 1944, and had wide repercussions. Early in the morning of that day hundreds of homeless people, who could no longer bear with their semilegal status of lodgers in the crowded shanties of Orlando or even illegal status in white homes, where they worked as servants, marched in the direction of Phefeni to vacant municipal land near the railway. The march was led by James M. Mpanza, described as an "eccentric township demagogue" by Mary Benson.[7] These desperate people, who had nothing to lose, sang "Sofasonke[8] nenguewu baba!" ("We will all die together with our father!").

Upon reaching their destination the people began building huts and shacks with crates and pieces of scrap iron, i.e., with what they could find on scrap heaps. An entire township was built within a single day. Thousands of other homeless people streamed to this spot from other townships around Johannesburg.

The alarmed city authorities had to take urgent steps to regain control and prevent the appearance of more slums. The production of slag-blocks was organised from the waste of the nearest power station, and these were used to build so-called shelters; the slag-blocks were simply laid on top of one another without mortar to form walls, and the structure was given a roof of asbestos sheets. It was planned that all this (some 4,000 of these "shelters" were erected) would be temporary. But, in fact, the Orlando shelters existed for many years. In 1947 they housed some 20,000 people. At the close of 1960, when the Johannesburg municipal authorities pulled down the last of these cabins, tiny brick dwellings—dubbed "matchboxes"—were built in their place and became standard housing for most of Soweto's population. Here is a description of these locations by John Gunther: "Most houses in these locations, if they can be called houses, are crumbling, crooked structures of rusty corrugated iron, bits of wood, cardboard or even reeds." Some of the houses were a little better: "Floors are of cement, which gives people rheumatism... There are, of course, no toilet facilities whatever in most houses, or even running water... lining 'streets' full of rocks and flowing with slime."[9] James Morris, who also saw these locations with his own eyes, writes: "In summer they are blazing·hot; in the winter a bleak wind howls through them, and the people huddle themselves in ragged blankets... Some of these camps have been there for 20 or 30 years."[10] But perhaps the most eloquent description is in the report of the governmental Native Laws Commission of 1948: "The majority of such locations are a menace to the health of the inhabitants... disgrace... quite unfit for human habitation... mere shanties, often nothing more than hovels... dark and dirty... encumbered with unclean and useless rubbish... one could hardly imagine more suitable conditions for the spread of tuberculosis."[11]

The growth of these shanty-towns around Johannesburg increasingly troubled the City Council. "The slums were a breeding ground of fatal contagious diseases," writes the South African journalist Joyce Sikakane. "With no sanitation, smallpox and tuberculous diseases took their toll. Such outbreaks alarmed the white government who feared the spread of deadly diseases to the white community."[12] The City Council's negative attitude to slums mushrooming on the outskirts of Johannesburg was thus quite understandable. Various plans and projects were suggested for tearing down the shanties and providing the inhabitants of the townships with better housing, and something was even done. But even these pitiful improvements and changes were soon discontinued.

The National Party came to power in 1948 and put its apartheid doctrine into effect—blacks were given no role save that of labour serving the cities and the industries concentrated in them. "It is accepted Government policy," says a circular issued by the Bantu Affairs Department, "that the Bantu are only temporarily resident in the European areas of the Republic, for as long as they offer their labour there."[13] The former Prime Minister Hendrick F. Verwoerd said: "The native residential area in the town is simply a place where the European in his part of the country provides a temporary place of residence for those who require it from him because they work for him and earn their living in his service."[1 4]

One of the new government's first acts was to deprive the township inhabitants of 99-year leases for their dwellings, replacing these in 1949 with 30-year leases, and then in 1968 abolishing long-term leases altogether and replacing them with monthly rent.

Since the end of the 1940s the nightmarish shanty-towns continued to be seen as an evil that had to be combated, but the Verwoerd government's main thrust was not against them. It was directed against something much more dangerous for the racists—the townships where blacks felt they were permanent residents.

Sophiatown—A Condemned Township

Sophiatown was located in the western part of Johannesburg, at a distance of only seven kilometres from the city's centre. It was there because it no longer exists.

Sophiatown's existence—it had a population of almost 60,000—was incompatible with apartheid, being inconsistent with its dogmas. In Sophiatown (as in another location—the township of Alexandra) blacks were allowed to buy the land on which their dwellings stood, and also the dwellings themselves. Precisely this circumstance was what condemned the township.

Sophiatown appeared at the beginning of the present century. A certain Mr. Tobiansky, charmed by the beautiful view afforded by this hilly site to the west of the then small town of Johannesburg, purchased it and planned to build a suburban neighbourhood for whites. After giving the new neighbourhood the name of his wife and the future streets the names of his children, Mr. Tobiansky got his project off the ground and expected that it would be a success and bring him the corresponding profits. Possibly with the passage of time there might have been a suburb such as the Johannesburg suburbs of Parktown or Houghton. But Mr. Tobiansky was unlucky. The City Council decided that the sewer system for Johannesburg, which was

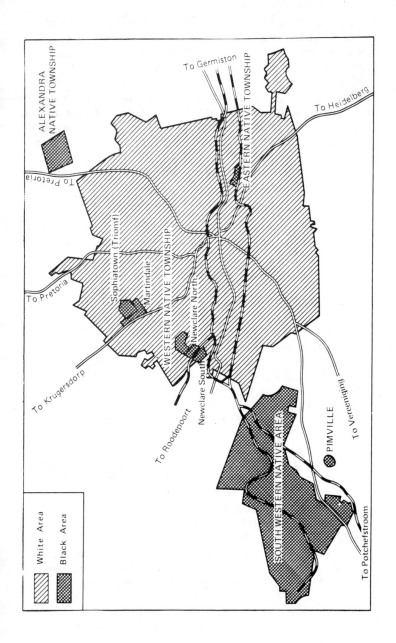

To Germiston

To Heidelberg

To Pretoria

To Pretoria

To Krugersdorp

To Roodepoort

To Vereeniging

To Potchefstroom

ALEXANDRA NATIVE TOWNSHIP

EASTERN NATIVE TOWNSHIP

Sophiatown (Triomf)

Martindale

WESTERN NATIVE TOWNSHIP

Newclare North

Newclare South

SOUTH WESTERN NATIVE AREA

PIMVILLE

White Area

Black Area

expanding, should be built in a western direction, i.e., where Tobiansky was planning his neighbourhood. Naturally, none of Johannesburg's white residents wanted to purchase a house in such an uncongenial environment.

The First World War was raging at the time, and South Africa's industry was showing a boom-inspired growth. The new factories that sprang up in the Johannesburg area required labour, mainly black labour. In this situation the City Council had no alternative to permitting one more township to be built for black workers. This gave a start to the Western Native Township that was to accommodate 3,000 workers and their families. The nearness of the sewer was no obstacle in the given case. Mr. Tobiansky got the opportunity of selling plots of land to the black newcomers, especially as such transactions were as yet not prohibited by the law. The name of the township and of its streets were all that remained of Tobiansky's ambitious plans.

In Sophiatown the houses differed greatly from each other in size and conveniences—this depended on what their owners could afford. By the early 1920s this was a township in the true sense of the word, with hundreds of houses. Along the western perimeter there thus arose a cluster of practically interlocking townships called by the general name "Western areas" that, apart from Sophiatown and the Western Native Township, consisted of Martindale, Newclare (North and South), and Pageview. Altogether, some 70,000 people lived in this cluster. The centre of this group of locations, Sophiatown, was not a location but, to the extent the conditions in South Africa permitted, an almost normal town.

It had a territory of about 100 hectares and consisted of 1,694 plots of land. The structures built on these plots ranged from sturdy brick cottages with several rooms to hastily put-together huts. In 1950 Sophiatown had a population of 39,200. In 1955, when the dismantling of Sophiatown was started, of the 10,000 black families living there only 350 owned land. These families felt more or less confident, for they regarded themselves permanent urban residents. And looking at them, hundreds of other people aspired for the same thing. This was possible, of course, but only if one had the money. This situation was distasteful to the political party that had come to power—

the National Party with its apartheid doctrine. Sophiatown was doomed.

As a first step, the government laid the judicial, legislative foundation. This was not difficult to do because in South Africa the affairs of the black majority are managed by a parliament all of whose members are drawn from the country's white minority. Besides, the levers of power were in the hands of the National Party. The Group Areas Act, passed in 1950, empowered the government to proclaim specific areas as the homelands of this or that racial group and expel from these areas all who belong to some other race. Accordingly, the Western areas of Johannesburg were proclaimed "white" areas. In 1954 one more law was enacted—the Native Resettlement Act, under which the government set up a Resettlement Board with the clear-cut authority to expel blacks from Sophiatown and other townships along Johannesburg's western perimeter. The authorities then began the "lawful" forcible eviction of blacks and the destruction of the above-mentioned townships.

The government was doing all this under the pretext of putting an end to slums and resettling people to the new locations of Meadowlands and Diepkloof, which, they said, were more suitable for dwellings. Indeed, these locations were in line with the requirements of apartheid. They were situated far to the southwest of Johannesburg and were now, to all intents and purposes, a part of Soweto.

In fact, dilapidated houses and shanties predominated in Sophiatown and other townships on the west side of Johannesburg. But, as it turns out, this was not the point. Let us look at the evidence of a person who lived in Sophiatown for many years— Father Trevor Huddleston: "I do not weep for the destruction of the material which was Sophiatown. At least two-thirds of it would have had to be destroyed in any sheme for the renewing of that area which we had always dreamed might come to pass... Sophiatown was a slum. Those of us who lived there would never wish to deny that... But slum conditions can be removed without the expropriation of a whole area... Sophiatown could have been replanned and rebuilt on the same site: a model African suburb." Further, Trevor Huddleston quite rightly notes that in "the 'Shelters' at Orlando and the

Moroka Emergency Camp... at least 90,000 people were living under slum conditions quite obviously worse than anything in Sophiatown."[15] Yet it was Sophiatown that was put first on the hit-list.

John Gunther, who toured Sophiatown in the early 1950s, writes: "Here some 60,000 Africans lived in circumstances considerably better than in Moroka or Orlando. Part of Sophiatown was, it is true, a slum, but part was not. Here was the only place in the whole Transvaal where Natives were permitted to own their own homes... The government defends the Sophiatown removals on the ground of 'slum clearance'. The real motives go deeper. The evictions will serve to make Johannesburg a whiter city, and are the first concrete steps towards converting residential apartheid into a reality. Moreover it uproots and in effect destroys the most prosperous, stablest, and best educated Native community in Transvaal. If the government had genuinely wanted to do a bit of slum clearance it might well have given its attention to the shanty-towns."[16] "In nearby locations," writes Mary Benson, "tens of thousands of Africans were still living in shanties and in tin tanks, yet the Government ruled not only that these Sophiatown people living in overcrowded slum conditions must move, but also the thousands living in solid decent houses."[17]

And, lastly, here is how blacks themselves see it: "Sophiatown, where Africans owned freehold rights," Joyce Sikakane notes, "had to go because in the eyes of the apartheid regime such rights for Africans symbolized a permanency that was incompatible with the concept of Africans being temporary sojourners." She goes on to quote a pronouncement by an African leader: "We deny that this is a slum clearance scheme, because to eliminate slum conditions you do not have to condemn the good with the bad, you do not have to divest people of their property rights."[18]

The assault on Sophiatown began early on the misty morning of February 10, 1955. It was to destroy this township, and did destroy it, for apartheid permitted the existence exclusively of locations with blacks living temporarily in them; Sophiatown did not fit the bill. A description of those events, which were a tragedy for blacks, is given by Father Trevor Huddleston: "...it is the beginning of the end of Sophiatown. Today the great removal is beginning...

A light rain is falling. A detachment of African police under European command marches raggedly but purposefully down the hill... It was beginning to get light, but the rain was coming down hard... On the broad belt of grass between the European suburb of Westdene and Sophiatown (we called that strip 'the Colour Bar') a whole fleet of Army lorries was drawn up: a grim sight against the grey, watery sky. Lining the whole street were thousands of police, both white and black: the former armed with rifles and revolvers, the latter with the usual assegai. A few Sten guns were in positions at various points. A car, containing the Commissioner of Police and a mobile wireless unit (which we afterward discovered was in hourly contact with the Minister in Cape Town) patrolled up and down... Two thousand police, armed; a total ban on all gatherings. ... All this, to effect a slum-clearance scheme which would be a lasting benefit to the 'natives'."[19]

This operation took four years to complete. Most of the people were resettled against their will, forcibly, while their homes were levelled with the ground by bulldozers. In 1959 the authorities announced that the operation had been completed and that a total of 48,563 persons had been resettled; in addition, about 1,500 men had been given accommodation in "bachelor" quarters.[20] A white suburb with the meaningful name Triomf (Triumph) appeared later where Sophiatown had stood.

The Sophiatown operation attracted public attention. Much was written about it in progressive South African publications, and there were reports in media around the world. This inhuman action was widely denounced; naturally, the ruling circles were not at all pleased about this publicity. Later, to avoid such publicity they began to resort to more subtle methods.

Precisely such was the destiny of the Newclare township, which was part of the Western areas and was likewise destroyed in the 1950s. It was separated from Sophiatown by a single automobile highway running from the centre of Johannesburg to the west, to Krugersdorp. For many years this township was inhabited mainly by Sothos. Most of them had been urbanised and domiciled in Johannesburg.

In early 1952 the entire population of the southern part of the township was terrorised by a gang of criminals and hooligans. Many people were killed or wounded. The police did practically nothing to protect the inhabitants of Newclare from the gangsters. "Somehow or other, the police were never there when the gangsters were active; or they came when the immediate trouble was over... for some strange reason, which has remained unexplained to this day, the police did not disarm the gangsters."[2 1] In the rare case when the police intervened, it was not the gangsters but those they were trying to victimise who were disarmed.

People had to abandon their homes and move to the northern part of Newclare. About 2,000 refugees built make-shift shanties for themselves in Newclare's Reno Square. In spite of this exposure to frost and winds, the total absence of sanitation, people came here to save themselves from terror at the hands of gangsters.

Meanwhile, the city authorities used the police to evict these unfortunate people to an out-of-the-way rural area 50 kilometres from Pretoria.

Father Trevor Huddleston, who was in the thick of these dramatic events and tried to do something to save the people, writes that the authorities knew perfectly well where and who the criminals were, but did nothing to capture and punish them. "I was convinced at the time, and I am still convinced today, that this inertia was deliberate and calculated. The Western Areas Removal Scheme, involving the expropriation of all non-Europeans from Sophiatown, Martindale and Newclare, was crystallising into its final shape. Unrest and tension, therefore, were most valuable and potent propaganda weapons for the Government."[2 2]

The authorities used the tragic situation in Newclare to expel its inhabitants and tear the township down. The only thing that the champions of these helpless people were able to do was to ensure their resettlement not in the north, in a rural locality, which for city-dwellers would have signified the maximum calamity, the total collapse of all their hopes, but in the Moroka location. Thus, there appeared in Moroka one more shanty in which living conditions were, naturally, much worse than in Newclare.

Most of the inhabitants of Newclare and Martindale were resettled in Diepkloof. By 1968 a total of 22,500 families and 6,500 unmarried persons from the Western townships had been resettled in Meadowlands and Diepkloof. But the authorities had attained their objective: yet another step had been taken to demolish the Western townships, where Africans felt they were permanent urban dwellers.

Rebellious Alexandra Township

After they had levelled the western section of the black "ring" around Johannesburg, the authorities gave their attention to the northern section. The Alexandra township, or Alex as its inhabitants called it, was situated within the city, some ten miles from the centre, and adjoined the "white" suburbs.

This township had appeared early in the present century. Africans who came to earn a living in Johannesburg began to settle near a highway linking Johannesburg with Pretoria. There was much to attract them to this location: the nearness of the city—commuting was cheaper and consumed less time; but the principal attraction was that they could purchase a plot of land and, as in Sophiatown, build their own house. This gave people a sense of security that they felt would extend to their children and grandchildren. Of course, this was achieved by a few, but it was the hope of many.

There was another circumstance, an extremely important one in South Africa, drawing Africans to Alexandra township: until November 1956 it did not fall under the system of influx control, in other words, there were no constraints of blacks coming to this township and taking up permanent residence in it. The loophole for this was that although the township was in fact on the territory of Johannesburg it was not part of the city's "white" neighbourhood and its inhabitants were not regarded as Johannesburg residents.

The foundations for the discriminative system were laid in 1923 with the passage of the Native Urban Areas Act. This was reinforced with the Bantu (Urban Areas) Consolidation Act of 1945, which enlarged upon the provisions of the previous act. This Act introduced strict limits of the influx of blacks into cities and thereby formalised the discriminating racist principle that blacks could live in a "white" city only temporarily, as long as their labour was needed by their white employers.

It so happened that Alexandra was among the last townships to come under the operation of this Act. It therefore became the destination of those who could not count on getting permanent residency rights upon arriving in Johannesburg or any other city in the Witwatersrand. By the close of the 1950s Alexandra had nearly 100,000 inhabitants.[2 3] All of them had jobs in Johannesburg although officially they were not regarded as residents. "Without the Alex 'natives' the northern suburbs would have to go servantless, and not a few commercial concerns in the city would be hard put to it to find labour."[2 4]

Alexandra occupied a small square territory, with one of the edges abutting the Johannesburg-Pretoria highway. This was where the main road into the township began and where the Public Utility Transport Corporation had garages for its buses that provided transportation for the bulk of the people working in the Johannesburg down-town. The central bus terminal was right in the centre of the township, in the vicinity of 12th-15th Avenues. The township had 22 avenues, each of which had a number, and these were crossed by nine streets with pompous names such as Vasco da Gama Street, Roosevelt Street, London Street, and so on.

The township had upwards of 2,500 registered plots of land with houses, each of which was owned by one family. Up to 90 persons lived on each such plot 80 by 140 feet in extent. Some rented rooms, "corners", or cots from the owners, while others were allowed, for a price, to build shanties on the same plot.

In Alexandra there were no businesses that could offer jobs, but this "bed-room" city had almost everything that people required after working hours: retail outlets, more than ten schools, one of which was a Higher primary school, a cinema, sporting grounds, community centres, several churches of different denomination, two post-offices, a dial-telephone (a unique service in black townships), a cemetery and, of course, a police station.

The inconceivable overcrowding, the many shanties totally unfit for human habitation, and the mass of other inconveniences, for instance, the absence of electricity, were the same as in the other locations. Nevertheless, Alexandra's inhabitants loved their town. This was where their life had shaped, where they had acquired the sense of fellowship, of solidarity with the other members of the community. The township was home for thousands of people. At times, for instance, when banditism was running amuck, when gangsters were terrorising the people, this was a frightening and dangerous home. But it was the only home they knew. The well-known poet Wally Mongane Serote, who was born in Alexandra, expressed the feelings of the township's inhabitants in the following lines:

> *Were it possible to say,*
> *Mother, I have seen more beautiful mothers,*
> *A most loving mother,*
> *And tell her there I will go,*
> *Alexandra, I would have long gone from you.*
> *But we have only one mother, none can replace,*
> *Just as we have no choice to be born,*
> *We can't choose mothers;*
> *We fall out of them like we fall out of life to death...*
>
> *... Alexandra, I love you;*
> *I know*
> *When all these worlds became funny to me,*
> *I silently waded back to you*
> *And amid the rubble I lay,*
> *Simple and black.* [25]

Like the people in other locations, the inhabitants of Alexandra suffered from racial discrimination and police terror. And like them, they protested and fought back.

On May 1, 1950, there were turbulent demonstrations in many South African townships and cities protesting against the discriminative laws. The police responded with repressive measures and even fired at the demonstrators. The following passage is from a book by Lionel Forman, a prominent figure of the liberation movement in South Africa, describing the events of those days: "At Alexandra, Third Avenue, a very narrow lane, was the scene of the shooting. A pick-up van and troop carrier were passing through and the people had dispersed. One solitary stone was thrown by a woman as the pick-up van passed. It bounced harmlessly from the roof. There was no other stone-throwing or threat. But immediately the police opened fire with Sten guns. In a few seconds eight people were dead, including one fifteen-year-old schoolgirl... As the people gathered during the weekend at the funerals of those who had been killed it was clear there was very great bitterness in their hearts. At the funeral in Alexandra Township... one speaker said: 'We have not made this a political funeral, but the people know that those whom we are burying did not die of taking poison.'"[26]

In the South African people's resistance movement bus boycotts have been a major weapon. These were a way of protest used on several occasions by the people of Alexandra. The first of these boycotts took place as long ago as in October 1939. For eight long months the township's inhabitants boycotted buses and walked to work in protest against the penny rise in bus fares. They won their fight. There was no change in the fares charged in the Public Utility Transport Corporation's buses. This victory was largely owing to the organised manner in which the campaign was conducted under the leadership of a committee elected by the township's inhabitants themselves.[27]

Another attempt to raise the bus fare was made in 1943, and once again the people of Alexandra took action to protect themselves. But this time the bus boycott lasted only nine days, beginning on August 1, which proved sufficient to compel PUTCO to beat a retreat. The following description of the boycott is by Mary Benson: "It was midwinter, and in the bleak cold of the highveld, Alexandra lay under a thin grey cloud of smoke from the braziers on which the night meal had been cooked. Every morning early from thousands of small, iron-roofed houses the people emerged and set out along the steep main road towards the city. 15,000 men and women trudged the nine or more miles to work; cleaners and messengers and clerks, washerwomen and maids. Some were given lifts but most of them walked. Again, in the chill of nightfall they walked the nine miles back home."[28]

In November 1944 PUTCO tried again to raise the bus fare, and again the people of Alexandra responded with a boycott, which this time dragged out for seven weeks. As one eyewitness put it, "Alexandra walked... old men, tiny children, washerwomen loaded with their bundles, industrial workers doing a 50-hour week 20 miles from home in war industries walked through sun, wind and rain for seven weeks before the deadlock showed signs of breaking."[29] Once more the boycott was successful. On January 4, 1945, the people of Alexandra went to work in Johannesburg in buses, paying the old fare.

In 1957 yet another bus boycott was staged by the inhabitants of Alexandra as a tested way of protecting their interests. In January PUTCO announced again that they were raising the fare in their buses. Having repeatedly failed to raise the fare, the management was unquestionably hoping to use the overall political situation in South Africa to get what it wanted. Shortly before this announcement was made, the South African government had mounted a massive police-terrorist operation. On December 5, 1956, the police arrested 156 persons, among whom were leaders of all the main progressive organisations. All were charged with high treason. A "marathon trial", as it was called in South Africa, began, and it went on for four and a half years. It was blue-printed by the government to intimidate the resistance movement, to break the spirit of the people, and to defuse the powerful liberation movement of the 1950s whose culmination was the 1955 Congress of People that adopted the Freedom Charter. The trial was to mark the start of a counter-offensive by the government.

However, the bus company's management miscalculated. Instead of the submission and tractability expected of them the people of Alexandra confronted the bus company with powerful resistance despite the orgy of reaction and police terror. This struggle for the vital interests of the township's inhabitants merged with the nation-wide movement of protest against the racist regime.

The boycott commenced in January by decision of a general meeting of the township's inhabitants. This meeting was addressed by Alfred Nzo, now the ANC General Secretary. Tens of thousands of people unanimously pledged to boycott the buses: "Azikwelwa!" ("We Won't Take the Buses!") Nobody broke this pledge for four months, up until the day in April when it became known that the people had won the fight.

This time the boycott had powerful support: in token of solidarity it was joined by the inhabitants of Sophiatown and the townships in the vicinity of Pretoria, Port Elizabeth, East London, and Randfontein. "The mass response to the boycott exceeded all expectations. It underlines something more, too—the seething political tension and unanimity of the people in their opposition to Government evident since the treason arrests."[30]

In analysing the character and substance of this powerful action of Alexandra's working people, who had the support of thousands of people in other townships, Lionel Bernstein, a prominent figure in the liberation movement, wrote in the next issue of the same journal: "The issue flowed far beyond the matter of a penny on the fare that was the trigger that fired the boycott, but all the pent-up bitterness against a system of inferior, apartheid services, constituted the rest of the charge. The boycott was never, at any time, just a protest about the penny. It was more than that. It was a declaration to PUTCO, and through PUTCO to the white people and the government and city councils they had elected, that the cup of bitterness was running over. It was an assertion by the African people of their manhood; and of their determination to be considered and consulted on matters that concerned them... What is happening amongst the boycotters tells of a ferment and development that is taking place everywhere amongst the non-European people in every corner of the country; because here in embryo are emerging the forces that will shape a new South Africa."[31]

The bus boycott was a battle in every sense of the word: hard-fought and exhausting. On the side of PUTCO was the entire machinery of state with its police apparatus and media. Abuse was heaped upon the boycotters, public opinion was misinformed, and the boycott itself was portrayed as inspired by "terrorists" while the boycotters themselves were described as victims of intimidation. All of this was a futile exercise. "There was the usual talk in the press of intimidation—as though a few picketers could intimidate a township of a hundred thousand people at bus stops where the police were active to break the boycott... The boycott was essentially a movement of the common people," wrote the ANC President Albert J. Luthuli, who is one of the most esteemed persons in South Africa.[32]

The police went to all lengths to break the boycott, to force the people into submission. In fact, this was not merely a matter of protecting the interests of a government-subsidised private company. The bus boycott was a massive demonstration of the working people's strength and unity, an open action against the racist regime and the entire system of oppression and exploitation in South Africa. This was why the police response was so savage.

The 9-10-mile stretch between Alexandra and the centre of Johannesburg was turned into a battlefield. The police harassed the people as they walked to work. Everybody's passes were checked, and many were arrested there and then on account of some inaccuracy or an omitted formality. The names of taxi-drivers and passengers were taken as a warning of subsequent dire consequences. Those few who had bicycles on which to go to work had their tyres punctured.

The bus boycott was a severe trial for its participants, but it added a glorious chapter to the record of struggle against racism and oppression. No wonder Albert Luthuli wrote so highly of the militancy and sacrifices of Alexandra's inhabitants: "What heroism there is! For a strong, 25-mile walk on the top of the day's work, is a sufficient test of endurance. But what of the weak? What of the sick widow with five young children whose only income comes from backbreaking labour?.. The weak walked too, setting out before there was a hint of sunrise, and arriving home long after dark, exhausted."[33]

The unanimity and unity displayed by the people of Alexandra during the bus boycott of 1957 as, in fact, during the previous three boycotts gives a lucid idea of the atmosphere of active resistance to the authorities that reigned in the township.

Mention must be made of yet another circumstance that characterises life in the township: there was no racial intolerance, let alone racial hatred. One in five of the longest-established residents was coloured, and all had normal relations with the blacks. As a matter of fact, there were coloureds on the township's Health Committee, which was the sole administrative body until 1958.

Father Trevor Huddleston provides striking evidence of the normal race relations in the township. He writes of Helen Navid, one of the few progressive, sober-minded whites, who performed useful work for a long time on the Entokozweni, a voluntary committee helping destitute families. Helen Navid has to cease this work because in pursuing their apartheid policy the authorities made all dissenting progressives a target of persecution. This compelled Helen Navid and many others to emigrate. Trevor Huddleston describes a meeting organised by blacks to protest against this persecution: "Two or three hundred people on dry and desolate veldt at Alexandra on a Sunday morning: the police in the car, lounging and listening at the same time. A small group of men appearing unexpectedly with the black, green and yellow flag of the ANC. It was not a very impressive gathering by any standards. Yet how wonderful that here in Nationalist South Africa, in the heart of a 'black spot', in a place where African nationalism itself is at its strongest, a protest meeting should be held: a protest called and addressed by Africans because a white woman was being forcibly removed from amongst them after only three and a half years in their midst."[34]

Alexandra, like Sophiatown, did not fit into the pattern of the times, being a thorn in the flesh of apartheid. But it proved to be impossible to deal summarily with this section of the "black belt" by levelling the houses with bulldozers and resettling the inhabitants elsewhere. Johannesburg needed a source of cheap labour precisely in that locality. Were it to be destroyed, all the northern districts, populated by whites, would be left without servants, while many industrial facilities and retail outlets would find themselves without labour. The whites felt this keenly during the long bus boycott of the 1950s. To avoid this from happening (every white household employed three or four servants), white employers at the time transported their workers and servants themselves, thereby indirectly contributing to the success of the boycott.

Another solution was found, and it was to convert the township into a huge hostel complex for migrant labour. The authorities planned to turn it into an ideal location (from the apartheid point of view) that would serve exclusively as a hostel for "unmarried" workers, i.e., for persons called "economically useful". The rest—wives and old people designated as "unqualified"—would be expelled to the homelands. The few who were permitted to live with their families in suburban areas moved to Soweto or Tembisa townships.

On February 2, 1979, *The Star* carried a report about the government's plans for the township under the heading "Alexandra Makes Way for Hostel City".

Enforcement of these plans began at the close of the 1950s. At first the intention was to limit the number of persons living with families to 30,000, and to add 15,000 "singles", mostly women, accommodated in hostels. The authorities had recourse to a trap to endorse out "idle or undesirable" people. Alexandra township was formally under the jurisdiction of the district administration, not of the Johannesburg City Council. But because it was located on the city's perimeter and was, to all intents and purposes, a part of it, most of the township's inhabitants worked in the city. This circumstance was used by the authorities: it was decided that those working in the city would be subject to eviction. Those regarded as single were also moved to hostels in Diepkloof and Meadowlands.

The World reported that massive evictions from Alexandra began in June 1960. The statistics of a census taken at the time were used to determine which of Alexandra's inhabitants had families and learn where they worked. As a result, many families were divided because married persons had been declared "unmarried"; they were moved to hostels for "singles". The newspaper cited the case of Ephraim Chepape as typical. When the census was being taken his wife went on a holiday to rural area. He was now moved to a hostel in Meadowlands as having been registered as unmarried in the census.

Checks at workplaces yielded even a bigger "catch". The police undertook massive raids to check passes. This was usually done in the mornings, when people were on their way to work, and in the evenings, when they were returning home. If the police found that a person worked in Johannesburg, he or she was immediately resettled in Meadowlands or Diepkloof. In this way almost 24,000 persons had been evicted from Alexandra by the beginning of 1963.

In parallel, new legislation was enacted to limit the term of residence in the township. In 1963 the government announced that no more family houses would be built in Alexandra. In the next year, 1964, the township was proclaimed a "designated" area—under the act on upgrading the administration of designated areas this empowered the government to take steps to evict people from that area. It was decided to build seven hostels for approximately 20,000 "singles" in Alexandra. In the meantime, people continued to be expelled en masse from the township. By August 1972 their number had reached 65,000.

But none of this yielded the results expected by the Pretoria regime. There was practically no diminution of Alexandra's population. Many of the evicted returned and lived in the township in spite of the law. Moreover, new people came from the homelands. There was nothing the authorities could do to reduce the population.

In this context increasing attention was given in Alexandra to building hostels on the site of cleared family homes. In 1972 a decision was taken to build 20 hostels for 60,000 persons. This housing project envisaged 15 hostels (10 for men and five for women) in the first stage.[35] A new plan for the "hostel city" was adopted in 1978: the township was to be divided into seven districts, with eight hostels in each. This significant increase in the planned number of hostels (to 56) was due to a decision not to build large hostels.

The first two hostels, one for men (2,642 beds) and the other for women (2,727 beds), were opened on August 1, 1972. Construction of a third hostel (3,000 beds) was started in January 1979.

Francis Wilson describes the men's hostel in Alexandra. It is impressive with its sheer size. Varying in height from three to five storeys, the buildings measure 250 metres in length and formed an elongated hexagonal. The bedrooms, leading off common corridors, are furnished with from four to eight single iron beds and with the same number of iron lockers for clothes and food. The windows are just under the ceiling, much above eye-level. There is no heating although the winters are quite cold in the Johannesburg area. The cooking is done in a common kitchen where there are clusters of gas rings and sink for washing up, but there is no space for the men to sit and eat. There are no dining-rooms, either. Nor are there any tables or chairs in the hostel. The intention is that the people would eat out, but most cannot afford this. Outside the heavy iron gates closing the entrance to the hostel there is a row of single-storey structures that house administrative offices, a few shops, and a bar-cum-beerhall, which is the only recreation premises. There is one wash basin for 11 persons and one bath or shower and toilet for 14 persons. To get to work by 7.30 in the morning people have to—as most do—queue up at the wash basins and toilets at 4 a.m. From the standpoint of sanitation and hygiene the conditions are clearly unsatisfactory.[36]

In spite of all the shortcomings, living conditions are better than in the old privately-run hostel compounds in Alexandra. Sixteen such compounds are regarded as "temporary", and for that reason their owners do not bother to create normal conditions. Francis Wilson visited one of these compounds. It measured roughly 100 feet by 20 feet and contained 40 rather wobbly double-decker iron beds (i.e. space for 80 men). It is hot in summer and cold in winter, and food is cooked on primus-stoves on the earthern floor.

In comparing the old and the new hostels and finding the new ones better, Francis Wilson notes "one fact whose existence lays bare the potential explosiveness of the whole plan".[37] The thing is that amongst the administrative offices outside the gates of the hostel are three rooms: a police charge office, a thickly-walled cell, and a control room with a switchboard controlling steel doors that can seal all corridors and exits from the building to the court-yard. At the touch of a button any group of rooms can be locked off and the men incarcerated. "Strikes or riots will, it is believed, be more easily contained by such methods,"[38] Wilson writes.

The hostels for women are of the same type but the rooms are smaller—each is for four beds.

The journal *Sechaba* compared this innovation with a concentration camp. "The new set-up in Alexandra is beyond human conception, something completely rootless, artificial and static, an enforced, unnatural existence. Here a city with 60,000 people stripped of all basic human rights, with no married couples, no families and no children, has been established. The people here are going to be deprived of a clearly defined concept of social identity, self-respect and human dignity."[39]

Formerly, hostels were built mainly for migrants who came to the city to work for a specified period: their roots were in the homelands. The hostels were more like mine-head compounds, and their inhabitants were workers employed in the mines on short-term contracts. In the 1970s it became evident that the South African regime was planning to force the majority of urban blacks into hostels of the concentration-camp type.

But far from everything went as the authorities wanted. After the 1976 revolt (it will be discussed below) the government had to reconsider its plans for Alexandra township. In May 1979 the Minister for Cooperation and Development Piet Koornhof declared that the government had decided to leave the family houses in Alexandra untouched.

Upon learning that Alexandra was saved, many of its inhabitants danced in the streets on that day. But it soon transpired that it was too early to rejoice. The authorities had reserved the right to decide who could or could not live in Alexandra. This meant that the evictions would continue. The regime believed that by permitting a section of the inhabitants to remain in the township it would thereby split the population of Alexandra that had hitherto been united in demanding an end to evictions.

Moreover, the regime stripped the inhabitants of Alexandra of the right to own the land on which their houses stood. The most that they could count on was to take out a 99-year lease for their houses without their children having the right to inherit this lease. For the majority of the people this meant that they would be tenants or subtenants.

According to the 1970 census there were 57,040 registered inhabitants in the township: 54,292 blacks, 2,700 coloureds, 23 Indians, and 25 whites.[40] In addition, there were some 10,000 persons living in the township without official permission. Later, they were joined by over 8,000 persons, including more than 2,800 women, who were accommodated in the three hostels for "singles" built in the 1970s. In 1979 there were 5,661[41] black families in Alexandra, but towards the beginning of 1985, i.e., five years after the authorities dropped their plan for turning the township into a hostel complex, the number of these families exceeded 14,000, while the population reached a total of about 80,000.[42]

The Alexandra Liaison Committee headed by the Reverend Sam Buti was formed with official approval in 1972. The functions of this Committee largely coincided with those of the puppet "councils" in other ghetto-townships, but during the first few years after it was set it enjoyed considerable support in the township on account of its efforts to preserve the township in its original state. This committee even organised a Save Alexandra Party and published the newspaper *The Alexandra News*. The Save Alexandra Party, led by Sam Buti, won the 1979 elections, while the 1981 elections reinforced this party's position: it won all the seats on the local council, ousting its rivals belonging to the Alexandra Action Committee and the Alexandra People's Action Party. A total of 5,179 persons went to the polls in the 1981 elections.[43]

Despite this electoral triumph, the committee's popularity began to wane. The reason for this was that after it won some concessions from the authorities it slipped into collaboration with them. In the opinion of the African National Congress, the Alexandra Liaison Committee made two errors that undermined the support it was getting from the people. The first of these was that it helped to determine who among the population was entitled to live in the township and who was thus liable to be evicted. Its second mistake was its consent to replace land ownership rights in the township with 99-year leases for this land. "The rights which the people of Alex demand cannot be won by collaboration with Koornhof, but by struggle," the ANC journal *Mayibuye* wrote.[44]

After they had backed down from their intention of turning Alexandra into a ghetto-township inhabited exclusively by "singles" living in barracks-type hostels, the authorities decided to tighten control over "rebellious" Alexandra in another way. In 1979 they announced a programme for the township's "renewal and development". This was to include a large sports stadium, tennis courts, and even a park with side-shows. At first little was reported about housing construction; more was said about pulling down existing houses and clearing and replanning territory. This programme was to be implemented in 11 phases and no deadline was indicated. There was a lot of hoop-la about the new programme, and this public relations campaign was joined by the township's "saviour" Sam Buti.

Only 49 houses were built during the first three years after the programme was launched, and in 1984 the number of new houses rose to 56. But all of these were houses built privately, by well-to-do families: each such house cost from 36,000 to 42,000 rand.

This sort of "development" could in no way resolve the housing problem in the township, where the monthly incomes of 76 per cent of the families (in 1984) was between 100 and 400 rand; consequently, they could not pay more than 30-40 rand for housing. Thus, 79 small standard single-family houses were built, but the rent was unaffordable (125 rand and higher) for the majority of the people. In the meantime, the demolition of old housing continued on a steadily growing scale. People moved into temporary "zincs" on Third Avenue and decrepit buses or were expelled from Alexandra altogether.

The actual design of the architects of this "renewal and development" gradually came out into the open; it was, after all, their intention to destroy the old Alexandra and replace it not with a hostel complex but a new township inhabited mainly by relatively well-to-do people, who would, consequently, be more compliant and inclined to reconcile themselves to the regime. This is also the opinion of those who had the opportunity to observe the "renewal" at first hand: "... it seemed the township was being redeveloped not for its present population, but for some other—far wealthier—group, the priority being given to middle-class housing in the renewal of Alexandra," such was the conclusion offered at a conference of the Black Sash organisation in Johannesburg.[45]

To protect their interests the majority of Alexandra's population united in the Alexandra Resistance Association, and this organisation likewise saw through what the authorities were doing: "the scheme only benefits the rich, while the majority of residents will be driven out by the high rents".[46]

By the close of 1985 710 new houses and flats were built, and of these only 167 were sub-economic. Altogether, 6,500 new houses are to be built under the "renewal and development" programme. With the consummation of all of the programme's 11 phases roughly half of the families now living in the township will not be resident in the new Alexandra.

Despite and largely as a result of the "renewal" life is growing steadily harder in Alexandra. "Our problems are worsening," a member of the Alexandra Liaison Committee acknowledged in 1982. "Everything in Alex is deteriorating, particularly the conditions of housing... Conditions were bad before but now they are rapidly getting worse."[4] [7]

Alexandra's population has not resigned itself to the situation. In January-February 1984 they responded with another boycott of PUTCO buses when the company announced a coming fare rise. Moreover, they made clear their attitude to Sam Buti. Upon becoming the "mayor" and head of the "town council", which replaced the ALC, he no longer played at resistance to the regime. In early 1984 his house was shaken by two explosions, and in February 1986, when Alex revolted (see Chapter Five) and its inhabitants engaged the police in battle, the "mayor" and his "councillors" and personal police simply fled from the township under the escort of white troops.

---

[1] *Poets to the People. South African Freedom Poems*. Edited by Barry Feinberg, Heinemann, London, 1980, p. 162.

[2] In the South African context the word "township" is used for several types of such ghettos: "location" built in an officially designated place for blacks working in a given city or district; "shantytown" or "bidonville", appearing spontaneously on the perimeter of a city and side by side with an existing location; "compound", a group of shanties for workers of a given industrial facility or farm. In the 1970s, the word "township" began to be used more commonly than "location".

[3] Brian Bunting, *Moses Kotane—South African Revolutionary*, Inkululeko Publications, London, 1975, p. 496.

[4] Ezekiel Mphahlele, *Down Second Avenue*, Faber & Faber, London, 1973, p. 162.

[5] John Gunther, *Inside Africa*, Hamish Hamilton, London, 1955, p. 497.

[6] Hilda Bernstein, *The World That Was Ours*, Heinemann, London, 1967, p. 24.

[7] Mary Benson, *The African Patriots*, Faber & Faber, London, 1963, p. 113.

[8] Since then Mpanza has used the word "Sofasonke" as a pseudonym and even as the name of an organisation he later set up in Soweto and pretentiously called a party.

[9] John Gunther, *op. cit.*, p. 497.

[10] James Morris, *South African Winter*, Faber & Faber, London, 1958, p. 35.

[11] Cited in: N. Phillips, *The Tragedy of Apartheid*, G. Allen & Unwin, New York, 1960, pp. 25-26.

[12] Joyce Sikakane, *op. cit.*, p. 18.

[13] Cited in: Hilda Bernstein, *For Their Triumphs and for Their Tears*, International Defence and Aid Fund, London, 1975, p. 121.

[14] Cited in: *South African Freedom News*, Dar es Salaam, August 2, 1963, p. 8.

[15] Trevor Huddleston, *Naught for Your Comfort*, William Collins Sons & Co., Ltd., Glasgow, 1977, pp. 142-143.

[16] John Gunther, *op. cit.*, pp. 499-500.

[17] Mary Benson, *op. cit.*, p. 203.

[18] Joyce Sikakane, *op. cit.*, p. 21.

[19] Trevor Huddleston, *op. cit.*, pp. 133-135.

[20] *The World*, Johannesburg, March 5, 1960.

[21] Trevor Huddleston, *op. cit.*, pp. 78-79.

[22] Ibid., p. 86.

[23] *The World*, Johannesburg, September 24, 1960.

[24] Trevor Huddleston, *op. cit.*, p. 22.

[25] *The Star*, Johannesburg, October 14, 1977.

[26] Lionel Forman and E. Solly Sachs, *The South African Treason Trial*, John Calder, London, 1957, p. 136.

[27] *Mayibuye*, Lusaka, December 21, 1968, p. 12.

[28] Mary Benson, *op. cit.*, p. 100.

[29] *Mayibuye*, Lusaka, December 21, 1968, p. 12.

[30] *Fighting Talk*, Johannesburg, February 1957, p. 9.

[31] Ibid., March 1957, p. 7.

[32] Albert J. Luthuli, *Let My People Go*, Collins, Fontana Books, London, 1962, pp. 175-176.

[33] Ibid., p. 176.

[34] Trevor Huddleston, *op. cit.*, p. 112.

[35] Francis Wilson, *Migrant Labour*, S. A. Council of Churches, Johannesburg, 1972, p. 42.

[36] Ibid., p. 43.

[37] Ibid.

[38] Ibid.

[39] *Sechaba*, London, Nos. 10-12, 1973, pp. 48-49.

[40] *Population Census 1970. Report No. 02-05-10. Geographical Distribution of Population*, Department of Statistics, Republic of South Africa, Pretoria, March 1976, p. 32.

[41] *Financial Mail*, Johannesburg, May 4, 1979.

[42] *Weekly News Briefings*, London, No. 5, 1985, p. 9.

[43] Ibid., No. 38, 1981, p. 13.

[44] *Mayibuye*, Lusaka, No. 8, 1979, p. 1.

[45] *Weekly News Briefings*, London, No. 14, 1984, p. 11.

[46] Ibid., No. 9, 1985, p. 9.

[47] *Financial Mail*, Johannesburg, January 22, 1982.

Chapter Two

SOWETO AND THE SOWETANS

Apartheid Creates Soweto

At the outset of the 1950s the South African government and the Johannesburg municipal authorities set about putting into effect their plans for creating a large complex of townships, which was subsequently called Soweto. This complex was to accommodate the bulk of the labour needed by Johannesburg. Hitherto, the Africans working in Johannesburg lived in locations forming an almost unbroken ring around the city. The authorities felt it would be more expedient to concentrate black workers in one district that could be easily controlled.

Incidentally, the name Soweto was officially endorsed by the municipal authorities only in 1963 after a special committee had sat for a long time, considering various names, including Apartheid Townships and Verwoerdstad.

As the authorities saw it, the new townships would bear no resemblance to the old locations. There would be no place for the free-thinking that had turned Sophiatown and Alexandra into centres of resistance to and struggle against racist white minority rule.

The site for the new complex had to meet certain requirements: it had to be as far away from the city as possible and there should be total control by the Johannesburg City Council.

The fact that Soweto sprang up to the southwest of Johannesburg and not anywhere else was not accidental. In the first place, there already were several locations such as Pimville and Orlando. It was assumed that these scattered townships would merge into a single large complex and, at the same time, that there would be qualitative changes in them compatible with the requirements of apartheid. Second, on the southwest Johannesburg was bounded by industrial districts and, consequently, no new suburbs for whites would be built there.

Two railways and an automobile highway, which could be used by the inhabitants of these locations to get to work, ran across the southwest area.

Another important circumstance from the standpoint of

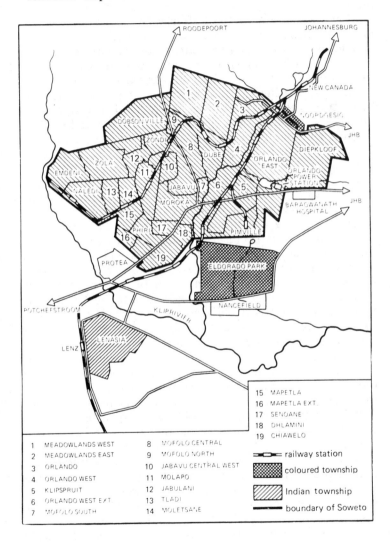

			15 MAPETLA
			16 MAPETLA EXT.
			17 SENOANE
			18 DHLAMINI
			19 CHIAWELO
1	MEADOWLANDS WEST	8	MOFOLO CENTRAL
2	MEADOWLANDS EAST	9	MOFOLO NORTH
3	ORLANDO	10	JABAVU CENTRAL WEST
4	ORLANDO WEST	11	MOLAPO
5	KLIPSPRUIT	12	JABULANI
6	ORLANDO WEST EXT	13	TLADI
7	MOFOLO SOUTH	14	MOLETSANE

⊐▭⊏ railway station

▨ coloured township

▨ Indian township

━━ boundary of Soweto

apartheid was that there were an industrial district, mines, and wasteland forming a sort of buffer zone between the white neighbourhoods of Johannesburg and the black locations. "The disposition of the southwest areas was ideal for the grand apartheid strategy of rehousing the African people."[1]

There was more to the buffer zone than a way of separating residential areas in accordance with the colour of people's skins. In such cases buffer zones enable the authorities to exercise physical, military control over African townships. *The Times* of London carried an article on these townships, writing: "These new townships stand at a distance from the city, fenced in, and forbidden to Europeans. Between them and that city there is a good field of fire. In the arbitrament of force ruthlessly applied, as it would be, the Bantu can stand little chance."[2] An analogous assessment is given by the American researcher of South Africa's problems Gwendolen M. Carter, who writes of "townships separated from white areas by open land that is easily controlled by machine-guns and helicopters".[3]

The following description is by Father Trevor Huddleston: "Today it is necessary by law that there should be a buffer strip at least five hundred yards wide between any location and the town it serves... Nothing must be erected on the buffer strip—not even a pair of football goal-posts. It must mark that tremendous and vital distinction between civilisation and barbarism upon which the doctrine of white supremacy rests. No one of either race may linger on that strip of land, for in that way it might become a meeting-place. It is, in exact and literal terms, a no-man's land: and it is meant to be just that... Sometimes, with the older locations, tall iron fences were erected and gave the impression not only of a kind of imprisonment but of a fortification, as though the location were totally alien to the life around it and had to be defended at all costs from any contact with it. Today the buffer strip serves the same purpose and is less expensive." Further Huddleston is more explicit, probably unravelling the regime's inner-most design: "And, in the sphere of broader strategy, it is also wiser to have the natives living in one large but easily recognisable camp, than scattered around the town in smaller groupings. If there is trouble in Johannesburg, for instance,

Orlando can be 'contained' by a comparatively small force. It is not a bad target from the air either. And its buffer strip ensures that no European suburb will be hit by mistake."[4]

In preparing to carry out its design, the government rushed bills through parliament that would ensure the forth-coming large-scale project with funds and cheap labour. The Bantu Building Workers' Act permitting Africans to learn building trades and work in black townships was passed in 1951. A tax on employers who did not provide their workers with housing was introduced in 1952; it amounted to a weekly 30 cents for each worker employed by them. And, lastly, the practical implementation of the plan for a single complex of locations was started in 1953.

The first step in this direction was to mark out 35,000 0.034-hectare lots of land. A standard single-story three-room house with a kitchen and a useful floor-space of 43 square metres was to be built on each lot. Subsequently, these standard houses amounted to 98 per cent of the dwellings built in Soweto.

Construction proceeded on a grand scale: 11,074 houses in 1957-1958, 10,500 in 1960-1965, 3,000 in 1965-1969,[5] 3,703 in 1970, 1,089 in 1971, 954 in 1972,[6] and 1,009 in 1974.[7] Thus, more than 31,000 standard houses were built in Soweto within a span of 18 years. Other sources say that nearly 50,000 houses, 88 schools, and three hostels for 14,000 persons were built between 1954 and 1969.[8]

Outwardly, this had the appearance of concern on the part of the authorities: many houses were being built, and these were of brick and unquestionably better than the shacks made of mealie-stalks, hessian, poles, biscuits-tins, old iron, anything that could provide shelter for the bulk of the people of the townships. However, some circumstances gradually came to light that disappointed those who had looked forward to moving into new houses.

Most of the resettlers were from Sophiatown, the Western Native Township, and some other locations that were being pulled down around Johannesburg. In addition to the fact that many of them lost the right to own houses and became simply tenants, people were quickly disappointed by the houses themselves. In 1961, i.e. when construction was in full swing in Soweto, *The World* wrote of the Africans' impression of the new houses. When a delegation from the

Western Native Township was brought to Moroka township to inspect the future homes, "quibbling and quarreling broke out". The mood of the future inhabitants changed sharply when they were shown the foundations of the houses under construction. "We have been tricked," members of the delegation said, "these are just lavatories. No twin-beds will go into these rooms." The delegation protested that the yards were too small. There was a stir when a member of the delegation said that he had seen a builder using mud in the foundations instead of cement. Other foundations were inspected and the delegates found that they had been built of mud, not cement.[9]

During the initial years of the Soweto project most of the building was in the townships of Meadowlands and Diepkloof situated on either side of Orlando, which had expanded by that time. Unlike the other townships, Meadowlands and Diepkloof were at first formally not part of Soweto because they were administered not by the Johannesburg City Council but by the Bantu Resettlement Board. Spread over an area of 1,800 hectares, these two townships were built specially for Africans evicted from Sophiatown and other western areas of Johannesburg and also from Alexandra township. The first of the resettlers were brought to these townships under a police escort in February 1955, when the authorities began the demolition of Sophiatown. In December 1968 they had a population of 22,516 families and 6,494 unmarried persons. Ellen Hellmann estimates that in 1970 three-fourths of the Sowetans were living in townships administered by the City Council and one-fourth in townships under the jurisdiction of the Bantu Resettlement Board. In June 1970 there were 403,165 people in townships that were formally part of Soweto, and 155,533 persons in the townships administered by the Resettlement Board, with the latter including Meadowlands and Diepkloof, which had a population of 150,896. Actually, all these people were residents of Soweto.

These statistics are from official censuses, which the Africans feared and endeavoured to evade. The official figures for the population of Soweto are, as has already been pointed out, understated by roughly 17 per cent. The actual population of Greater Soweto, including Meadowlands and Diepkloof, numbered between 1.3 million and 1.4 million in the 1970s.

Here we have a description of Meadowlands written in 1958 by James Morris: "One damp misty evening my African host stopped his car on a ridge above Meadowlands, and we surveyed in silence the expanse of African Johannesburg below us. As far as I could see, stretching interminably away into the dusk the houses of the township lay there blankly. A few candles flickered here and there (there was no street lighting, and no electricity) and a car or two moved urgently through the mist: but mostly the location lay there torpid, numb and sullen, 'Our black metropolis!' said my host, with an ironic twist of his mouth. 'You see how they have cut us off? If there was any trouble they would isolate us here, this side of the railway line, and then bomb us and shell us until we surrendered'." [10]

The dull monotony of the endless rows of matchbox houses has been noted by all who saw the Soweto townships. James Morris writes: "It is the deliberate impersonality of the locations that is most terrible... In Johannesburg you cannot escape the suspicion that this severe barracks-like order is intended to subjugate the African, to impress upon him his inferior status, to prove that he is not in white South Africa by right, but only on sufferance. He must never be allowed to feel a permanent resident, but must be branded as a migrant, a visiting servant whose only home is in his distant tribal territory." [11] This is the impression of a white man from overseas. The opinion of the African about the new locations is much more explicit. Jordan K. Ngubane writes: "A new factor becomes observable in the locations—the systematic crushing of individuality. The locations are not designed as residential areas for human beings with different temperaments and preferences; they are meant to be reservoirs of labour in which the enlargement of the personality will be kept to a minimum. The houses are built according to one monotonous pattern, with straight streets to facilitate troop movements; and the hut in which the university lecturer lives is like that of his neighbour, the grave-digger." [12]

Central to the plans and intentions of the South African government was the objective to degrade the urban Africans psychologically. They were not merely resettled from old to new townships—they ceased to feel themselves masters of their own homes in both the literal and figurative senses. They had to become a faceless mass of docile workers, disinherited and inarticulate. The atmosphere was designed to debase their human dignity and trample their individuality. This is seen even in what would seem to be an irrelevant circumstance: during the first few years most of the streets had no names. There were only the numbers of standard matchbox houses. Subsequently, when some of them were finally named people had become so accustomed to this deprivation of identity that they would say, for example, that Kambula lives in 6002-A Orlando, and Marite lives somewhere in the 4000s.

In the locations people could not feel at home either in their houses, which they do not own, or in the townships as such. The Urban Bantu Councils[13] are less than consultative bodies of local self-government. The white authorities did not make even a pretence of "consulting" them on serious matters concerning the locations. After the bloody events of 1976 in Soweto when the helplessness and ineffectiveness of these "councils" became starkly evident, they began to be called "Useless Boys' Clubs". [14] Joyce Sikakane writes that this nickname indicates the total impotence of these "councils" and characterises their members, who earned the label "boys" by their collaboration with the white authorities.[15] The "councillors" themselves admitted in hearings before the Cillie Commission[16] that young people "call us the Useless Boys' Club and lack confidence in us because they know we have no power".[17] The only purpose of these puppet bodies was to create the semblance of self-administration in order to calm public opinion and divert blacks from the struggle for genuine self-administration and independence.

Real and total rule over the townships inhabited by hundreds of thousands of blacks working at the industrial facilities in Johannesburg and serving the city's white residents has always been exercised by those who lived outside these townships—first by the Johannesburg City Council and then by the government in Pretoria.

In the 1950s and 1960s all of Soweto's affairs were handled by the Johannesburg City Council, which exercised its authority in the townships through the Non-European Affairs Department, which had offices in every location, where its officials administered all affairs and had the African Community Councils at their beck and call.

With the hardening of the apartheid regime, the government found it necessary to place Soweto under its direct control. By a decree passed in 1973 the government set up the Bantu Affairs Administration Board, giving it administrative jurisdiction over all locations in South Africa. Soweto came under the jurisdiction of the West Rand Administration Board.

The organisations and boards administering Soweto and controlling the life of its inhabitants change, but one thing remains unchanged, and it is that the black township is ruled by the white official. Each township has a superintendent with an apparatus of officials and police, both white and black. The whites have not only all the formal, judicial levers of power but also the material means of control: for instance, the water and food supply. These means are used time and again to pressure the inhabitants and break their resistance. Such was the case, for instance, in 1960 after the Sharpeville massacre,[18] which rocked the whole country with shock. It was then that Cape Town authorities attempted to break the resistances of Langa township, who as those of other townships participated in a general strike. On top of police repressions the water supply to the township was cut off.

The white masters control all aspects of life in the locations. They determine who may or may not live in them, what houses people may occupy, who may teach children in the schools—in fact everything up to where the inhabitants may or may not brew their traditional beer. This is permitted in Meadowlands and Diepkloof, but not in the other Soweto townships.

The following statements by representatives of the white authorities are extremely indicative. One is by the Manager of Non-European Affairs: "We are going to do you good, whether you like it or not; for we alone know what is good for you!"[19] It is hard to say what motivates such words: cynicism or arrogance. Speaking in Soweto in 1968 Deputy Minister for Bantu Affairs Blaar Coetzee declared that Johannesburg should not make it attractive for black people to live there because then they would have no incentive to move to the homelands.[20]

Official propaganda described the houses being built in the new locations as sturdy and comfortable, asserting that Africans were willingly moving into them. The demolition of the old townships and the removal of their inhabitants to Soweto were presented as a magnanimous act by the authorities, as evidence of their concern for Africans. *The Times* of London, for instance, wrote of "a really spectacular improvement of the appalling conditions to be met with a visitor in the recent past".[21] To say nothing of official South African publications lauding apartheid and, in particular, the housing projects in Soweto, the claim that there has been a significant improvement of the life of Africans in the new Soweto locations is to be found in the writings of students of South African problems approving or sympathising with apartheid.

One of them, Heribert Adam, writes of "a more hygienic civilization here in new locations".[22] Tom Hopkinson notes that "since 1948 the Nationalist Governments have built or subsidized vast new housing developments for Africans" and claims that "this massive resettlement had a beneficial by-product".[23] In an effort to refute Trevor Huddleston's consummately competent and warranted judgment of the new locations, A. Steward writes of "a new promise which Apartheid holds out: a Bantu building contractor, a Bantu grocer, a Bantu artisan and Bantu homes at a cost which Bantu can afford".[24] True, as A. Steward himself writes, he drew his conclusions from a brief tour of one of the new townships and a short conversation with the building contractor and the future owner of a house.

Granted, the standard houses are better than the squalid hovels built hastily of any material lying about. At least they have walls and a roof. In Soweto the waiting list for a matchbox house is growing ever longer. On this list there were 13,056 families in 1970, 17,225 in 1975, 22,000 in 1977, and 25,000 in 1978.[25] Most of these people have official permission to live in Soweto, but since they have no dwellings of their own they are compelled to rent a room or a "corner", or build a temporary shelter on the land of the tenant of the given house. The sub-tenant has practically nothing and for that reason it is indeed a boon to move into a matchbox house. Thus, only those are content to get one of these houses who previously had no housing

66

at all or lived in a dilapidated shanty.

Very few of those who have been living for some time in these houses are content with their dwellings. Each house is designed for one family. This is the only condition for a more or less normal life in it. But this is not the case in Soweto. "Almost all Soweto houses are overcrowded."[2 6] "Almost every dwelling had more than one family, or sub-tenants."[2 7]

The natural population growth in Soweto requires at least 2,000 new houses annually, but in the early 1970s only about 1,000 were built. The main reason for the over-crowding in Soweto is not, of course, the natural population growth but the continuous influx of labour.

The average family in Soweto consists of five persons, and in 1970 there were over 65,000 persons on the waiting list. Moreover, 23,800 applications for a place in the hostels for unmarried men and women were not granted.[2 8] In 1977 the number of families on the waiting list for housing exceeded 100,000. These statistics give an idea only on the number of people with official permission to live in Soweto. To these must be added those who live there without per-mission or are waiting for such permission, and these, judg-ing by unofficial estimates of Soweto's population, number hundreds of thousands.

In the 1970s only one in every four houses in Soweto had running water. The people living in all the other houses had to get their water from street pumps; only 3 per cent of the houses had hot water.[2 9] There is electricity in 15 per cent of the houses; candles or paraffin lamps are used for light-ing in the rest of the houses. Only a few streets have light-ing, and even this is provided by weak, dim lamps. These were streets leading to police stations, administrative of-fices, and beer halls. Most of Soweto plunges into dark-ness as evening draws near. David Thebehali, the "mayor" of Soweto, had himself declared: "Right now we are told that electricity is available to residents of townships like Orlando East, Orlando West, Orlando West Extension, Du-be, Moroka, Naledi Extension, Emdeni Extension and Molapo Extension. This is a false report and the worst scan-dal I have ever encountered. The people of places like Naledi, Emdeni, Molapo and Dube will be surprised to learn that they have electricity. These places have no electricity and no attempt has ever been made to supply them with power."[30] This was an incontestable reply to those who made believe that 15, 20, or even 31 per cent of the houses in Soweto had been electrified.[31] The fact that electricity is unavailable in the vast majority of the houses was noted by *The World* newspaper in its coverage of the launching of television broadcasting in South Africa: "While white South Africa switched on to television last night, the black majority remained in its black-out mainly because of our low earnings and the lack of electricity in our townships. The black population of the country has to wait—all because of the lack of electricity in areas as vast as Soweto, which is only fractionally electrified. Unfortunately few schools in Soweto have electricity."[32]

Nor was there normal telephone communication in Soweto. In 1976 there were only 39 public telephones. Very few houses had telephones. Soweto's first and only pharmacy was opened as late as 1981. There was not even one bakery; this was acknowledged in 1977 by none other than the Minister of Bantu Administration and Development.[33] All this is not merely to make life miserable for the Sowetans. It is meant to keep black Soweto dependent on "white" Johannesburg, to give the white overlords the means for dictating conditions and keeping the black inhabitants of Soweto under control.

Thus, the matchbox houses comprising 98 per cent of all the dwellings in Soweto lack the conveniences making for a normal life.

But the conveniences or inconveniences of the standard houses are not the only factor shaping the emotional state of the black in a "white" city. Also vital is the circumstance that under the racist apartheid regime the Africans cannot, when they find themselves in "white" districts, choose where and in which house to live. This is decided by the white authorities—not even by the city councils but by the government that acts through its respective agencies. The African is usually settled where this is permitted by the apartheid system and the interests of the racist regime.

There is yet another psychological factor that influences the attitude of the black to his dwelling and his life in the city generally. Racial discrimination is to be seen in all aspects of life in South Africa, including the housing question. Unlike seasonal and migrant workers (housed in the city), permanent African city-dwellers compare their housing not with the housing in the rural localities of the homelands but with the housing of whites in the same city. The Sowetans know well how the white residents of Johannesburg live and how their homes are furnished. For that reason they cannot help being envious and bitter, feelings that solidify into anger. These sentiments are conveyed to some extent in Mongane Wally Serote's poem *Johannesburg*, an excerpt of which was quoted earlier: [3 4]

> *And as I go back, to my love,*
> *My dongas, my dust, my people, my death,*
> *Where death lurks in the dark like a blade in the*
> *flesh,*
> *I can feel your roots, anchoring your might, my fee-*
> *bleness*
> *In my flesh, in my mind, in my blood,*
> *And everything about you says it,*
> *That, that is all you need of me.*
> *Jo'burg City, Johannesburg,*
> *Listen when I tell you,*
> *There is no fun, nothing, in it,*
> *When you leave the women and men with such frozen*
> *expressions,*
> *Expressions that have tears like furrows of soil erosion,*
> *Jo'burg City, you are dry like death,*
> *Jo'burg City, Johannesburg, Jo'burg City.*

The Elite of Dube and the "Bachelors" In Hostels

It would be wrong to say that all Sowetans live in similar conditions, eat similar food, wear similar clothes and, most important of all, think along similar lines. All of them suffer from racial discrimination and apartheid and all have the same humiliating status relative to whites, and yet each has his or her own individuality and lives differently.

Along its southern side the township Meadowlands is bounded by the township Dube, which has been in existence since 1945. It is situated along one of the railways running through Soweto. There is a railway station at Dube.

Soweto consists of many townships and basically they resemble each other, but Dube is visibly distinctive. It is inhabited by the elite of Soweto, by the urban middle classes: shopkeepers, small businessmen, teachers, priests, police sergeants, medical nurses, factory workers with permanent jobs and receiving relatively good pay, and clerks. Such people also live in other townships: Orlando, Moroka, Pimville. But there they are sooner exceptions, while in Dube they constitute the principal category of residents. There is one more distinction: in the other townships such people have been living for a long time, ever since these townships were population centres in themselves and there was no Soweto. But Dube began expanding in the mid-1950s, when the demolition of the locations west of Johannesburg was started.

Dube acquired its present shape at the time Sophiatown was razed. Most of Sophiatown's inhabitants who owned the houses they lived in and, consequently, had money removed to Dube, where they were allowed to rent pieces of land (but not to own them as in Sophiatown) and build their houses on this land. While they stripped the blacks of the right to own land, the authorities nevertheless sought to preserve an elite among the African urban population, counting on the collaboration of this elite as a means of splitting the united resistance to apartheid. "The creation of Dube Township in 1955," Joyce Sikakane writes, "was a result of a tactical manoeuvre by the government so as to succeed with its segregated housing policy."[3 5]

With the demolition of the locations where blacks could have property in land and their removal to Soweto, where such property rights were denied, the blacks found that they had in fact been deprived of the right to own land. However, they still had the right to lease plots of land for a term of 30 years. Those who had such leases felt they were established citizens.

The changes in housing policy were linked to the changes taking place in the domestic political situation. The latter half of the 1960s was marked by a reactionary counter-assault, an intensification of police terror, and a temporary decline of the national liberation struggle. The government was banking on strength and believed that it did not have to throw any sops to the urban middle classes and the

70

bourgeoisie in order to wean them away from the united front of struggle against apartheid. An indication of this attitude of the government was the directive of the Department of Bantu Administration and Development instructing local authorities to stop Africans building houses on plots for which they had taken 30-year leases and place a limit on the issue of such leases. Those who had already built houses were not to be harassed "until further notice". But a house could be sold by its owner to nobody except the authorities. If the owner of a house died this house could not be inherited.[36] This curtailing of the rights of urban blacks was one of the many steps that were taken to stiffen the administration of black townships.

In the mid-1970s, when resistance to the racist regime began to mount again, the South African government once again used the long-term lease as bait for the urban middle classes and bourgeoisie in the black townships. It was felt that this manoeuvre would cause divisions in the united front of discontent with and resistance to apartheid that were maturing in the townships. In May 1975 the Minister of Bantu Administration and Development promised that the restrictions imposed in 1968 would be lifted. This promise was followed in October of the same year with a very significant explanation: the right to lease land and the right to own the houses built on it would be granted only to those who had agreed to become "citizens" of a Bantustan.[37] This divested the right of leasing land plots and building houses on them of all sense: one had to declare oneself a foreigner in order to live permanently in the city and feel more or less firm ground under his feet. Naturally, this "boon" inspired no enthusiasm even among the most compliant members of the black elite.

It is quite possible that the authorities would have made no further concessions and would have ignored the discontent of the black elite in the townships, had resistance to apartheid not continued to grow. In June 1976 a revolt erupted in Soweto and spread throughout the country, marking the start of a new stage of the struggle. On August 13, 1976, the government announced that Bantustan "citizenship" would not be a mandatory condition for permission to take out a 30-year lease.[38]

But in the given situation a concession of this kind was worth nothing. Discontent went on mounting. The government had to find some other solution, make new promises and, finally, in 1978 authorise 99-year leases for land plots on which to build privately-owned houses.

What more could be desired? This lease meant owning land practically in perpetuity, giving the person concerned a sense of security and a sense of having provided security for his children and grandchildren. However, under the regime of apartheid and racial discrimination the right to a 99-year lease cuts an entirely different picture than in other countries. In South Africa this right is not granted to all who desire it. Only those who qualify under Section 10 of the Urban Areas Act are eligible for this right; the number of such people is limited. Small wonder that a comment on the 99-year lease bill published in *South African Digest*, mouthpiece of the South African Ministry of Information, spoke of blacks of the middle and higher classes and of "selected blacks on merit".[39]

Moreover, there are many limits on the inheritance of this right, and these limits nullify the attractiveness of a 99-year lease. It cannot be willed to children by those who have become "citizens" of a Bantustan (the government wants all blacks to be such "citizens"); this right cannot be inherited by the widow or adult unmarried children of the lease-holder. Discontent with these limitations was openly articulated by "influential members of the black community",[40] i.e. by the very people the South African government counted it could depend upon. There is yet another significant circumstance: possession of the right to lease land is not automatically accompanied by the right to reside in a given area or a given house.[41] This deliberate judicial muddle enables the authorities to evict the legitimate heirs of the lease-holder by denying them permission to reside in a given place. The authorities can always easily find a pretext for eviction. Moreover, the white superintendent of any township has the authority to invalidate, at his own discretion, the title to possession of a house. As grounds for such a decision *The World* names, among others: if, in the opinion of the superintendent, the owner of a given house ceases to be "a fit and proper person" to reside in the area; if he has been absent from his house for more than 30

days without the written permission of the superintendent.[42]

Thus, the permit for a 99-year lease made conditional
upon various limitations does not signify much for the African under the apartheid regime. A black owner of a house
built on leased land cannot be certain of his status of a
South African urban dweller. This has been eloquently
illustrated by a cartoonist who portrayed an African inscribed with the word "Soweto" and sitting in an arm-
chair and smoking an unlit pipe inscribed with the word
"Home ownership", while a match with the word "Freehold" is held by Minister Connie Mulder, who does not give
it to the African. The caption reads: "Smoking an Unlit
Pipe."[43]

Speaking to South African televiewers (mainly white)
about the government's policy in relation to real estate
ownership Mulder, who headed the Ministry of Cooperation and Development (it was formerly the Ministry of Bantu Administration and Development), said that not a single African would be permitted to own land in "white"
South Africa as long as he was Minister. "If we grant the
blacks title to property," he declared, "they are also entitled to political rights, and I am not prepared to endanger
the future of the white people."[44] B. J. Vorster, the then
Prime Minister, told the parliament that "blacks could not
own land in the townships" and that "township land would
continue to belong to the city councils".[45] Thus even the
relatively well-to-do inhabitants of Dube, who own the
houses they live in and have a bank account, cannot be entirely certain of what the future holds out for them.

Dube is regarded as a "chic" township in Soweto. Foreign
tourists are sometimes brought here by the authorities to
see the showcase comfort in which Africans live. Some of
the houses may even be described as handsome. Blue-printed individually, they have green courtyards, lawns, and
flower-beds. There are several two-storey houses. One of
these, costing £ 10,000, belongs to B. Mabuza, a businessman
who at the close of the 1950s ran a restaurant in the centre
of Johannesburg. True, the land on which this house stands
does not belong to Mabuza, who, as all other Africans,
leases it from the City Council.

The Dube inhabitants are counted the elite of the urban

black population and the government promises them something from time to time. However, these promises are in sharp contrast to actual life under apartheid and racial discrimination. No blacks, not even the most privileged and well-to-do, are guaranteed against arbitrary action by the police. *The World* newspaper reported that Richard Maponya, a home owner and well-known Dube shopkeeper, was arrested in his own shop and taken to the township superintendent's office in handcuffs. His only crime was that he was in arrears with his service payments, and this in spite of being the president of the African Chamber of Commerce at the time and having a business, which he himself assessed as worth over 60,000 rand.[46] Nothing has changed over the years—home owners are handcuffed and humiliated, being treated like ordinary tenants in arrears with rent and service payments.

Such is the reality: the urban black elite—doctors, lawyers, teachers, office employees, and even businessmen—cannot say "my home is my castle" even though they live in comfortable houses built on their own money. Like all other Sowetans they have no say in the affairs of the township and are not masters in their own homes. Their only consolation may be that financially they are better off than people in other Soweto townships; besides their township is named after John L. Dube, one of the first black enlighteners who was director of a teachers' training college. He was also the first President of the African National Congress, which was founded in 1912.

In Dube there are also people regarded as being on the bottom rung of the social ladder. These are the inmates of hostels (6,272) for "bachelors" or "singles", although many of them are married, with families in the homelands. In Soweto there are ten such hostels housing some 45,000 persons.[47] The largest of these is called Mzimhlope and is located in Meadowlands. It accommodates 10,316 persons. The other big hostels in Soweto are Diepkloof (5,428 persons), Mapetla (5,072 persons), Nancefield (4,976 persons), Jabulani (4,352 persons), and Dobsonville (4,228 persons). The hostels are usually for men, but there are some for women. For instance, in Orlando West there is the Mzimhlope women's hostel with 800 beds. The figures cited here indicate that such hostels are a widespread phenomenon and that a fairly large section of Sowetans lives in them.

Most of the hostel inmates are migrant workers. Many return to their families after working in the city (and living in a hostel) for 10-12 months or less. They then come back to look for earnings in the city. There now seems to be a trend towards a stabilisation of migrant labour numerically, especially in the Johannesburg industrial area. One outcome of this is that a steadily growing number of workers living in the hostels are becoming permanent inhabitants in them. Moreover, the official policy relative to African labour is, in particular, to turn a considerable segment of the workers into migrants or, at least, into "bachelors" residing in hostels, i.e., denied the possibility of living a normal life. The Dube hostel strikingly bears this out: up to 95 per cent of its inmates are, to all intents and purposes, living permanently in it, and only 5 per cent are working under temporary contracts. Some persons have been living in this hostel ever since it was opened in 1956. The annual renewal rate in the Dube hostel is only 4.8 per cent, Francis Wilson notes in a study of migrant labour in South Africa. By way of comparison he writes that at the Nancefield hostel the annual renewal rate was 48 per cent, i.e., ten times higher.[48]

Dube Hostel was regarded quite highly in Soweto. But the living conditions in it were wretched. Let us again refer to Francis Wilson, who visited it in December 1971. Unlike other hostels, which are housed in a single large building, Dube Hostel consists of a complex of single-storey barracks-like structures. These have two dormitories with eight iron beds in each and a kitchen. The kitchen has a single-plate coal stove, a concrete table, and benches large enough to seat about 10 men. The stove is for heating in winter: food is cooked on primus-stoves. The toilets, wash rooms, and common showers are located separately.[49] However, in July 1977 *Rand Daily Mail* reported that in Dube Hostel there were no showers, while the bathrooms were in disrepair. On the hostel territory were a common-room, an open-air floor for traditional dancing: because the popularity of such dancing has declined, this space is used for showing films. There also were a beer hall, a small restaurant, and six small shops.

The whole appearance of the living quarters, Francis Wilson notes, "was drab, not say bleak".[50] Because of the shops, women were allowed from the neighbouring streets but they were strictly forbidden to enter the living quarters. There were about 30 special police to maintain order and monitor compliance with the many interdictions on the hostel territory.

In 1971 the monthly rent was 2 rand 10 cents per person; this amounted to about 5 per cent of that person's monthly wage (40-45 rand).

The lodgers were of different ages—from 18 to 74, but the average age was 39, much higher than the average age of the miners in the compounds. This was also evidence that these were in fact permanent lodgers. Francis Wilson concludes his detailed description of life in Dube with the words: "The overall impresssion of Dube Hostel then is one of men—predominantly urbanised and 'detribalised'—living their working lives in spartan barrack conditions."[51]

In the other hostels the conditions were generally worse. The Johannesburg *Financial Mail* wrote in April 1977 of the "bleak existence of the men who live in Soweto's 'bachelor' hostels". The biggest complaint of these people was about the treatment they were getting at the hands of the police, which was characterised as "grossly inhuman". As regards the living conditions there were complaints that "there were bed-bugs, dirty walls, no hot water, and for some weeks there had been no lights in the grounds of some hostels. They had to cover themselves and their belongings with plastic sheets when it rained because of the leaks."[52] "The general condition is one of filth and squalor," another newspaper reported. Moreover, this report spoke of the overcrowding in the rooms and of a total lack of sanitation and hygiene in the hostels.[53]

Non-migrants living in hostels permanently or for long periods do not differ from the permanent residents of the Soweto townships. The only marked distinction is that they are "bachelors", "singles" compelled to live separately from their families. Of course, this influences their way of life and mentality. But these are not fundamental distinctions, especially as under the apartheid system the family life of the Sowetans is attended by obstacles and subject to various forms of arbitrary rules laid down by the authorities and to

discriminative legislation. Many hostel dwellers have relatives in Soweto and meet regularly with them. The contacts
between hostel dwellers and families living permanently in
Soweto are very diverse. The Johannesburg newspaper
Sunday Times noted that "at church level there was considerable mixing between hostel dwellers and residents".[5][4]

As in Dube, the majority of the dwellers of many hostels
in Soweto are migrant or seasonal workers intending to stay
temporarily. Most are illiterate or have little education,
find city life alien, and are oriented towards rural life. "By
and large these hostels are little pieces of rural South Africa transplanted into the city, for living in them are predominantly contract workers from various homelands[5][5] who
came to town on a temporary basis. They leave their families—and often their hearts too—in the homelands."[5][6]

In the 1970s the priorities in Soweto were for new "bachelor" hostels for "single" over family housing. This was
stated in the *Survey of Race Relations in South Africa*
for 1971, which spoke of further allocatons for the building of new and the enlargement of existing hostels in Soweto. For instance, the Dube hostel was enlarged in December 1971 and similar work was completed on the Orlando
West hostel for women in early 1972, and there were plans
to enlarge the hostels in Diepkloof and Meadowlands. The
large Mapetla hostel was completed in 1972.

Ellen Hellmann wrote in 1971 that the hopes generated
by the rapid growth of housing construction in the 1950s
were not justified. This construction failed to continue developing in Johannesburg or other cities. Hellmann noted
that at the time it was becoming ever harder for blacks to
obtain loans from the central government for family homes.
"Government priorities are bachelor hostels for 'single'
Africans in 'white' towns, and family housing in towns in
the homelands."[5][7]

Are Sowetans Well-Off or Poor?

It is considered that in Johannesburg, particularly in
Soweto, blacks have a better life and are more prosperous
than in other parts of South Africa. This is indeed true. The
average income of Sowetans in 1973 was 2.2 times higher

than the average income of blacks in the country at large (although it is only one-seventh of the average income of whites). Speaking at the Rivonia trial[58] Nelson Mandela said: "The highest-paid and the most prosperous section of urban African life is in Johannesburg. Yet their actual position is desperate."[59] Nelson Mandela made this assessment of the actual situation on the basis of statistics published by the City Council of Johannesburg. These showed that 46 per cent of the African families in Johannesburg were not earning enough in 1964 to make ends meet.

Even more eloquent statistics are cited by Muriel Horrell in the *Survey of Race Relations in South Africa* for 1966 The average monthly wage of a black worker residing in Soweto was 35 rand 62 cents. The monthly expenses of a family of five in 1966 were estimated at 55 rand 57 cents, this calculations being made on the basis of the poverty line. These included expenses for basics: food, clothes, rent, fuel, electricity, detergents, transport, and taxes. The conventional average family was thus short of the poverty line by the sum of 9 rand 26 cents, and where there was only one breadwinner the family was short of almost 20 rand for bare necessities. This survey noted that compared with 1958, the gap between the income of the average family and its expenses narrowed in 1966 in relation to the poverty line, in other words the situation improved somewhat.

The poverty line budget did not include expenses on medical care, furniture, and household items, let alone "luxuries" such as recreation, books, writing materials, and tobacco. All these expenses were components of another budget calculated on the basis of the "minimal effective line", which was 50 per cent above the poverty line budget and fixed in 1966 at 83 rand 35 cents.[60] In this case, the average family in Soweto was monthly short of more than 37 rand.

The various South African statistical agencies, the Johannesburg Chamber of Commerce, and some universities annually compiled the budgets of the average family in Soweto. The poverty line and "minimal effective line" budgets grew steadily with the rise of inflation, prices, rates, and rents. In 1976 the poverty line budget was set at 129 rand 05 cents.[61]

The most vital section of the budget consisted of expenses on food. In 1966 these expenses amounted to 31 rand 50 cents,[62] and in 1976 to 67 rand, i.e., they more than doubled, but the diet did not become better. This money was spent mainly on bread and stamped maize. This is the food of most of the Soweto families living at or even below the poverty line. "The food eaten is dependent upon wages earned," Monica Hunter wrote in 1961. "Those who can afford it eat European food—bread with butter or jam, and tea or coffee for breakfast; meat, potatoes, rice, and greens at midday; and bread, tea, and meat or maize in the evening. The poorest live on stamped maize, or porridge and have at the most two meals a day. The average unskilled labourer's family eat stamped maize, bread and tea or coffee, with meat once or twice a week, possibly some sour milk, and potatoes or rice on Sundays."[63]

In 1962 the Bureau of Market Research of the University of South Africa conducted a selective study of family incomes in Soweto. It was found that 56.8 per cent of all families (the survey covered 1,409 families) were those of unskilled labourers. If to these are added families with still lower incomes (families headed by housewives, unemployed, or pensioners), it will be seen that 66.2 were ekeing out a hungry existence.[64]

The hardest hit by the unceasing rise of the cost of living caused by inflation, whose rate averaged 9.3 per cent in 1970-1975, were the poorest black families in the townships. Food prices grew the fastest, particularly the prices of staple foods of the majority of the blacks—bread and mealie. "The rise in food costs is the highest in more than two years," the *Financial Mail* wrote in 1976. This growth of the expenses of black families, the *Rand Daily Mail* noted in 1976, corroborating the findings of the former newspaper, "was due mainly to the acceleration of the rise in food prices".

The wage rise won by the workers in a sustained strike struggle was visible in the early 1970s but it was whittled down by the inflation, the soaring prices, tariffs, and rents. In the period from 1948 to 1970 the average per capita income in the black townships rose by almost 5 per cent annually, but this was almost paralleled by the increasing cost of living. Moreover, in the townships food was dearer than in Johannesburg. "African shoppers in Soweto are paying more than 20 per cent more for their groceries than their white counterparts."[65]

How then does the average family survive on a budget below the poverty line? Laura Longmore, who has studied the life of blacks in the townships around Johannesburg, concludes: "Many Africans manage to keep up an outward semblance of well-being by making drastic reductions in essentials such as food."[66] The same conclusion is offered in the *Survey of Race Relations in South Africa* for 1967: "The shortfall is probably met in most cases by economising on food." Joyce Sikakane, who lived in Soweto before she left South Africa, is much more explicit and emphatic on this point: "On wages of six rand to ten per week how much can the Sowetonian in the barest income bracket spend on food? Rent and train ticket [daily commuting.—*V.G.*] come first, then food. The agonising pain about apartheid in South Africa is that when white Johannesburg shoppers produce several rand notes to spend on food the African shopper scratches the bottom of his purse for a few cents to buy staple food like mealie-meal, milk, eggs and meat."[67]

In the 1950s and 1960s most of the inhabitants of the townships around Johannesburg lived in want. Workers, particularly unskilled labourers (the latter forming the majority), earned so little that their families could not afford a normal diet. It was in these years that Laura Longmore wrote: "Perhaps the most outstanding characteristic of the urban African community is its poverty."[68]

There was some improvement in the economic condition of Soweto's inhabitants in the 1970s. This was due not so much to the wages (which, anyway, were absorbed by the inflation) as to certain changes in Soweto's population structure. The principal change was in the proportion of unskilled, semi-skilled, and skilled workers. The proportion of the first group diminished, while the proportion of the second and third groups increased. The following figures show the proportion of unskilled labourers in industry (with the exception of mining) (per cent):[69]

1936 — 89.5
1960 — 84.0
1970 — 68.2

In the Johannesburg industrial region these changes, within only two years, were more marked (per cent):[70]

	1967	1969
Unskilled workers	66.8	42.8
Semi-skilled workers	24.9	44.8
Skilled workers	8.2	12.3

Because of the considerable disparity in the wages of these groups of workers (according to statistics for 1973, in the Johannesburg region the weekly wage of an unskilled labourer was 13 rand 46 cents and that of a skilled worker was 32 rand 06 cents,[71] i.e., two and a half times more), the addition to the budget of many Sowetan families was quite significant.

Another circumstance affecting the average family income upward was the number of wage-earners in the family: children grew up to be adults and went to work. Statistics take the average family to consist of five persons: two adults and three children. The number of wage-earners in such a family was 1.3 units in 1956, 1.7 units in 1962, and 2.2 units in 1968.[72] Subsequently, the average number of wage-earners probably continued to grow while, according to one study made in Soweto in 1972, the average statistical family consisted of as many as 6.7 persons.[73] Many such families have three or more wage-earners. These changes, which took place over the last years, brought essential alterations in family income. The above-mentioned study of 1,409 families in Soweto in 1962 showed that the head of the family accounted for an average of 67.4 per cent of its income. The wife contributed 10.8 per cent; and the family's other wage-earners contributed 21.7 per cent.

Nevertheless, food prices, rent and transportation expenses are growing faster than the incomes of even a family with adult children. A study of 800 families conducted in 1973 showed that the statistically average family (6.7 persons), including four adults, had a per capita average monthly income of 16 rand 70 cents, i.e., a total of 112 rand. According to computations made by the Johannesburg Chamber of Commerce, the poverty line budget in February 1973 amounted to 128 rand,[74] in other words, each family was short of 16 rand every month for life at least on the poverty line.

In the Soweto of the 1970s there was no longer the

universal and glaring poverty that was to be seen in the 1950s. Most of the families were somehow managing to make both ends meet. And yet in early 1976, i.e., just before the uprising, 43 per cent of Sowetan families were living below the poverty line, set at 130 rand per family of six, and roughly 80 per cent of the families were living below the minimal effective line.[75] In 1981 the minimal effective line for the black urban family in Johannesburg rose almost three-fold to 363 rand 2 cents.[76] The unchecked inflation, the rise of prices and rents, nullified the wage increases sought by the black workers. The newspaper *Rand Daily Mail* reported that the 20 per cent wage rise of the Sowetans in the period 1978-1980 was accompanied by a 38.64 per cent rise of the cost of living. As a result, the proportion of families living below the poverty line in Rockville, one of the more prosperous of the Soweto townships, grew from 29.4 per cent in 1978 to 37.3 per cent in December 1980.

Such are the mean statistics: average statistical family, average budget, average wage, and so on. They give an overall picture of the economic condition of the Sowetan population: it had become somewhat better than earlier, but is still such that the bulk of this population lives closer to the poverty line than to the minimal effective line.

Johannesburg's central dump is in Maraisburg (a district on the city's western outskirts), an hour's walk from Soweto. A stream of people is to be seen going in that direction daily, not only elderly people and children, but also men and women in the prime of life—these are the unemployed. They go there to scavenge for food amid the garbage from the white neighbourhoods of Johannesburg. A widow, the mother of ten children, talked to a newspaper reporter who came to see the dump, saying: "It's shameful because it is hard for a proud person to accept such a way of life, but you must tell our story."[77] The West Rand Administrative Board, which administers Soweto, and spokesmen of the city councils of Krugersdorp and other cities of this region attempted to deny that there were cases of this kind. In reply to this attempt a new report appeared in May 1979, this time carried by *The Star* newspaper, which sent not only a reporter but also a photographer to a garbage dump in Diepkloof. The newspaper wrote that women and children dig in the garbage, collecting not only empty bottles and bits of wood and coal but also food waste, and that this is taking place at garbage dumps throughout the Rand.[7][8]

And here is still another account carried by the Christian Institute magazine *Pro Veritate*: "... over 1,000 black children aged between seven and fourteen fend for themselves in the Johannesburg streets, daily. They live on what they can beg or steal, and often die from the effects of malnutrition."[7][9]

Statistics bear out that this is no chance observation of a sensitive journalist. A study conducted in Diepkloof has brought to light that undernourishment is the lot of 29 per cent of children aged from two to five, of 39 per cent aged from six to nine, of 45 per cent aged from ten to twelve, and of 38 per cent aged from thirteen to sixteen.[8][0] Thus, one in three children does not eat enough. Dry statistics corroborating that in Soweto children are indeed dying of starvation give the most definitive reply to the question of how people live in Soweto.

The poverty of some, the privation of others, and the unsatisfied requirements of those few in Soweto living above the poverty line or even the minimal effective line are all factors generating and exacerbating social problems, making Sowetans discontented with their life under the apartheid regime. This impels them to rise against existing practices, against the authorities and the regime that marks out and implants such a way of life.

Urbanisation's Ugly Grimaces

Having penetrated all aspects of the life of Sowetans, poverty and privation are dictating a well-defined pattern of behaviour and thinking and aggravating existing problems. One of these is the rampant crime in black townships, particularly juvenile crime. In Soweto many children practically do not know the meaning of a home because their mothers have to work in Johannesburg and leave them unattended throughout the day. Soweto has very few children's institutions, and it does not have enough schools to accommodate all children of school age. Besides, many families

83

cannot afford to pay the high tuition fees. In Soweto there are almost no elderly people who could look after children while their parents are at work. As a consequence, a considerable number of children turn to crime, first as juveniles and then as adults. Gangs of these criminals, called *tsotsis*, virtually terrorise the townships, especially on Fridays when workers return home with their weekly pay.

Unemployment is an equally serious cause of the appearance of *tsotsis*. "The development of a class of permanently unemployed young men in the cities of South Africa, notably the tsotsis of Johannesburg," M. J. Herskovits writes, "affords us the most extreme example of how settlement in the city can bring on its own particular forms of social pathology."[81]

The *tsotsis*, classified as personifying a form of social pathology, emerged as a backlash to the specific socio-economic conditions prevailing in South African townships, Soweto being the outstanding example. Paradoxically as it may seem, the *tsotsis* even play an economic function in families living in the township. According to the observations of Laura Longmore, a son who has become a *tsotsi* often brings his loot to the family, and in some cases it amounts to 50 pounds a week.[82] The shortfall in the budget of a family living in these ghettos, may be augmented also in this fashion.

Mention must be made of one more socio-pathological phenomenon in the black townships. It is prostitution. Laura Longmore, whom we have quoted quite a few times, notes that "many married women supplemented what monies their husbands gave them by occasional or frequent prostitution".[83] She writes that prostitution is practised extensively in the black townships: "Many parents encourage their daughters to go in for the business in order to raise money for rent, food, clothing, and so on. I found that some married women practised it with the cognizance of their husbands, who keep watch outside the house while the wife is entertaining a client, in case the police are on patrol. Prices range from five shillings to twenty-five."[84]

This widespread practice was due to the imbalance in the sex composition of the black population of industrial areas, caused by the imposition of the system of migrant labour.

84

For example, in the early 1960s the black male population of urban areas between the ages of 20 and 49 was almost twice as large as the female population of the same age group.[85] According to the 1970 census this ratio showed a tendency towards levelling out, reflecting the process of urbanisation, but the imbalance remains: in 1970 the number of males between the ages of 20 and 49 in urban areas exceeded the female population of the same age group by nearly 580,000.[86] It should be noted that official statistics mention only those who are permitted to live in the townships. The actual situation, taking into account the number of unregistered persons, mainly men, is much more acute. This applies fully to Soweto as well.

Thus, despite the certain improvement of the Soweto inhabitants' material position, their poverty is the central factor of social disorganisation in the black urban community, the mainspring of the extremely acute and painful social problems.

Alcoholism is widespread in the Soweto townships. The reason for this is principally social: poverty, an unsettled way of life, the constant threat of eviction from the city, police harassment, and racial discrimination. Another major factor is that many township inhabitants, particularly the temporary workers, who live in hostels, have not adapted themselves sufficiently to city conditions and have very little self-confidence. Further, apart from church services or a football match there is practically nowhere to spend leisure time.

Soweto has innumerable beverage outlets run by the West Rand Administration Board: beer halls, bars, wine shops. An insight into Sowetan life is given not by these establishments, which are run chiefly for profit and encourage imbibing, but by the shebeens or speakeasies run by Africans themselves. They give their owners (mostly women, called shebeen "queens", but there also are "kings") the possibility of augmenting the family budget.

The shebeens are a sort of club that spring up on the soil of the ugly urbanisation taking place under apartheid and racial discrimination. They play a dual role in the life of the Sowetans: on the one hand, they are a source of evil (of alcoholism and its social and spiritual consequences) but, on the other, they give township inhabitants their fairly rare opportunity for a social life, for meeting each other.

They date them with the appearance of the townships themselves. And from the outset they were illegal. Urban blacks were prohibited from brewing and selling "um-qombothi", the traditional African beer. But the ban on the sale and consumption of "European" hard liquor was even stricter. Nevertheless, both were widely available in the townships. Although the shebeens were routinely raided and their owners and regular clients arrested, the police can hardly be credited with being concerned about enforcing sobriety. Their main objective was most likely to keep the blacks in a state of constant tension and even fear, to deny them the possibility of having their own, even if not the best, places where they could gather and have some semblance of social life.

The following description is by Lewis Nkosi: "Johannesburg 'shebeens' or speakeasies—twilight underground world of urban African life where all classes met... In the shebeens one met teachers, businessmen, clerks, show-girls, payroll robbers, 'nice-time girls' and occasionally, even renegade priests." Noting the popularity of the shebeens and their impact on Africans, Nkosi compares them to English pubs as centres of urban life. "Interminable talk went on there about politics, business, love, literature. Anything."[8 7] In the opinion of a well-educated Soweto man quoted by Jim Hoagland, the "shebeens are important for crushing down tribalism. They bring people of the same class together and let us talk about developing an urban African culture. Perhaps that is why the police don't like them."[8 8]

The sale of "Kaffir" or, as it was later named, "Bantu" beer (the Africans call it "tamele") has been and is a monopoly of the authorities. This yields huge and ever growing revenues that go to the state treasury. In Soweto alone these revenues amounted to 1.3 million rand in 1960, 2.8 million rand in 1969, and 5.6 million rand in 1970 (i.e. doubling in a single year). The ban on "European" alcoholic beverages was lifted in 1962, and their sale was likewise made a government monopoly, of course. In 1970 the sales of these beverages amounted to 6.4 million rand in Soweto.[8 9] The government publicly declared that these large sums of money would be spent on social programmes for Africans, but apartheid confines black "legal" residence to the homelands, not in the urban areas, where blacks are only "tolerated" as long as their labour is required. For that reason most (80 per cent) of this "beer" and "alcohol" money is used for the "development" of the homelands, i.e., on the implementation of the selfsame apartheid policy, rather than on the development of public services and amenities in the townships.

As regards the officially licensed beer halls, eye-witness accounts say that initially they resembled cattle pens. They were premises surrounded by corrugated iron, with no conveniences, and with the inevitable policeman at the entrance. "The sense of animal degradation is overpowering."[90]

These "cattle pens" subsequently gave way to cleaner and tidier beer halls, but even in these sterile conditions the atmosphere of degradation continued to prevail. And, as always, there was a policeman at the door.

Despite the bans and the competition from licensed beer halls, the private shebeens flourish on account of the more amenable atmosphere in them. Little wonder that the ANC adopted a resolution in support of the shebeens. At a conference of the ANC Transvaal division in 1959 it was decided to conduct a compaign to demand the legalisation of beer-brewing and oppose the opening of municipal beer halls in African black townships.

The shebeens have become an inalienable part of the Soweto life. There are about 1,000, and most are in private homes where their status depends on how much the owner can afford to spend on them. The mistress is the shebeen's "queen". There are various types of shebeen in Soweto reflecting the socio-economic structure of the population.

The lowest-class are shebeens where fellow tribesmen living in Soweto gather to drink home-brewed beer and talk in their native tongue. Unlike the vast majority, these "ethnic" shebeens are nests conserving tribalism under urban conditions. Here the "queen" is an illiterate woman whom nobody employs even as a servant. The husband is usually an unskilled labourer earning miserable wages. "If the wife didn't sell beer, they would starve to death," one of these labourers is quoted as saying.[91]

One step higher on the ladder are shebeens, whose "queens" are unmarried women with some experience of city life. In the half year before they are spotted by the police they usually have put together enough money to feed themselves and their children and pay the fine, or to pay a bribe to the police. The clients are mostly urban young people, mainly *tsotsis*. These serve hard liquor and have the added attracting of recorded jazz music.

There are shebeens with a more respectable clientele—industrial workers, who come to talk over a glass of beer or wine. They usually come in groups so as to be in a position to fight off *tsotsis*, who may likewise come here. Women frequent all save "ethnic" shebeens.

White collar workers (clerks, teachers) have "clubs" of their own. The "queen" of one of these is, for example, the wife of a shopkeeper. She had had a good job—saleswoman in a shop but she quit it. She and her husband want to buy a car and for that reason opened a shebeen in their home. They hope to raise the money before they are caught by the police.[92]

Lastly, there are top-class shebeens for the elite of Soweto: businessmen, lawyers, doctors, school headmasters. In these one finds a wide range of drinks and European beers, good music, classy glassware, sprucely attired serving girls, and no arguments and no fights, as often happens in other shebeens, particularly where the *tsotsis* are regulars. One of these top-class shebeens is in Zondi township and it is presided over by old Mathoko. And Mathoko, writes Peter Becker, "is more than a shebeen queen. She's the majesty of Shebeenland."[93]

Regardless of the class of their shebeens, all the "queens" live in fear of a police raid. True, it is possible to bribe one's way out, but none feel secure. Even the clients do not sit long over their drinks. "We know the police could come at any minute, and we don't want to be found with anything," a Soweto man said. "At least the shebeen is ours. We have little else. In the white schools, the children are taught what the flag is. To me it is just a piece of cloth. How can it be anything else."[94]

In the 1970s the "alcohol problem" in Soweto acquired a new dimension. The increased sale of hard liquor, formerly banned for Africans, was seen as a double advantage by the authorities: large revenues and making alcoholics of Africans. Drinking establishments mushroomed throughout

88

Soweto, especially at railway stations, i.e., places that no working Sowetan could avoid passing. Every Friday people returning home from work with their pay packet let themselves be caught by these alcohol traps. In the officially licensed beer halls they were in no mood for friendly talk; they had come to drink, even if it meant spending their last penny. "The SA Government has built numerous bottle stores... and beer halls... next to the stations," said Tebello Motapanyane, a Sowetan youth leader. "We believe that they are there to misdirect the black people. Most of the bottle stores are next to the stations so that when our fathers and mothers come from work, they drink and forget about their surroundings."[9][5]

During the 1976 uprising, when young people began smashing hated institutions that personified the apartheid regime, the wine shops built by the Sowetan authorities were one of their chief targets. These were destroyed by young people chanting "They give us drunk parents!" and "Less drinks, more education!"[9][6] One only bottle store survived, all the others were wrecked or burned down.[9][7] The loss was estimated at 22 million rand.[9][8]

In their anger against these hotbeds of apathy and degradation they decided to put an end to alcoholism throughout Soweto. In regard to the shebeens they chose a different tactic: they did not wreck them but demanded their voluntary closure. The youth leaders heading the uprising put this demand in the form of an ultimatum. By the deadline set by them—October 31, 1976—all illicit drinking establishments in Soweto were indeed closed.

But after the period of mourning proclaimed by the youth organisations came to an end, everything returned to the old ways. Private shebeens reappeared, and throughout Soweto the municipal beer halls and bottle stores were restored or rebuilt.

In 1979 the Soweto Shebeen Owners Association, subsequently renamed the Soweto Taverns Association, began to negotiate the legalisation of the shebeens. To get this concession from the authorities the shebeeen "queens" and "kings" had recourse to a tested tactics—boycott. They ceased to buy their liquor from the state wholesale wine stores in Soweto. Moreover, they urged Sowetans to boycott municipal bottle stores. This campaign produced a newspaper, *Espotini*, that counted on shebeen owners for its circulation.

The authorities countered with their unchanging tactics: police raids, round-ups, arrests, and fines. But, in the end, they had to yield. In 1981 the parliament cleared the way for shebeen owners to apply for licences for the sale of alcoholic beverages provided they complied with a number of reservations.

As regards the municipal bars and bottle stores in Soweto, a notable innovation has been added to them. They are now windowless buildings, and clients are separated from the management by bullet-proof partitions and steel doors; moreover, they have radio communication to police stations in parallel with telephone communication. Each such "alcohol fortress" cost 120,000 rand to build.[99]

It seems that the shebeens are doomed all the same. It is getting harder for them to adapt to life in present-day Soweto and, besides, they are themselves undergoing a change. They are ceasing to be clubs with a distinct clientele and becoming ordinary bars at railway stations. The attitude to them on the part of most Sowetans is likewise changing. Three-fourths want to see an end to the shebeens.[100]

Soweto is thus a complex of townships set up by the apartheid regime for the workforce required by "white" Johannesburg. But in fact it is a huge ghetto in which poverty and denial of rights reign aggravated by racial discrimination.

[1] Joyce Sikakane, A Window on Soweto, p. 20.

[2] *The Times*, London, March 6, 1961.

[3] Gwendolen M. Carter, *Confrontation on Southern Africa. The African Experience*, Vol. 1, *Essays*. Edited by J. N. Paden, Northwestern University Press, London, 1970, p. 571.

[4] Trevor Huddleston, *op. cit.*, pp. 94, 95.

[5] Ellen Hellmann, *op. cit.*, pp. 3, 7.

[6] *A Survey of Race Relations in South Africa (Annual)*, Johannesburg, 1976, p. 84.

[7] *Sunday Express*, Johannesburg, March 19, 1977.

[8] N. Mandy, *A City Divided. Johannesburg and Soweto*, St. Martin's Press, New York, 1984, p. 183.

[9] *The World*, Johannesburg, May 20, 1961.

[10] James Morris, *op. cit.*, p. 34.

[11] Ibid., pp. 34-35.

[12] Jordan K. Ngubane, *An African Explains Apartheid*, Greenwood Press, New York, 1963, p. 124.

[13] Set up in Soweto in 1968 under the Urban Bantu Councils Act No. 79, 1961. Prior to this the townships had advisory boards. In 1978 the Urban Bantu Councils were replaced with Community Councils.

[14] *The Cape Times*, Cape Town, September 7, 1976.

[15] Joyce Sikakane, *op. cit.*, p. 51.

[16] The Cillie Commission was formed by the South African government to inquire into the events linked to the Soweto revolt in June 1976.

[17] *A Survey of Race Relations in South Africa (Annual)*, 1977, p. 184.

[18] A peaceful African demonstration protesting against the pass system was shot down in the township of Sharpeville on March 21, 1960.

[19] Cited in: Trevor Huddleston, *op. cit.*, p. 96.

[20] N. Mandy, *op. cit.*, p. 188.

[21] *The Times*, London, March 3, 1960.

[22] Heribert Adam, *Modernizing Racial Discrimination*, University of California, Berkeley, 1971, p. 99.

[23] Tom Hopkinson, *South Africa—Life World Library*, Time Life International, New York, 1964, p. 94.

[24] A. Steward, *You Are Wrong, Father Huddleston*, The Bodley Head, London, 1956, p. 69.

[25] *A Survey of Race Relations in South Africa (Annual)*, 1972, p. 164; 1976, p. 84; *Financial Mail*, Johannesburg, November 11, 1977; *Rand Daily Mail*, Johannesburg, August 12, 1978.

[26] Joyce Sikakane, *op. cit.*, p. 24.

[27] *A Survey of Race Relations in South Africa (Annual)*, 1976, p. 84.

[28] Ellen Hellmann, *op. cit.*, p. 7.

[29] Ibid., p. 9.

[30] *The World*, Johannesburg, January 30, 1976.

[31] Heribert Adam, *op. cit.*, p. 99.

[32] *The World*, Johannesburg, January 6, 1976.

[33] *Rand Daily Mail*, Johannesburg, June 21, 1977.

[34] *Poets to the People*, pp. 162-163.

[35] Joyce Sikakane, *op. cit.*, p. 9.

[36] Ellen Hellmann, *op. cit.*, p. 6.

[37] *A Survey of Race Relations in South Africa (Annual)*, 1976, pp. 186-187.

[38] Ibid., p. 187.

[39] *South African Digest*, Pretoria, May 26, 1978.

[40] *Post*, Johannesburg, May 25, 1978.

[41] *Financial Mail*, Johannesburg, June 16, 1978.

[42] *The World*, Johannesburg, July 13, 1977.

[43] *South African Digest*, Pretoria, April 14, 1978.

[44] Ibid.

[45] Ibid., April 21, 1978.

[46] *The World*, Johannesburg, May 27, 1961.

[47] *Rand Daily Mail*, Johannesburg, July 22, 1977.

[48] Francis Wilson, *op. cit.*, p. 33.

[49] Ibil., p. 34.

[50] Ibid.

[51] Ibid., p. 35.

[52] *Financial Mail*, Johannesburg, April 15, 1977.

[53] *Rand Daily Mail*, Johannesburg, July 22, 1977.

[54] *Sunday Times*, Johannesburg, September 5, 1976.

[55] The South African authorities prefer to use the word "homeland" for the rural reservations that were being turned into Bantustans.

[56] *Sunday Times*, Johannesburg, September 5, 1976.

[57] Ellen Hellmann, *op. cit.*, p. 6.

[58] This was the 1964 trial of leaders of the liberation movement arrested in the small town of Rivonia.

[59] Nelson Mandela, *No Easy Walk to Freedom*, Heinemann, London, 1965, p. 185.

[60] *A Survey of Race Relations in South Africa (Annual)*, 1967, p. 210.

[61] *Financial Mail*, Johannesburg, July 30, 1976.

[62] *A Survey of Race Relations in South Africa (Annual)*, 1967, p. 209.

[63] Monica Hunter, *Reaction to Conquest. Effect of Contact with Europeans of the Pondo of South Africa*, Oxford University Press, London, 1961, p. 447.

[64] Monica Hunter, *op. cit.*, p. 447.

[65] *Rand Daily Mail*, Johannesburg, November 20, 1976.

[66] Laura Longmore, *The Dispossessed. A Study of the Sexlife of Women in Urban Areas In and Around Johannesburg*, Corgi Books, London, 1959, p. 19.

[67] Joyce Sikakane, *op. cit.*, pp. 34-35.

[68] Laura Longmore, *op. cit.*, p. 108.

[69] *The African Communist*, London, No. 53, 1973, p. 51.

[70] Ellen Hellman, *op. cit.*, p. 9.

[71] *Rand Daily Mail*, Johannesburg, September 12, 1973.

[72] *A Survey of Race Relations in South Africa (Annual)*, 1969, p. 85.

[73] *Rand Daily Mail*, Johannesburg, January 12, 1974.

[74] *International Defense and Aid Fund. Southern Africa Information Service*, London, January-June 1974, Part I, Table 672.

[75] John Kane-Berman, *op. cit.*, p. 54.

[76] *Rand Daily Mail*, Johannesburg, December 30, 1981.

[77] *Sunday Express*, Johannesburg, December 10, 1978.

[78] *The Star*, Johannesburg, May 28, 1979.

[79] Cited in: Joyce Sikakane, *op. cit.*, p. 35.

[80] John Kane-Berman, *op. cit.*, p. 54.

[81] M. J. Herskovits, *The Human Factor in Changing Africa*, Knopf, London, 1962, p. 276.

[82] Laura Longmore, *op. cit.*, p. 166.

[83] Ibid., p. 140.

[84] Ibid., p. 143.

[85] Sheila T. van der Horst, "The Effect of Industrialisation", *Industrialisation and Race Relations*. Edited by G. Hunter, Oxford University Press, London, 1965, p. 110.

[86] *Population Census 1970. Report No. 02-02-02. Sample Tabulation, Bantu Age, Occupation, Industry, School Standard, Birthplace*, Department of Statistics, Republic of South Africa, Pretoria, March 1973, pp. 3-4; *Addenda*, Table 4.

[87] Lewis Nkosi, *Home and Exile*, Longmans, Green & Co., London, 1979, p. 14.

[88] Jim Hoagland, *South Africa: Civilization in Conflict*, Mifflin, Boston, 1972, p. 95.

[89] Ellen Hellmann, *op. cit.*, p. 5.

[90] James Morris, *op. cit.*, p. 36.

[91] Jim Hoagland, *op. cit.*, p. 96.

[92] Ibid.

[93] Peter Becker, *Tribe to Township*, Panther Books, Herts, 1974, p. 207.

[94] Jim Hoagland, *op. cit.*, pp. 96-97.

[95] *Sechaba*, London, Vol. 11, 2nd Quarter 1977, p. 57.

[96] *The Times*, London, January 19, 1977.

[97] *A Survey of Race Relations in South Africa (Annual)*, 1977, p. 191.

[98] *Rand Daily Mail*, Johannesburg, March 27, 1977.

[99] Ibid.

[100] *Sunday Post*, Johannesburg, October 14, 1979.

Chapter Three

A SYNTHESIS OF TRADITIONALISM AND CONTEMPORANEITY

Detribalisation and Adaptation

Capitalist development in South Africa has brought about the urbanisation of Africans and an inexorable and accelerating erosion of their traditional lifestyle throughout the country, while in the fast-growing cities it has fostered the development of a new way of life in which traditional customs and norms are receding into the background. Will Carr, Manager of the Non-European Affairs Department in Johannesburg, noted in the 1950s that even ordinary peasants coming to the city "very rapidly throw off their rural affiliation and allegiances... it has often astonished me how quickly they become, shall I say, assimilated, integrated, into an urban environment".[1]

In ethnic terms the black population of South Africa consists of Zulu, Xhosa, Tswana, Pedi, Sotho, Shangaan (Tsonga), Swazi, Venda, and Ndebele. But these divisions are applicable mainly to the rural population.

In the cities, to be more exact, in the numerous suburban townships ethnic distinctions are disappearing: a single African community with new social relations is taking shape. In the present-day capitalist city with its industries there is no room for ethnic isolation or division among the people living and working in it. The city shatters and destroys the ethnic partitions in the consciousness of the new urban blacks. Lenin wrote that New York is like a mill that "grinds down national distinctions. And what is taking place on a grand, international scale in New York is also to be seen in *every* big city and industrial township."[2] The same was occurring in South African cities, particularly Johannesburg and the nearly industrial area of Witwatersrand. There "one finds the tendency, typical of industrial areas throughout the world, towards the eradication of specific ethnic distinctions".[3] The intensified planting of apartheid has somewhat slowed this process but it has not stopped it.

This obliteration of tribal and ethnic partitions is described by Ronald Segal, a South African civic personality and writer: "Ever increasing numbers of Africans from every tribe and from every village were drawn to labour on the white farms, in the white mines, and—most dynamically of all—in the white factories and homes of the fast-growing cities. Their shared subjugation speedily and inevitably widened African loyalties from district and tribe to people, or as white South Africans would have it—race. In kitchen and labour barracks, Xhosa and Zulu became together 'Kaffirs', then Natives, recently Bantu, always Africans."[4]

The tendency towards the disappearance of ethnic distinctions in urban areas has been noted by many researchers, including the South African sociologists J. C. de Ridder and Ellen Hellmann. The latter has noted that the loosening of tribal affinities was leading to marriages between people belonging to different tribes.[5]

Urbanisation is not the only cause of detribalisation. Tribalism is on the retreat in the countryside as well: rural inhabitants are coming under the impact of capitalist society. However, in the cities the detribalisation processes are much faster and yield more tangible results. This is seen, in particular, in the fact that the black settling in the city acquires a new mentality that either rejects tribalism generally or adapts its individual features to the new, city conditions.

Considerable attention is focused on the detribalisation processes for they are the most characteristic feature of South African reality, all aspects of which are steeped in apartheid, which, in turn, is a bid to slow down detribalisation and promote retribalisation. Detribalisation is taken to signify also a more general process, namely, the relinquishment by city-dwellers of traditional values, of which tribalism is one. But this is a slower process than the departure from tribalism. Traditional customs are extremely viable even in cities, but they are nonetheless gradually disappearing.

Detribalisation processes are seen very clearly also in the renunciation of traditional values in the Witwatersrand industrial district, where cultural-psychological urbanisation is proceeding most intensively. People of virtually all the

95

ethnic groups inhabiting South Africa live in the townships around Johannesburg and other cities. No single ethnic group is predominant there in numerical terms (as distinct from the Cape Town area, where Xhosa are predominant, or the Durban area, where most of the Africans are Zulus), and this is one of the main factors prompting the eradication of ethnic distinctions. For instance, in 1976 the Soweto population included 176,000 Zulus, 116,000 Tswana, 61,600 Xhosa, 88,200 Sotho, 56,500 Pedi, 40,000 Swazi, 40,000 Shangaan, and 2,000 Venda.

It is symptomatic that ethnic affinities are steadily crumbling in Soweto, which was set up as a complex of locations consistent with the apartheid doctrine. A 1966 study in Soweto showed that 83 per cent of those polled were opposed to keeping the population grouped ethnically.[6] This was also shown by a selective poll in 1970 among high-school graduates in Soweto: 88 per cent of the 200 graduates questioned said they favoured the formation of a single nation regardless of ethnic origin and were opposed to Soweto's division into ethnic zones.[7]

The South African scholar Philip Mayer, who studied the social and ethnic conditions of the African population of the Johannesburg area in the early 1970s, offers the conclusion that "exclusive tribal patriotism seems to have almost died in Soweto".[8]

One of the most abiding customs is that of burying fellow-tribesmen among the graves of ancestors. However, the Pedi, for example, did not insist on compliance with this custom when a fellow-tribesman Elias P. Moretsele, an ANC veteran, died. They agreed with the ANC leaders, who said that Moretsele was profoundly respected by Pedi, Zulus, Xhosa, and other peoples and that he should be buried by all Africans among Africans.[9]

The South African sociologist Monica Hunter (Wilson) writes that "the values in town are European, not tribal. Status depends largely upon wealth and education... The influential men in the town community are the eating-house owners, the teachers, the ministers, and the police sergeants. Knowledge of tribal law, skill in talking cases, renown as a warrior, and even the blood of a chief's family count for comparatively little in town".[10]

Nor are traditional chiefs esteemed by city-dwellers as

they used to be. This negative attitude to them on the part of their fellow-tribesmen and now—of city-dwellers is due, to no little extent, to the fact that chiefs have to have their titles endorsed by the South African government, and this presupposes, naturally, total loyalty to the racist regime. Those who act in opposition to apartheid are deprived of their titles, as was the case with the late Chief Albert J. Luthuli, who was ANC General President.

In 1959 the South African newspaper *New Age* carried an account of a meeting in a Johannesburg township between fellow-tribesmen with the Pondo and Ngkika chiefs Zwelidumile Sigcau and Velile Sandile, who were brought from the Transkei. At first this meeting was postponed from 9 a.m. to 3 p.m. because of the poor attendance. And when people were finally rounded up for the meeting they gave voice to their scorn although they had been warned not to ask questions. Velile Sandile was unable to hold their attention, for the people shouted that they wanted to have nothing to do with chiefs appointed by the government and then sang ANC songs. The chiefs were welcomed solely by a handful of miners brought in a truck from the City-Deep mine compound, where they were working under a short-term contract. These were seasonal workers and had not yet broken their ties with their native village: they were only taking their first steps towards detribalisation and their overall attitude to traditional chiefs was changing slowly.

As for Sowetans, they did not show a different attitude to traditional chiefs in subsequent years either. Nimrod Mkele, director of the Institute for Black Studies, said in 1976 that the Zulu Chief Gatsha Buthelezi, who holds one of the top positions in the tribal hierarchy, visits Soweto (where, as we have already noted, there are some 200,000 Zulus) only if he is provided with a police escort.

Practically all the men and most of the women living in the South African townships work at modern industrial facilities, business offices, and commercial firms. They associate with each other and with Europeans daily in the sphere of capitalist relations. In the course of this regular and long association they see what is for them a new world and accept its realities and values. The South African sociologist Sheila T. van der Horst writes: "Many have shown great eagerness to participate in the new society. They have shown great adaptability, surprising willingness to travel hundreds of miles and to learn its ways, from the complicated ritual of domestic service to the handling of machines and materials in mines and factories. They have quickly learnt the use and value of money, the necessity of punctuality and continuous daily appearance at work. Many have adopted Christianity, achieved some Western education and are asking for more."[1] [1]

Africans (men and women) working as servants in white homes are adapting to city life as, if not more, quickly as factory workers. Many live in the same houses in which they are in contact with whites. In 1964 there were over 57,000 persons (of whom 78.5 per cent were men) employed as servants in Johannesburg alone.

Many of the Africans coming to the cities in search of employment and remaining there for a long time or as permanent residents go through the phase of service in homes. One who went through this stage was the late General Secretary of the South African Communist Party Moses Kotane. His biographer, the South African Communist Brian Bunting, notes that during this period of his life he loved to read, acquiring a hunger for knowledge and extending his mental outlook.[1] [2] For the level of cultural-psychological urbanisation, the African servant in the white home has gone much further than many workers, let alone the migrant workers who come from the villages to work in the mines.

Life in the city constantly exposes the African to European culture and the corresponding lifestyle. Monica Hunter writes in her study: "They [Africans.—V.G.] are about the streets of the European town, buy in European stores, and attend European bioscopes. Many are acute observers of European life, and have a far more intimate knowledge of the round of European daily life, of European interests and ideas... In towns it is smart to be as Europeanized as possible. In their dress men and girls follow European fashions... European titles 'Mr.', 'Mrs.', 'Miss'—are liked and used as respectful terms of reference or address in Xhosa conversation... European games are fashionable. Houses, furniture, and food are all as European as earnings permit."[1] [3]

Urban Africans come under the influence of the mass

media, the more so that their literacy rate is very high. In the early 1960s one in eight Africans in the Johannesburg region read newspapers. According to the 1970 census the literacy rate of the Africans countrywide was 49.5 per cent, and that of urban Africans was 70 per cent. The number of African radio listeners is growing rapidly: within just two years (1967-1968) the proportion of Africans owning radio receivers rose from 26 to 48 per cent.

A significant number of urban Africans prefer to read English-language newspapers and journals, although many read local African-language periodicals as well. A 1968 survey of African readers in South Africa as a whole produced the following data: English-language publications—daily newspapers had 378,000 readers (13 per cent); Sunday newspapers, 442,000 readers (15.2 per cent); journals, 372,000 readers (12.8 per cent); publications of the same category in African languages had respectively 340,000 (11 per cent), 814,000 (28 per cent), and 692,000 readers (23.8 per cent). It should be borne in mind that in the cities the contingent of readers in English is larger than in the country as a whole. The same survey showed that films were viewed by 230,000 people (7.9 per cent).

An extremely interesting and indicative view is offered by *The South African Journal of Economics* about the feelings and tastes of African shoppers: "The greatest inflow is to retailers whose largest percentage of sales is ascribed to whites.They do in fact also attract the African with their wider selection, high-quality goods and lower prices, but their greatest attraction is the very fact that their customers are mainly whites. And what is good enough for whites, is good enough for Africans." Another attraction, the journal says, is that in these shops the Africans can, if only for a fleeting moment, shake off the township atmosphere.[14]

A 1970 poll among Soweto high-school matriculants showed that 68.7 per cent preferred the modern European to the traditional lifestyle.[15] Urban youth are very much inclined to imitate the American lifestyle. The sociologist J. C. de Ridder notes an indication of this: traditional African nicknames are yielding to American, for instance, "California" Serote, "Baby Face" Sebidi, and "Killer" Kumalo. Musical groups adopt unmistakably American names: Boston Boys, Harlem Swingsters, Manhattan

Brothers. The same may be said of sports teams and the names of sports stars. The *tsotsis*, too, have their idols—American gangsters—emulating their manners and methods.

Afro-American socio-political schools of thought exercise a perceptible influence on the political and public life of the black townships. One outcome of this influence was the emergence of the Black Conscience Movement in South Africa in the 1970s.

Many of the urban Africans educated in the West are closer to Afro-Americans in their lifestyles and thinking than to fellow-countrymen living in rural localities.

The Christian religion has been a major factor in the adaptation of Africans. About one-third of the black population of South Africa professes Christianity. Of the various denominations, those with the largest following are first the Methodist Church (more than one million), with the Anglican and Roman Catholic churches in second and third place. A large role in adapting the Africans to European norms of life was played by the missionary schools, which prevailed in the country until the Bantu education system specially designed for Africans was introduced in 1953. In 1951 the different churches were in control of 84.5 per cent (4,961 of a total of 5,870) of the schools for Africans. Many African intellectuals of the senior generation, including prominent leaders of the liberation movement, got their secondary education at missionary schools. The Christian church was widely involved in philanthropic programmes and ran many medical institutions (there were 75 missionary hospitals in 1949).

An indication of the extent the Africans have adapted to life in a modern city is how often they use the services of financial institutions. In 1969, for instance, 24 per cent of the urban Africans, or almost one in four, had a bank account. Ten years earlier only 7 per cent had such accounts. According to polls, other financial operations (insurance and so on) involved from 3 to 11 per cent of the blacks in 1969.

Another major indication is the consumption of modern foodstuffs by Africans: of the total number of surveyed families 78.4 per cent were buying canned and powdered milk, almost 38 per cent—canned fruit, 31.5 per cent—canned vegetables, and almost 40 per cent—canned meat.

The diet of a majority of urbanised Africans (63.4 per cent) includes canned fish although the eating of fish is prohibited among many African peoples. In 1969 *The Times* of London printed data showing how many Africans in South Africa owned durables: 48 per cent had radios and radiolas (only 26 per cent in 1962), 38 per cent had sewing machines, and 3 per cent had electric stoves and refrigerators. In 1979 there were 38 privately-owned cars per 1,000 persons (20 per 1,000 persons in 1956). The South African economist Hobart D. Houghton estimates that in South Africa the vast majority of Africans "have assimilated Western culture to a greater or lesser extent, or have rejected in varying degree their tribal beliefs and practices".[16]

Detribalisation and adaptation are mutually-complementing social processes determining the way of life of urban Africans. The results produced by these processes depend on many circumstances and the conditions of the life of individuals. These are, mainly, economic status, education level, length of residence in the city, character of production activity, and age. Their effectiveness differs not only in the various classes and strata of the black urban population, but also in the case of individuals, for a large role is played by the mentality and worldview of the individual.

Detribalisation processes are to be observed also in the reserves and homelands, where blacks live in accordance with archaic customs. John Gunther noted in 1955: "Ten years ago the gap between university-educated Africans in the towns—doctors, preachers, teachers—and tribal Africans out in the remote veld or the reserves appeared to be unbridgeable, but it is being bridged rapidly. The pace of African advance, despite all obstacles, has been astonishing."[17]

Detribalisation and adaptation processes are going on in diverse areas of the life of urban Africans. They are seen in family relations, the evolution of religious views and the work of religious organisations, culture and, lastly, sociopolitical life.

The Urban Family and Its Problems

The family is a unit of society and, quite naturally, its forms and functions are predicated by the character of the prevailing social relations. For its part, the family influences the life of society, including the cultural development and socio-political consciousness of its members. Under the apartheid regime the urban African family is disadvantaged and this affects the mentality of its members and, in the final analysis, their attitude towards this regime.

The urban African family faces not only discrimination. It is denied many rights. The racist minority ruling the country and holding that all cities are "white", denies to the African family even the right to live in the cities. This springs directly from apartheid's basic postulate, which says that the black lives in the "white" city temporarily, only as long as his labour is needed there. But the family is a serious stabilising factor, reinforcing the African's urban status, fosters his cultural and psychological urbanisation and, consequently, comes into conflict with apartheid. Back in 1929, the then Prime Minister Jan C. Smuts spoke against permitting the families of black workers to migrate to the "white man's" town, saying that "the tribal bond is snapped and the traditional system falls into decay" when this happens, adding that "it is this migration of the native family, of the females and children, to the farms and the towns which should be prevented. As soon as this migration is permitted the process commences which ends in the urbanized detribalized native."[18]

In 1970 there were 75,307 officially registered families in Soweto,[19] while the actual number of members of these families was close to 500,000. In addition, there were at least another 500,000 persons, many of whom came under the category of "bachelors", although these were people with families. Some left their families in the homelands, while others lived with their families but their residence in Soweto was not permitted officially.

The numerical growth of black families living in the cities—Soweto being a prime example—is artificially constrained by racist discriminative legislation. Those families that have taken shape and been able to remain in the city are under constant harassment and face the threat of eviction—of the whole family or one of its members—and this is a factor causing families to fall apart. "In the face of these restrictions and harassments normal family life has become a luxury which few enjoy."[20]

The basic instruments of the apartheid system to prevent black families from migrating to the cities or to evict from the cities those families that have settled there is the system of Influx Control and the Pass Laws.

In 1970 there were over 140,000 "bachelors" and "singles" (of whom about 100,000 were men) in Johannesburg and its suburbs. Ellen Hellmann writes "that there are many men who would like to have their wives and children join them but are prevented from doing so by the pass and influx laws is incontestable... The necessity for some form of influx control may be debatable. But there cannot be any debate about the gross injustice of denying a man who is legally qualified to be in Johannesburg the right to have his wife join him. A country that does this gives the lie to its professed concern for the sanctity of family life."[2][1]

A man marrying a woman with official permission to live in the city may bring her to the city only if he has a home for a family. Given the acute housing shortage in Soweto, this is a serious problem. If the wife had formerly lived in a rural area, even if it was "white", it is extremely difficult for her to obtain permission to join her husband. This is practically impossible if she is from a reserve. On top of this, to obtain permission to settle in a house in Soweto a man must be married. This forms a vicious circle. Many men married in accordance with traditional custom find a way out by contracting a new marriage with a woman who is permitted to live in the city. In Soweto these were called "shilling" marriages (the payment made to the office of the Bantu Affairs Commissioner for formalising this marriage). The existence of such "marriages" (the number of which, for understandable reasons, it is impossible to establish) does not contribute to the durability of the family bonds of urban blacks.

There are many families who have lived in Soweto for years and brought up their children there, but the wife, the children, and aged parents have no legal status and are constantly under the threat of eviction to a homeland. In many instances it turns out that even there they have lost the right of legal residence. Some instances of this are given by Francis Wilson.[2][2]

"Mrs. E. N. was born in Nqutu, Natal. In 1961 she married Mr. K. B. who qualifies to live in the prescribed area of Johannesburg in terms of Section 10 (1) (b) of Act No. 25 of 1945. In 1963 she came to Johannesburg to live with her husband and has lived with him ever since. There are three children of the marriage, all born in Johannesburg. One is six years old, one four years old and the youngest fourteen months.

"In 1963 when she first came to Johannesburg her husband applied for permission for her to remain with him in his brother's house in Orlando East. This was refused and on 14th May, 1963, her reference book was stamped that she was not permitted to remain in or work in Johannesburg. She then went to Nqutu on a short visit but says that she was told there that she could no longer live there and should go to her husband in Johannesburg. She came back to Johannesburg and lived unlawfully here with her husband.

"In 1968 her husband applied for a house of his own in Soweto. This was refused because his wife had no permission to live in Johannesburg. Her reference book was endorsed to the effect that she was warned to leave the prescribed area of Johannesburg within 72 hours on 30th July, 1968.

"However she remained in Johannesburg with her husband. In 1970 her husband went to Nqutu to see the Bantu Affairs Commissioner there. He says he was told verbally that his wife and children cannot live there.

"Mrs. N. and her children are displaced people. They have nowhere to go. They wish to continue living with their husband and father but the law forbids them to do so. Although the children were all born in Johannesburg Mr. B. cannot put their names on a house permit. He cannot have a house of his own because his wife is not lawfully in Johannesburg. His children will have to face grave difficulties when they reach 16 years of age and have to take reference books."

"Mrs. M. P. L. was born on a farm in an area which is now part of Soweto. She cannot prove the fact of her birth there but has a letter from the daughter of the white owner of the farm who knows she lived on the farm as a very small child until the Johannesburg City Council bought it. She lived there from her birth in 1936 until 1952. She then moved to the Moroka Shelters with her sister. She can prove employment in Johannesburg from 1952 to 1960 and thereafter has a variety of receipts and doctors' letters showing that she has been continuously resident in Johannesburg from 1960 until the present date. She is lawfully married to a man who qualifies to remain in the prescribed area of Johannesburg in terms of Section 10 (1) (b) of the 1945 Act and she ordinarily resides with him in Soweto where he has a lodger's permit. When she married him in 1962 they tried to get permission for her to live with him and her book was stamped that she was not permitted to remain in or to take up employment in the proclaimed area of Johannesburg. There are two children of the marriage."

"The three sisters Agnes, Maggie and Joyce are the daughters of a man and a woman who both qualify to remain in the prescribed area of Johannesburg in terms of Section 10 (1) (b) of the Act. They are 25, 23 and 18 years old respectively. They were all born in Sophiatown in Johannesburg which is now demolished and there is no way of proving this statement but they lived with their mother at her employers' house from the time they were born until they each in turn reached school age when they were sent to school in Rustenburg. They came back to their mother during school holidays and the mother's employer has certified to this in writing. Their parents were eventually allotted a house in Soweto but failed to put their daughters' names on the residential permit. All the girls have lived continuously in Johannesburg since the time of their birth except when they were at school. On 28th July 1971 they were all warned to leave the area within 72 hours. An endorsement to this effect was stamped on the temporary identification certificates when they applied for their first reference books."

In accordance with the apartheid doctrine, the racist discriminative laws are designed to deurbanise Africans, to turn them into homeless and familyless migrants. Their operation is such that even if a black family lives in the township there will always be a loophole for evicting this family, destroying it by the eviction of any of its members, or at least permanently bringing administrative pressure to bear upon it. One of these laws, as we have already noted, allows denying widows or divorcees the right to rent or own a home. It the words of one such woman, "some officials demand that the widow must come to their offices a day after the funeral of her husband to discuss the question of the house... The widow is not entitled to the tenancy of the house."[2 3] At best, such families may continue living in the township as subtenants. Even if a widow or divorcee is permitted to remain in the city, her children and other dependents must be sent to a reserve.

In the townships there are very many families whose only breadwinner is the woman (widow, divorcee, or unmarried mother). At the close of the 1960s women were the heads of 41 per cent of the families in the Eastern Native Township, which was one of the oldest suburbs of Johannesburg (this township was likewise being demolished).

Even in Soweto, where families without men are subjected to harsher harassment, such families formed 14 per cent in 1962 and 22 per cent in 1970 of the total number of families. It is indicative that only one-fifth of the one-parent families are tenants of houses, while as many as one-third of such families are subtenants. This is also confirmed by Joyce Sikakane in her book about Soweto: "In Soweto alone there are thousands of one-parent families. Some are separated from their spouses by the influx control laws; some are widows--men are the main victims of murder; and some are local women who have become pregnant by those thousands of migrant single-sex hostel dwellers... The rigours of apartheid laws have so disrupted normal African life that the dignity of marriage has lost its deeper meaning in the eyes of the youth of the ghetto."[2 4]

Thus, in addition to the serious economic difficulties encountered by the black family in cities governed by apartheid laws aimed at uprooting this family, it has to cope with practically insurmountable obstacles. The unrest caused by this situation among blacks is, naturally, directed against the entire apartheid system, against the racist white minority, which so obviously and ruthlessly denies Africans the right to a normal family life in the city.

The shaping of the worldview of urban blacks today, the restructuring of their way of mentality in the course of urbanisation also depend on the process by which the traditional family becomes a modern urban family. This is also to be seen in the changed forms and functions of the family---this concerns the family as a whole, its individual members, and the relationship between them.

First and foremost, it should be noted that black urban family is, as a social unit, entirely different from the former extended or large family of tribalist society. It is no longer a traditional family, a unit of a large traditional group, with its members having clearly defined duties and linked to each other by kinship. As a rule, the urban family is small (five or six persons). This is a nuclear family consisting of the mother, the father, and children; it is a separate unit among many thousands of similar units.

The changes in the forms of the family and in the functions of its individual members are due chiefly to changed economic conditions in which the black family finds itself. The large family has disintegrated on account of the widespread system of migrant labour. Relatives go to various places in search of earnings, and the links to them weaken or, as is often the case, break off altogether. People belonging to different kindred groups live in close proximity to each other in urban areas. Neighbours form haphazardly, regardless of their wish to preserve and maintain relations of kinship, for the acute housing shortage does not give people the opportunity of choosing where to live. Nor is anything changed by the "ethnic zoning" in the new Soweto townships, the purpose of which is to retribalise the urban population. Even in such townships families are usually nuclear and separated from each other despite belonging to one and the same ethnic group.

In the townships affinity to a kindred group loses much of its significance. Here the modern family becomes the predominant social unit. Yet if bonds of kinship remain, the functions of these bonds undergo a modification in the new conditions and are expressed in, for example, mutual assistance in looking for a job or in the striving to associate with people having similar interests.

The changes that have taken place in the functional relationships between members of the family are even more glaring. While in the traditional black family there was economic mutual dependence among its members and balanced mutual duties ensuring the viability of the entire family, the situation is entirely different in the modern urban family. Economic mutual dependence has given way to economic independence, which now largely determines the relations between members of the urban family.

In the city the economic factor determines the life of the family and of the black community as a whole. "Every requirement has to be paid for in money, which has become the basic determinant of Soweto living."[2][5] Those who have the opportunity, work and earn money and thereby acquire a measure of financial independence in the family. "Money has provided the impulse for urban African individualisation, individualisation of the bonds of family and kin, as well as individualisation of the individual. Financial independence has caused a rapid dissolution, so marked that some of the fundamental elements of traditional life seem to have vanished in the new setting of the urban environment, while remnants of the old institutions, where they still survive, may have become destitute of their original meaning and character, or been modified to reconcile African and European divergences in tradition."[2][6]

Entirely new relations have taken shape between the members of the urban family—between the husband and wife, and between parents and children. These changes, springing from the new economic conditions in which the African family has found itself, must be considered in some detail, because the new relationships within the family differ basically from the relationships in the traditional family and have led to the appearance of new forces in public and political life in South Africa.

In the city the black woman has acquired the opportunity of working for a wage, of earning money. To be more exact, this has become indispensable. In most African families one breadwinner, as we have noted, cannot provide a minimum or even poverty-line living. This compels women to look for employment. The number and proportion of working women are growing in the townships, and this reflects the deteriorating economic condition of the Africans and, to some extent, the emancipation of women. The 1960 census showed that 15 per cent of the total number of African women were economically active, but in 1970 the proportion of economically active women rose to 25 per cent. In the cities a large proportion of women work for wages (37 per cent); true, the majority are in service in white homes (65 per cent). The manufacturing industry, in which modern technology permits using female labour, employs 8 per cent of the total number of black urban women. Most of these women are employed in the food, sewing, and textile industries. Seven per cent of the women are teachers or nurses (in surveys they are classified as professionals).

"The possibility, or necessity, of wage-earning for women has raised their status and given them a considerable degree of independence and authority."[27] While the male has always been the dominant figure in the traditional family, in the city his power and authority have visibly declined. "Today in urban areas women do things that in tribal areas they would never be permitted to do. For example, a wife in town sits in the dining-room with her husband and converses with visitors on all subjects. She attends parties, cinemas, meetings, and even takes part in labour strikes; she does everything that her husband does. She belongs to clubs and associations. She goes out to work, and may be absent for days on end, only returning home during the weekends. She earns good money, often more than her husband. She may open her own savings account without his knowledge. If she is a professional woman such as a nurse, a teacher or a social worker, she may marry a man of inferior education, even a labourer, and she certainly never abides by his decisions in such cases."[28]

Unquestionably, not all women (nor to one and the same extent) have freed themselves from the traditional power of husbands and become equal members of the family and the urban community. The extent of emancipation enjoyed by women depends on many factors, the most important of which are the family's material condition and the education level of the woman concerned. Women of middle class families in Soweto are more independent. An equal or almost equal status of women in such families is regarded as normal and does not give rise to conflicts in the family or society. But in most urban proletarian families, that had not been long under the cultural and psychological influence of urbanisation, the situation is more complex. In these families the tendency towards the emancipation of women clashes with strong patriarchal traditions and this makes contradictions and conflicts inevitable.

The changes that have taken place in the status of women in the family are to be seen also in the role played by them in social and political life. Since the late 1940s and the early 1950s, black women have been increasingly active in the common struggle against racial discrimination and the racist regime. The scale of their actions grew visibly in the mid-1950s when the government made it mandatory for African women to have their passes on their persons at all times. In October 1955, for example, 2,000 women demonstrated in Pretoria against the pass law. In the following year, on August 9 (subsequently, this became South African Women's Day), 20,000 women protested in the same city, Pretoria. Many of the African women's actions against racism and apartheid were organised by the ANC Women's League. After the ANC was banned, the Federation of South African Women began to play a prominent role in the progressive women's movement.

African women have been active also in the trade unions, especially in the 1940s-1950s. In those years they were not required to carry a pass, and this circumstance gave them the opportunity to set up trade unions. The fact of the matter is that the basic law regulating labour relations in industry, including the formation of trade unions—the Appeasement in Industry Act No. 11 of 1924—excluded from its jurisdiction those obliged to carry passes, in other words, African men, thus denying them the right to organise in trade unions. That was when trade unions were formed in the textile and sewing industries.

Approximately the same socio-economic factors that changed the status of women in the black urban family led to a change in the relations between parents and children, to be more exact between fathers and children, even children of school age. Two main factors are debilitating if not totally eliminating the traditional power of fathers over their children. These factors are financial independence and the level of education, and they undercut paternal control. "Economic changes are at the root of the loss of parental control but there are other supplementary causes. The fact that young people have learned more of European ways than their parents, either through attending school or working in towns, is apt to make them feel superior, they understand things which their fathers do not understand; therefore, they are 'wiser'."[29]

The decline of parental authority is the result of the dying away of the ancestor cult. In the traditional family obedience of juniors to seniors was mandatory and, to some extent, based on the fear to anger or displease the *ithongo* ("ancestral spirit"). But in town "the ancestor cult has considerably less influence than under tribal conditions".[30] In Soweto most of the young people do not recognise the authority of their parents as set by tradition and have, to one extent or another, gone out of parental control. This is now true not only of the middle classes, who are firmly settled in the towns, but also for working-class families that are usually less sedentary.

In the townships it is no longer obligatory to pay *lobolo* (bride money). Urban young people speak out openly and quite sharply about this custom. *The World* carried a letter from a reader named S. T. Rapopo, saying: "Lobolo impoverishes young African couples and robs them of what little possessions they may have. Gagarin's space flight shows the world is heading towards progress. So why do we Africans drift backwards. Love is not bound to lobolo."[31] In 1963 12 per cent of the marriages (of a total of 1,514) did not involve the payment of bride money.

Polygamy, which was widely practised under traditional conditions, is now becoming rare. A survey made in Soweto in 1962 showed that only three marriages out of 151 were polygamous, and that in only one family in the entire township did the husband have more than one wife.

The condition of the African urban family is characterised by, above all, instability and a greater proneness for conflict. The disintegration of traditional family life in the modern city is exacerbating social troubles and injustices. The apartheid regime and racial discrimination are aggravating these problems.

Christianity and Traditional Cults

A study of cultural-psychological urbanisation and the formation of urban blacks' mentality, must necessarily take note of religion, which is one of the important forms of social consciousness.

111

Preached by white missionaries, Christianity failed to draw Africans entirely to itself. Blacks converted to Christianity began leaving the white man's church as early as the close of the nineteenth century. The first sects and independent churches appeared, one of which was the Ethiopian Church, which has many followers to this day.

The religious sectarian movement was, in a way, a form of anti-colonial protest at a time when black political organisations were lacking or only just emerging. There were about 30 African independent churches or Afro-Christian sects in South Africa in 1913 and as many as 78 only five years later. In the closing years of the nineteenth and early years of the twentieth century independent African churches or, in any case, some of them performed the functions of the earliest political organisations.[32] Political objectives were a high priority in their programmes.

Subsequently, in South Africa as a whole these denominations and sects basically abandoned the political struggle and began to adjust to the racist state of the white minority in order to win the government's recognition. Official recognition brought quite a few benefits, for example, the possibility of occupying a plot of land for a church in an urban area.

The number of Afro-Christian sects and churches in South Africa continued to grow. By 1971 there were over 2,500 and these had a total of nearly four million followers.[33] Other estimates place the number of followers at six million.[34] J. C. de Ridder writes that in the Johannesburg area there were 2,254 officially non-recognised religious sects in 1961.[35]

It is not hard to explain this swift growth of independent Afro-Christian sects. In the officially recognised churches the majority of the congregation consists of whites, and the teaching preached in such churches is permeated with the ideology of racism. This is to be seen most vividly in the activities of the Dutch Reformed Church, which is in a predominant position in South Africa. The white man's Christian churches have proved to be alien to the Africans, particularly to the urban blacks. "Many of the younger generation consciously associate Christianity with white supremacy and see Christianity as a form of exploitation. They refer to ministers as shrewd businessmen who live off the blood of poor widows."[36]

The importance and role of the official churches have fallen in the eyes of urban Africans. Joyce Sikakane writes: "Because of racial discrimination and the fake policy of Africanisation of the churches, the established churches like the Lutheran, Anglican, Roman Catholic, Presbyterian and others are losing out and failing to attract new members. Sowetonians as workers reserve Sunday as a day to do household chores like washing and cleaning, visiting the sick and attending weddings and funerals. Today, if a Sowetonian priest wants to eat he must conduct more weddings and burial services. At such services the Sowetonians willingly contribute to the family of God."[37]

This view about the influence of Western Christian churches being on the wane is shared by other researchers. "Christianity holds a prestige value because of its association with the white community; but at the same time it is resented because of the exclusiveness of white culture. Many African Christians feel a vague sense of betrayal: if it is slavery to speak the conqueror's language then is it not slavery of a much higher order to worship his God? And the Christian God is unmistakably a white God."[38]

The attitudes of the various Christian churches to apartheid are by no means indistinguishable and, besides, with the passage of time they had undergone significant changes. The situation where in one form or another the Christian churches favoured white supremacy, where, as the ANC President Oliver Tambo put it, "for generations, the church and apartheid in South Africa have been compatible bedfellows",[39] has gradually receded.

Many churches have gone over from making individual statements with cautious or half-hearted condemnations of apartheid and racial discrimination to denouncements of apartheid and even calling it a heresy. Anti-apartheid sentiment among church circles was reflected in an appeal to South African churches signed by 151 theologians at the close of 1985. Known as the Kairos Document, this appeal calls apartheid an unjust system and the Theology of State, which vindicates and asserts that system, "heretical and blasphemous". Whereas formerly only a few religious leaders—for example, Father Trevor Huddleston, Bishop Ambrose Reeves, and Canon John Collins—spoke out against racial discrimination and apartheid, today the majority of clergymen are opposed to apartheid. Even in the Dutch Reformed Church there is now an African "daughter" church that censures apartheid. An article in the journal *Mayibuye* says that "there is a new breed of church leaders, mostly black, who seek and are determined to live by the rules of their professed faith. Those rules have always been wholly irreconcilable with rules which define and regulate the apartheid system".[40] These leaders include Bishop Desmond Tutu, Alan Boesak, and Beyers Naude. In June 1977 when Africans marked the first anniversary of the Soweto revolt, special services were held in some churches in Soweto for the victims of police terror. At least 2,000 people were packed into the Regina Mundi Church. "You hear them singing in there?" remarked a reporter assigned to the commemoration story. "That's no hymn. It's a freedom song. This is a carbon copy of what happened last year."[41] A young patriot named Solomon Mahlangu was executed two years later, in 1979. This crime roused unmitigable indignation. Once again the Sowetans decided to gather and express their feelings where they were still permitted and where they used to gather—the Regina Mundi Church. But this time there was no service, and it had to be held elsewhere. The reason for this was a special decision by the Roman Catholic Diocese of Johannesburg "to be selective in its granting permission for prayer meetings to be held at Regina Mundi Church in Soweto and particularly to restrict the use of the church to religious purposes". The *Rand Daily Mail* reported that this decision shocked Soweto's residents and quoted P. Mzaidume, a veteran Soweto educationalist, as saying that "it was unfortunate that the catholic church had, at this point in time, taken the decision to ban secular meetings at the church. 'We regarded it as a progressive church, which we had identified with our struggle'."[42]

The influence exercised by the Western churches is nonetheless still quite strong in cities, including Soweto. A poll taken there in 1972 showed that 92 per cent of the people questioned belonged to a Christian Church. Out of every ten Sowetans, roughly three belonged to an independent Afro-Christian church, one or two to the Lutheran or Anglican church, one to the Roman Catholic or Dutch Reformed church, and yet another out of these ten was a member of a church society formed by whites. The same poll showed that "at most, 40 per cent of the community in Soweto in fact have active contact with the church".[43]

There are many churches in Soweto, their number having more than doubled during the seventies. In 1970 Soweto had 143 churches, but in 1981 there were 330. Denominations that have their own prayer houses are registered with the authorities, for otherwise they would not have been given the land plot on which to build their churches. This large number of churches is a sign not only of their popularity in Soweto but also of the benevolence of the authorities to them. In addition to registered denominations with their own churches there are in Soweto over 150 unregistered denominations and sects that usually gather in private houses or schools.

A. G. Schutte, a South African researcher, reports that in Soweto he found some 35 secret prayer groups (sephiri groups) and that there were many more. He believes that the number of such groups is particularly large in the townships of Senoane, Jabavu, and Diepkloof. Schutte located five leaders of such secret prayer groups by questioning the inhabitants of 108 houses in Moroka township. These groups are the selfsame African Christian sects with the distinction that they put a heavier emphasis on the African traditional element expressed in the practice of witchcraft. They see themselves as "the successors to the first secret prayer group founded by Christ and his Apostles".[44]

This abundance of churches and religious sects in Soweto, despite the departure of the Africans from the Christian religion of the whites (although this departure is partially responsible for the appearance of divisive denominations and sects), is due, in the first place, to the circumstance that people are looking for some moral comfort, for a distraction from their daily burden of poverty, unceasing racial oppression, police harassment, and chronic uncertainty about the future.

Religious rituals and customs provide them with such opportunity. Separatist or independent churches provide considerable information enabling one to understand the Sowetan way of life and the influences at work shaping the mentality of Soweto's inhabitants. In Soweto, as in other townships, they are the basic form of the people's religious unity. They make the biggest imprint on black urban culture.

At the early stages of their existence, the principal aim of the Afro-Christian churches was to be independent of the Western church of the whites. But the situation changed towards the middle of the twentieth century. For most of the present Afro-Christian sects a distinctive characteristic is no longer their striving to be separate (to say nothing of their political demands on behalf of Africans) but rather the opposite—conformism, a quest to adapt to white minority rule. These changes are due, in large part, to the pressure that is being constantly brought to bear on the Afro-Christian churches by the authorities and the official white churches.

Many of the present Afro-Christian sects are Pentecostal organisations (Zion and apostolic). The sects in Soweto are predominantly Pentecostal. Most belong to the Zion Christian Church, which is, in political terms, the most conservative force. It has a long history. The first Zion Church in South Africa was founded by one Büchler in 1895 in Johannesburg; other Zion churches sprang up in Orange Free State Province and in Zululand—these were also headed by whites. But the overall leader was the American missionary Daniel Bryant. In the 1970s and the 1980s this denomination attracted large masses of people, perceptibly whittling down the influence of the Ethiopian Church. It enjoys considerable influence in many places, including Soweto. To illustrate: a rally in Soweto in September 1981 drew nearly 25,000 parishioners. Its annual rally in 1985 in Moria, near Pietermaritzburg, attracted more than two million people and was addressed by the Prime Minister P. W. Botha himself.

The sect is headed by a "bishop", followed by a "vice-bishop", treasurer, priests, deacons, and preachers. Each sect has its own hierarchy with clearly defined functions at each level. Most of the sects have no premises. Prayer meetings are attended mostly by persons living in the vicinity, and for that reason sects are subdivided into congregations consisting of persons living in specific places. A congregation usually consists of between 20 and 30 persons. The female members of the sect (manyano) have

116

their own leaders. Women comprise the majority of the followers of Afro-Christian sects in Soweto.

Almost all sects have their "prophets", who "prophesy" and "heal". A study of 200 sects in Soweto showed that 175 of them each had at least one "prophet".[4][5]

The most typical function of all these sects is that of "healing"; the possibility of being "healed" is one of the biggest attraction. For example, two sects in Soweto owe 83 per cent of their membership to this attraction.[4][6] The search for healing or the failure to be healed often makes people leave one sect and join another. The composition of these sects thus changes quite quickly.

Martin West, who studied the activities of Afro-Christian sects in Soweto, gives an idea of the composition of a typical congregation of 25 adults: two-thirds were women; 72 per cent were over 41 years old; 11 said their native tongue was Zulu, seven Xhosa, five Sotho, one Tswana, and one Venda; 64 per cent lived exactly in this township or nearby, five had never gone to school, another five had studied for not more than four years, and none had a full high school education.[4][7] So, the members of the various sects are predominantly women, or people in the senior age groups, and their education level is low; ethnically they are heterogeneous, in other words, in urban conditions residence has become a more important factor uniting people in a sect than ethnic affiliation.

As we have already noted, most of the sects and churches in Soweto are Pentecostal, with varying degrees of syncretism, i.e., they combine Christian dogmas and rituals with traditional African beliefs and customs. This is the outcome mainly of the African's dual status in the capitalist city.

To one extent or another many Africans in Soweto adhere to their traditional tribal values. On the one hand, they have not been overly exposed to the cultural-psychological processes of urbanisation and, on the other, the situation created by the racist regime makes them cling to these values. A significant proportion of Sowetans are still unable or not prepared to renounce, for instance, ancestral worship. Unlike the Western Christian churches, the Afro-Christian sects do not require this of them. More, in these sects they find the possibility for combining Christian

dogmas about Christ, the Holy Spirit, and so on with tribalistic, pagan customs and rituals. "The independent
churches stand in a position somewhere between Western
Christianity and tribal beliefs."[48] Hundreds of separatist
sects practise "different forms of worship with varying
degrees of syncretism between Christian beliefs, ancestral
worship and magic".[49]

Magic is an important element of the religious practices
of the Afro-Christian sects and churches. B. I. Sharevskaya,
a Soviet author, is right when she notes that "magic... belongs... entirely to religion, of which it is a fundamental
and genetic element" and that "in African religious beliefs
considerable significance is attached to magic".[50] These
conclusions have been borne out by studies conducted by
South African scholars. On the basis of a survey of 2,500
urban blacks J. C. de Ridder writes of "the existence of
strong beliefs in witchcraft and the power of magic".[51]
Laura Longmore is of the same opinion: "Magic provides
a far more satisfactory outlet for the perplexities confronting him [the African urban dweller.—V. G.], and it is to
magic that he turns for aid in emergency."[52] Ridder's conclusions, drawn on the basis of statistics for the 1950s,
may be challenged as being obsolete. However, reports
about the Sowetans taking witchcraft seriously are received
in the 1980s as well. For example, the *Sechaba* reported in
October 1985 that a certain Pauline Ndou of Chiawelo
township was accused of sorcery. A crowd of 200, mostly
young people, actually believing that this woman was a
sorceress, manhandled her brutally.[53]

In some studies it is noted that far from diminishing, the
African's belief in magic and witchcraft grows stronger
when he comes into contact with Western civilisation
and culture. In the cities he encounters problems that are
new to him and the new and practically insurmountable
difficulties resulting from white minority domination.
J. C. de Ridder draws attention to the importance of African magic in urban areas: "... the witchdoctor, in his various forms, is a respected and valued member of urban society. Witchcraft and sorcery are powerful urban institutions.
The witchdoctor is consulted regularly by many Africans
who are dissatisfied with the results of European medicine
or legal judgments. Urbanization has had remarkably little

118

effect upon the practice of witchcraft: witchdoctors flourish in urban areas."[5][4]

This mention of medicine is not accidental. Sorcery is linked not only to the enduring worship of ancestors. As well as "prophets", who do their healing with their hands or in other, more complicated ways, and in addition to sorcerers and fortune-tellers--*dingaka* (men) and *sangoma* (women)--"prophesying and healing" by divine inspiration, there is yet another "branch" of sorcery that attracts urban Africans. It is "native" or "African" medicine prescribed by *nyanga*, who are medicine men specialising mainly in medicinal herbs. This treatment influences as much the patient's state of mind as his physical state, for it is accompanied by rituals, incantations, and so on.

The trust that many urban blacks put in traditional medicine and the *nyanga* is due not only to the force of tradition and cultural backwardness or distrust for European doctors and medicines (this is what Laura Longmore tends to believe).[5][5] There is a much simpler reason: the African just does not have the money to pay the doctor's and hospital bills. Soweto has only one hospital, the Baragwanath. It is acutely short of policlinics and doctors. The *nyanga* are always around and much cheaper.

In the cities African sorcery is undergoing modifications as it adapts to the new conditions. "New magic is developed to meet the new needs."[5][6] New materials are used alongside those in traditional usage, and these are now bought in European shops. The "technologies" of witchcraft are changing: a spell may now be cast by, for example, mail. But the most important thing is that there now are new aims and a need for more subtle sorcery. The urban black cannot influence the forces and factors on whose operation depend his wellbeing, economic status, residence in the "white" city, and even safety. Having no other way of influencing them he often resorts to sorcery, going for help to the *dingaka*, *sangoma*, or *nyanga*. Finding himself in a desperate situation, he believes that magic can help him get a good job, succeed in a small business, rent a room, in other words, get whatever is needed by an urban dweller.

For the African proletarian in the South African city the biggest problem is to find work, for employment not only gives the means of subsistence but legalises his residence in the city. Unemployment is, perhaps, the principal evil for him, and to counter this evil he has recourse to sorcery. The medicines used in this case, Monica Hunter writes, are comparable with those which give hope during drought. There are new applications for magic formerly used to escape danger in battle: it is now used to escape danger from the police, who are seen as a formidable menace to the African living in the "white" city.[57]

The sorcerers themselves have changed. *The World* carried an item, "Sangoma in High Heels", about a certain Beatrice Nkosi, then 35, who was described as "the most successful on the Reef". She wore smart European clothes, owned a stereo receiver of the latest type, and had a bank account. "A spirit came to me," she said, "and gave me as a gift to help people in distress... Until 1957 I was a smart factory girl." But then a "spirit" came to her in a dream and told her to go to a woman in Daveyton. She studied under that woman for a year, and now had her own business.[58] The same newspaper wrote about the "business" of another *sangoma* well-known in Soweto—Emma Maluleka of Orlando township.

The urban sorcerers are in many respects different from their colleagues of older days, when society was still traditional. To illustrate: seven witchdoctors and herbalists, headed by one Chauke, formed a registered company in 1961. They hoped they would eventually control and administer the affairs of *dingaka* throughout the country and determine the limits of treatment provided by them so that where necessary cases would be sent on to medical practitioners or hospitals. "We," Chauke said, "know there are some illnesses which must be dealt with by doctors trained to Western standards." He added that his company would advertise sorcery and for this purpose it would arrange lectures, demonstrations, and film shows of *dingaka* at work.[59]

An association of *dingaka* has been functioning in South Africa for many years (in the Transvaal it had 500 members in 1961[60]). In 1935 this association sent a delegation to a conference called by the African National Congress to consider the calamitous plight of Africans in South Africa and work out ways of resisting the enactment of new discriminative laws. Diverse public organisations championing the rights of the black population, including the Communist

120

Party of South Africa and an association of African trade unions, were represented at this conference, which was held in Pimville township.

The activities of officially recognised Christian churches, the innumerable unofficial Afro-Christian sects and churches with their bishops and "prophets", and the witch-doctors, sorcerers, and herbalists are a major factor shaping the urban black's mentality. The psychological influence that religion has on the African diverts him from actively protesting against the reality he lives in, reconciles him to the existing orders, and gives him no more than fleeting comfort.

In Soweto, as in other townships, the various Afro-Christian sects and churches provide the inhabitants of these ghettos with a religious-emotional diversion from the bitter realities of their day-to-day lives. Moreover, they bring people together to form cooperative groups, which fulfill diverse functions, including some outside the strictly religious sphere. Members of sects have some common interests. Religious services and prayer meetings are a form of association.

This is particularly the case with the smaller religious groups of 20-30 persons. The congregation is described as an "effective social group" by Monica Hunter, who, on the basis of a study of life in East London township, writes that "friendships tend to be made within these groups".[61] On the same subject, Laura Longmore notes that "many people no longer take church services seriously, but consider the church as a sort of club or association. It was a place for meeting friends and having a sort of respite from the daily round, where clothes and finery could be worn."[62] Congregations give their members not only the opportunity to communicate but, most importantly, provide them with mutual support both moral and material. Martin West believes that this is the strongest attraction of the sects and separatist churches, which thereby offer people the opportunity of forming "supportive groups in the urban situation". "Soweto," he writes, "is large and heterogeneous; its people are by and large poor and voiceless, and their surroundings are drab and uniform. The independent churches in this situation are important voluntary organisations which, because of the small size of their congregations,

121

are able to act as reference groups in relation to the wider society."[63]

Mutual aid in the congregation is particularly important and needed in extraordinary, critical situations in the life of its members, for instance, during an illness. Moreover, the congregation undertakes some of the functions that used to be performed by clans—marriage, burial, sacrifices to ancestral spirits.

The sects and churches give some people the opportunity to fulfill ambitions, to stand out among their fellows, to become leaders. Also, they find a place for themselves in the leadership hierarchy of the sects. This desire to stand out, to be a leader is, Laura Longmore believes, one of the reasons there are so many sects. "In the first place many people in the churches want to be leaders,"[64] she writes. Even in cases where the West European churches condemn racial discrimination, they remain white, missionary churches, in which most of the hierarchy are white. Many former African priests preferred to leave their subordinate position in these churches and become "bishops" or "vice-bishops" in independent separatist churches.

Thus, the spread of Afro-Christian sects and independent churches and the·role and character of their functions are a reaction to the distinctive urban situation created by the South African racist regime in the black townships, notably in Soweto. "Given a situation where all the main avenues of African political protest have been closed, the sects provide an opportunity of letting off steam and giving vent to racial resentments. It is a sociological process not unlike that which gave rise to the Black Muslim movement in the USA."[65] As a matter of fact, it is reported that Mohammedanism is becoming increasingly widespread among urban blacks, including Sowetans.[66]

The influence of separatist sects and churches, and also of Western missionary churches on the minds and hearts of urban Africans should not be overrated. Religiousity, mysticism, belief in magic, and the ancestral cult are all there. But what disturbs the inhabitants of Soweto (as of all other black townships) most is the ghetto way of life forced upon them by the apartheid regime. Neither the Christian churches nor the sects can give Sowetans comfort or make their life easier. During and after the rising in Soweto it was seen that some religious organisations supported this struggle. The factor of religion thus has only a limited influence on the worldview and spiritual life of the Sowetans. The central factor is the resistance to the hated racist regime with its discrimination and oppression.

Political and Public Organisations

Religious sects and churches are only one type of the diverse organisations in which urban Africans are seeking unity. "A striking feature of the urban African communities was the development of a rich and varied association life."[67] In addition to churches and sects Soweto has numerous other organisations that were set up by the people on the basis of common interests. They are sports, theatrical, and choral clubs; charities; associations of teachers, shopkeepers, businessmen, and herbalists; associations of houseowners and tenants; school committees; clubs uniting graduates of various schools or colleges; and diverse mutual aid groups. "It is the bonds based on association that today form the chief links of the people of Soweto... The new associations, the rapid proliferation of which is one of the features of Soweto life, form the growth points of today and tomorrow. It is their development which is, I suggest, giving Soweto the 'feel' of a community rather than that of the haphazard, unconnected aggregation which it once had."[68]

Monica Hunter found that religious associations—the independent churches and sects we have just described—are more widespread among the less educated, while political organisations and trade unions draw their membership mostly from the urban middle classes.[69]

Political organisations and trade unions play a large role in the life of the town-dwellers. With the authorities denying them recognition and with the trade union struggle inevitably becoming a struggle against the apartheid regime, the trade unions stand close to political organisations.

It would be no exaggeration to say that the African National Congress had been the most popular and largest political organisation in the long span from 1912 to 1960.

The ANC went deep underground in 1960 when it was out-lawed. Its members are selflessly conducting political work among the population, organising the armed struggle against the racist regime. Operating in secrecy in a new situation and performing new functions, it remains the vanguard in the liberation movement. Of course, having been banned it cannot register its mass membership; under the racist laws membership of the ANC is punishable with long terms of imprisonment.

For a short while at the close of the 1950s popularity was enjoyed in the Johannesburg townships, particularly Orlando, by the Pan-Africanist Congress, which was set up by a group of nationalists who had broken away from the ANC. It was also outlawed (in 1960) but, unlike the ANC, it failed to sustain its popularity and its unity.

In the long period of legal activity the ANC conducted many mass campaigns to protect the interests of the African population and there was usually a wide response to these campaigns in the black townships. The ANC led the Defiance Campaign against the unjust laws (1952), the Congress of the People, which adopted the Freedom Charter in 1955, several massive general political stay-at-homes and boycotts, the campaign against passes, and other mass actions. No exact statistics about the ANC's numerical strength in the period of legal activity were published, but it has been estimated that in the mid-1950s it had at least 100,000 members. It had 16,000 members in the Transvaal alone. An indication of the scale of its actions is given by the fact that 8,500 ANC volunteers were arrested during the Defiance Campaign (of these 1,900 were arrested in the Transvaal).

The method of enlisting activists, called "freedom volunteers", from among the membership and sympathisers was used by the ANC time and again. During the run-up to the Congress of the People in 1955 and while the Congress was in session there were some 5,000 freedom volunteers. These people were active in the work of the ANC, resisting apartheid and racial discrimination with fortitude in the face of brutal police harassment.

The impact of the extensive political work conducted by the ANC in the Johannesburg townships was seen vividly during the general political stay-at-homes that embraced South Africa's industrial areas. The oneday general work stoppage of March 28, 1960, a week after the Sharpeville massacre, virtually crippled the entire country. In the Johannesburg area it involved 90 per cent of black workers and office employees and paralysed industry and trade. It demonstrated the strength and potentialities of the African proletariat. Its form was purely South African: the workers simply stayed at home.

The ANC's important role in organising strikes was acknowledged even by *The New York Times*, which reported: "A new threat of racial unrest developed today in South Africa. Mimeographed sheets calling for a week-long work stoppage next week were distributed last night in African townships around Johannesburg. The circulars were signed by the Emergency Committee of the African National Congress. The leaflets, most of which were slipped under the doors of African dwellings, said the work stoppage would be 'our answer to the savage attack the Government has made on us and our leaders'."[70]

In the old Johannesburg townships, long before some of them merged in Soweto and others were destroyed, the ANC regularly held rallies and processions with freedom volunteers marching in the front ranks wearing the ANC colours: black, green, and gold. In Sophiatown, for example, the ANC usually held rallies in Freedom Square. One of these, attended by more than 5,000 people, was held on April 6, 1952 in honour of the Defiance Campaign. It was addressed by the then ANC President Dr. J. C. Moroka. Many ANC leaders lived in these townships at various time: Edwin Mafutsanyana, Walter Sisulu, and Nelson Mandela in Orlando; Moses Kotane in Alexandra; Robert Resha in Sophiatown.

Before it went underground the ANC united people of practically all the classes and strata of the black population of South Africa. The unity and national consolidation of this population were one of the tasks for which the ANC was formed in 1912. The broad social range of the ANC composition included, naturally, people living in traditional communities. If it is borne in mind that remnants of tribalism and traditionalism survived in urban areas, it will be seen why the ANC used traditional elements in its work as well. The highest title that can be won by an ANC member is *Isitwalandwe Seaparankoe* (hero of the national liberation struggle). Those awarded this title receive the traditional headdress of a Zulu warrior.

In the townships there were other political organisations, but they came to the fore only after the ANC was banned. They became active in the 1960s and 1970s, when they attempted to fill the vacuum left by the ANC. Of those that appeared earlier mention must be made of the Sofasonke Party, which was founded in 1944.

Formed in Orlando during a spontaneous movement of homeless people, this party evolved into an organisation whose aims had nothing in common with its initial objectives.

The Sofasonke Party leadership include the millionaire businessman Ephraim Tshabalala and the retailer Tolica Makhaya. To prevent its influence among the people from dissipating, the Sofasonke Party sometimes criticises the apartheid regime over particular issues. But its leaders, chiefly businessmen, are concerned mainly with seats on puppet bodies of township pseudo self-government bodies—first on the advisory board, then the Bantu urban councils and, lastly, the community councils. The office of "adviser" evidently satisfies the ambition of the black bourgeois who has a sizeable account in the bank. These people have thus made their peace with the racist regime and are obviously not intending "to die together", as is proclaimed in the party's name, for the interests of their party's rank and file.

This attention to the Sofasonke Party in the present volume is motivated not only by the fact that it is one of the oldest organisations of its kind and has, consequently, become firmly established in Soweto. Its genesis is typical of legal reformist organisations in Soweto. Their appearance is, as a rule, stimulated by the hardships and difficulties encountered by Sowetans in their day-to-day life. The common concerns and problems generated by racial discrimination induce people to unite spontaneously or semi-spontaneously. However, after the initial period of militant activity, of actions in defence of disinherited victims of discrimination, the leadership of these organisations is in most cases taken over by self-seeking, ambitious members of the African bourgeoisie and the elite of the urban middle classes.

Among such organisations, mention may also be made of the Asinamali Party, which appeared in the 1960s. The bus boycotts were usually staged under the slogan of *asinamali* (literally meaning: "We have no money!"). This slogan was used by skilled demagogues to attract people into the organisation allegedly capable of helping those in need.

The Masingafi Party ("We shall not let ourselves be killed") was formed in 1971 when the crime rate in Soweto reached a very high level (on average 80 murders were committed every month). This organisation was hardly able to do anything dramatic for the security of its members— there was practically no decline in the crime rate in Soweto. Yet it has continued to function. In answering a question about the party's political platform, one of its leaders Sipho Motha spoke of everything—a municipal status for Soweto, political rights, representation in parliament—except the purpose implicit in the party's name. He claimed that the Masingafi Party had a membership of 10,000.

There is yet another type of organisation uniting people on the basis of common problems. Among these in Soweto are the Residents Committee and the Tenants Association. The names of these organisations indicate the main problem they seek to resolve—housing and some matters linked to it, for instance, rent. These are among the most acute and painful issues in Soweto. In order to live in the city the urban African has to find a dwelling and the money for the rent. He has to contend with discriminative restrictions and obstacles erected by apartheid and the police. Hence the massive associations to provide mutual help in resolving these problems. The chairman of the Residents Committee A. Moerana said in January 1978 that his committee had the support of 65 per cent of tenants in Soweto. In October 1977 the Tenants Association had over 700 members.

It has to be noted that in tackling the housing problem organisations of this kind have to confront the entire government machine of the racist regime, and this makes their function a political one. It would be no exaggeration to regard them as even more political than such Soweto parties as the People's Party or the Progressive Party.

Despite their pompous names, these "parties" have nothing in common with mass political organisations. The People's Party represents a handful of sychophants and col-

127

laborators from among the bourgeoisie and urban middle classes who had earlier been "advisers" in advisory boards and had now united in order to get onto the community councils. Demagoguery brought these "representatives of the people" 34 of the 41 seats on the Soweto Community Council in 1964. Roughly similar tactics, albeit with lesser success, are used by the Progressive Party headed by the businessmen Lennox Mlonzi and Leonard Mosala.

A large organisation of the traditional mould, called *Makgotla* (a Sotho word meaning "groups of people gathered together"—a unit of which is called *Lekgotla*), functions in the Soweto townships. This is a well-organised system that includes vigilance committees or groups and traditional disciplinary tribunals. The Makgotla hierarchy in Soweto is headed by a president, Sigfrid Manthata. Like the Masingafi Party, the Makgotla appeared in the townships as a response to the growth of crime, especially among young people. Until lately the basic penalty meted out by the Makgotla was public caning, a punishment inflicted not only on juveniles of both sexes but also on adults.

Most of the Makgotla adherents are unenlightened, illiterate people totally committed to traditional, tribalistic practices. Incidentally, one of the leading lights in the Makgotla was the founder of the Sofasonke Party, James M. Mpanza.

The Makgotla has rather complicated relations with the authorities. Although the arbitrary traditionalist disciplinary actions and the entire Makgotla system are unlawful, the police have raised no objections and in many cases given their support. Back in 1960 it was reported that the police were protecting the Makgotla leaders. A case in point was that of T. J. Ramatibela, a Makgotla chieftain in Orlando. Another case was that of a woman named Sina Makume, nicknamed Madipere (Mother of Horses). She had been a policewoman assigned to escorting persons expelled from the city to a reservation. Joyce Sikakane wrote about her as being an agent of the authorities.

Prior to 1976 the racist government and the police tried to conceal their approval of the Makgotla, which had no popular support in Soweto and, in addition, irritated the top echelon of the urban middle classes who feared the rivalry of the Makgotla leaders in the drive for influence among the people. However, when the Soweto uprising was being crushed and the police did not stand on ceremony in their treatment of the young insurgents, the intimate links between the Makgotla and the racist regime's police came to the surface. Jimmy Kruger, then Minister of Justice, Police and Prisons, had a series of meetings with Makgotla leaders to consider the possible legalisation of that organisation, which had been useful to the authorities during the turbulent events of 1976. What formerly looked like the punishment of disobedient children with the permission of their parents now became a fight against insurgent youth. The backward, ignorant forces of traditionalism, which remained intact even in urban surrounding, thus made common cause with the "enlightened" racists and the police guarding apartheid and the supremacy of the white exploiting minority.

But far from everybody in Soweto condemns the Makgotla's actions. The Makgotla is opposed by the urban middle classes, intellectuals, and students. But there are many, chiefly with the lowest level of cultural development, who look to the Makgotla for some protection against their innumerable troubles. Playing on ignorance and fear, the Makgotla leaders have enlisted considerable support with their demagoguery, their appeals to traditional values. The leader of a Makgotla faction, Letsatsi Radebe, declared at the close of 1977 that his organisation had 6,000 members and was supported by another 10,000 persons. The support in this case is indisputably due to the hypocritical declarations that the Makgotla "will fight for full political rights for urban Africans".[7 1]

In spite of everything, the Makgotla failed to get official recognition. After the uprising in Soweto was crushed, the police cooled towards it: there is no further need for it, while its arbitrary tribunal rulings are resented by the township elite with whom the authorities are flirting. The Makgotla is now seen as secondary to the growing African bourgeoisie. It was planned to form a township guard subordinated to the community councils, in other words, to create an updated force to combat transgressions of the law.

Nevertheless, the Makgotla was active in Soweto, while in some quarters it retains or enjoys even growing influence and prestige. For example, support for the Makgotla was declared by David Thebehali, then mayor of Soweto and chairman of its Community Council and this marked a significant shift in the attitude of Soweto's leaders towards the Makgotla.

The Makgotla continues its efforts to win official recognition, notably from the Ministry of Police and the chief of police in Soweto, although, as we have already noted, the attitude towards it has grown cooler. In December 1978, for example, the police banned public caning, but the arbitrary tribunals found a new means of enforcing discipline: at midnight delinquents, regardless of age and sex, are now made to stand naked while water is poured on them for the edification of onlookers. They are also made to pay a fine. In fact, the Makgotla is running typical gangster rackets, one of which is "protection".

The Makgotla is "modernising" and evolutioning, now performing not so much the functions for which it was originally set up as those that tie up with the interests of its ambitious leaders. The latter are joining more and more actively in the in-fighting within the reformist and conformist organisations for the leadership of the Soweto Community Council. Mention has already been made of the Makgotla faction led by Letsatsi Radebe, which has its own "political platform". The Makgotla is in contact and has even concluded an alliance with another traditionally patterned organisation, the Zulu Inkatha. A "short conference behind closed doors" was held in May 1977 between representatives of the Makgotla of Naledi township and Inkatha representatives from Dlamini township. In the following year it was reported that leaders of these two organisations had met on a higher level and agreed on an alliance in the elections to the Soweto Community Council. It was also reported that some people were members of both the Makgotla and the Inkatha.

The Inkatha socio-political organisation carries considerable weight in Soweto, notably and quite naturally among the Zulus, who comprise about 33 per cent of Soweto's population. It was set up in 1975 in the Kwazulu Bantustan and has since been the ruling party there although the white minority remains the actual ruler.

It would probably be more correct to say that the Inkatha

was rather restored than set up in 1975. The Paramount Chief (or King) of the Zulus Solomon ka Dinizulu founded the Inkatha ka Zulu cultural association in 1928. But it hardly functioned until Gatsha Mongosuthu Buthelezi, Solomon ka Dinizulu's nephew, appeared on the political scene.

When the Paramount Zulu Chief Syprian Bekuzulu died in 1969, Gatsha Buthelezi became the regent for Bekuzulu's juvenile successor (Buthelezi has clung to the regency although the new Paramount Chief has come of age). At the same time he became Chief Minister of Zulu "Territory" which was later to become the Bantustan of Kwazulu. From the outset Buthelezi felt a need for an organisation that would give him command of a majority in the "legislature" and, as Baruch Hirson rightly notes, provide him with "a platform from which he could organise a movement throughout the country."[72] For this purpose the Inkatha ka Zulu was revitalised and, to keep pace with the times, renamed Inkatha Enkululeko Ye Sizwe, the latter two words meaning liberation of the people.

An adroit politician and demagogue, Gatsha Buthelezi attained his initial objective quickly, without any particular trouble, following which he set out to broaden his base of support. At first, before he was appointed Chief Minister of Kwazulu, he took a stand against apartheid and bantustanisation, but then toned down his criticism of apartheid, cautiously declaring that it was his policy to "protect Zulu interests within the system", i.e., the framework of apartheid. The Inkatha's membership grew rapidly: 120,000 in 1977, 200,000 in 1978, and (according to Buthelezi) 300,000 in early 1980. Naturally, propelled by his ambition to become a national leader of the first magnitude Gatsha Buthelezi made a special effort to win popularity in the Transvaal, where the bulk of the African proletariat is concentrated, in Soweto in the first place; Soweto's large Zulu community provides the Inkatha with wide scope for its activities.

The Inkatha is trying to supplant its political rivals, getting the support of some organisations and allying itself with others. With the view of making political capital out of the ANC's popularity and prestige, the Inkatha has repeatedly embarked upon manoeuvres to get the black population of South Africa to believe it is an ally and continuer of the work of the African National Congress.

We have already mentioned the Inkatha's links to the Makgotla. The Inkatha's drive for influence was also at the back of its participation in the puppet self-administration bodies in Soweto. In October 1979 Buthelezi told a rally of 30,000 Sowetans that he had links to the ANC and that he was Nelson Mandela's friend. For his legally functioning rivals in Soweto he had nothing but disparagement. For instance, he called Nthato Motlana, leader of the Committee of Ten,[73] a "political baboon" and a "political leper". Commenting on this and other Inkatha antics, *The Sunday Post* wrote: "Chief Gatsha Buthelezi's Inkatha movement is planning to capture control of Soweto. 'Contingency planning' has been under way since March and the movement's West Rand region, which includes its 24 branches in Greater Soweto, is expected to take a decision on the next community council election in the township. If successful, the takeover bid will give Chief Buthelezi an institutional power base in the country's biggest urban black township and among the largest single segment of its workforce."[74]

All the indications are that Buthelezi is using the Inkatha to move from the conquest of popularity to the conquest of power in Soweto. Despite his sharp attacks on the government and demagogic use of the ANC colours, Buthelezi is, for the time being, quite acceptable to the racist regime. As well as collaborating in the bantustanisation policy and denouncing the use of violence—the armed struggle against the racist regime—during the 1976 uprising in Soweto, Gatsha Buthelezi has in effect sided with the racist government, condemning the actions of the insurgent youth. In the province of Natal and in the Kwazulu Bantustan, where he was in control of the situation, Buthelezi cut short the maturing manifestations of solidarity with the insurgents. "In the event Buthelezi, who had been seen as a possible embarrassment to the regime, proved to be a valuable asset to the government forces."[75] Little wonder that this stand gave rise to a storm of indignation and resentment in Soweto, in that selfsame Soweto which was so vital for Buthelezi's ambitions. This possibly explains the Inkatha's futher invigoration in Soweto: it was a bid by Buthelezi to retrieve lost positions and even seize control of the township.

The evolution of traditional and tribalistic elements and their adaptation to modern, urban conditions is seen with particular clarity in the activities of organisations such as the Makgotla and Inkatha.

The mushrooming of a great diversity of organisations and associations in Soweto is due, in the first place, to the fact that the vast majority of Sowetans are at the stage of transition from one way of life to another. This transition from life in a traditional society with its established relationships to modern urban life which is devoid of customary relations, compels the African to form new relationships with persons he finds interesting and useful but who are not kinsmen or fellow-tribesmen.

Membership of this or that organisation gives the urban African a sense of confidence, security, and stability that he had formerly had in his traditional way of life ensured by the clan or the commune. For the urban black these organisations, at least many of them, compensate for the loss of the mutual aid and mutual support he had enjoyed as a member of a large family and of a tribe.

The diversity and intricacy of the urban problems encountered by the African account for the diversity of the organisations he can join in the hope of getting help to resolve these problems and cope with the hardships and perplexities of urban life. "The stimulus and complexity of urban living and the social distress also frequently associated with urban life," Laura Longmore writes, "have brought into being a number of voluntary organisations for economic, cultural, political, religious and recreational purposes. These associations perform an infinite variety of functions in satisfying human desires and meeting personal needs."[76] A point to be added here is that, because of apartheid and racial discrimination, membership of such associations and organisations not merely gives the opportunity to brighten the dreariness of day-to-day life, to spend one's free time among people with similar interests or united by common aims; it helps to survive in these ghettos. For instance, in mutual aid groups people take turns to use the money each regularly pays into a common fund.

Sports clubs are a form of association in accordance with interests. Football clubs are particularly popular, although in the whole of Soweto there are only three stadiums with normal football fields. In 1961 the Orlando African Football Association had 1,320 player-members.[77] In 1972 there were about a thousand amateur and 15 professional football teams in Soweto. Sports clubs do not confine themselves to sports activities: they usually arrange dance evenings.

Soweto has many diverse women's associations, most of which run charity, self-education, cultural, and recreational programmes. The Zenzele Young Women's Christian Association even has a cultural centre, which is located in Dube. This and other similar organisations such as the National Council of Women, the Housewives League, and the Association of Professional and Businesswomen draw their members from urban middle classes and the emergent bourgeoisie. Some are branches of the relevant international organisations. Meetings of these women's organisations take the form of dance evenings, tea parties, and fashion parades.

The aspiration of the Africans for unity in ghetto-townships sometimes acquires ugly forms. The innumerable gangs of juvenile criminals—*tsotsis*—are also a form of drawing together young people to whom apartheid has denied normal conditions for study and work.

In the townships there is very little opportunity for rest and recreation. A survey of 800 Sowetans showed that 72 per cent had never been to a movie theatre and simply had no facilities for rest and recreation. "Sowetonians are denied proper sporting and recreational facilities because, according to apartheid policy, blacks in urban areas are only there for the sole purpose of serving the white man and not to idle around."[78]

All of this takes a heavy toll among young people, above all. Some have no job, others have no opportunity for going to school. "...young people have nothing to do but to stand about or walk aimlessly looking for something to turn up to relieve the monotony, the dreary sameness of life, in an area where nothing happens unless you make it happen. What happens is gambling and fights, sex and drink."[79] This is the atmosphere in which groups of young people form *tsotsi* gangs.

Participation in the activities of socio-political, cultural-educational, sports, religious, and other organisations, clubs, or associations is an important aspect of Sowetan life. These activities are, as any other, a mix of traditional and modern ingredients. The traditional manifests itself usually in the external aspects, and the form of these activities. But their substance, their content is linked to various problems of the modern world: class conflicts, the national liberation struggle, ideological differences and clashes, and so forth. The urban African's aspiration to join an organisation or association in order to find protection for his or her interests in the complex conditions of a modern capitalist city, conditions that are compounded by apartheid and racial discrimination, is fostering the growth of socio-political awareness. This process depends upon the class affiliation of people and the level of their cultural-psychological urbanisation. For its part, the level of socio-political awareness determines the development rate of cultural-psychological urbanisation.

Cultural Life Despite Interdictions

The formation and development of urban African culture include the development of art. Works of art are strongly influencing the worldview of people and their attitude to life, their mentality.

In line with its apartheid doctrine the racist regime is determined to deny to urban blacks the opportunity to live a cultured life in the true sense of the word: to create and take delight in works of art. "Therefore although one of the main aims of apartheid is to develop the cultures separately, its effect is to ossify them separately, and to make them resistant to the entrance of new ideas."[80] This denial of and, in effect, ban on culture in the townships has been visibly pursued since the close of the 1940s when the racist National Party came to power in South Africa. An assault was mounted by the forces of reaction with the object of slowing down and halting the development of a truly people's, democratic culture, which was developing at the time. "In the past," Michael Harmel, a prominent figure in the South African liberation movement, wrote in 1965, "overcoming all the fearsome handicaps existing even under

135

the pre-Nationalist governments, such as that of Smuts before 1948, a handful of talented Africans managed to emerge as lawyers, writers, artists and composers, and even as university professors. Today, nearly all of these are either in prison for political 'offences' or living in exile; the doors to possible successors are locked and double bolted."[81]

A biographical reference book of Africans of the Transvaal for 1967 lists 89 writers. An autobiographical novel by Ezekiel Mphahlele, *Down Second Avenue*, was published in 1959. This book is about life in Marabastad, a Pretoria location where the author spent his childhood and youth. It ends with a description of life in Orlando where Ezekiel Mphahlele was a schoolteacher. The steady destruction of the individual under the apartheid regime is shown through the destruction of Sophiatown in an autobiographical novel by Bloke Modisane, another well-known South African author.[82]

Joyce Sikakane, the South African journalist we have quoted so many times, mentions Dorkay House on Eloff Street in Johannesburg which was the headquarters of the multiracial Union of South African Artists. "In its heyday [in the 1950s.—V. G.] it had been the Mecca of progressive African arts."[83] This Union gave a start to the famous King Kong ensemble, the careers of talented singers like Miriam Makeba and Letta Mbulu, and the actors Lyonel Ngakane and Bloke Modisane, who subsequently made his mark as a writer.

Athol Fugard's play *No-Good Friday* was staged at the Union in 1958; it was produced by, among others, the black intellectuals Lewis Nkosi, Nat Nakasa, and Bloke Modisane. This was followed by the production of the plays *Nongogo* and *Blood Knot* by the same author. The theatrical troupe formed in the Union of South African Artists staged avant-garde plays by European and American authors, including Jean-Paul Sartre, John Steinbeck, and Samuel Beckett. In those years theatrical life developed basically through cooperation between a small group of black intellectuals and English-speaking white liberals. The high point of the theatrical and musical life of that period was the staging of the musical *King Kong*, the scenario for which was written by Harry Blum and the music by Todd Matshikiza.

Little was drawn from traditional culture for plays and musicals. Traditional forms and subjects were used for, strange as it may seem, productions for white audiences, who were evidently attracted by their exoticism. Nevertheless, the then developing black urban culture absorbed also elements of traditional culture. This was seen, in particular, in Todd Matshikiza's music for *King Kong* in which melodies and rhythms of traditional Xhosa music are distinctly interwoven.

Jazz had a very large following in Soweto in the 1950s and 1960s. Songs were composed and played by Gideon Nxumalo and his orchestra. There were outstanding exponents of jazz like Chuck Chukudu, "Blues" by Ntaka, Mackay Davashe and, last but not least, the Manhattan Brothers, who, like Miriam Makeba, later won world-wide recognition.

In Soweto music developed much faster than other art forms. The reason for this is given by the South African writer and publicist Lewis Nkosi, who writes: "Music is an art that does not directly reflect reality. Unlike literature, it is free of restrictions. As a rule, interdictions do not extend to it. Moreover, it is less constrained in the choice of the creative forms for expressing the misery of its people. The popular urban African music is thus the most striking evidence of the subterranean processes hidden from the eyes of detached onlookers."[84] As regards the music itself, Lewis Nkosi says that "it is predominantly African ... but it is also eclectic; it mirrors the cultural diffusion in this part of the continent which could have become the finest laboratory for the reciprocal enrichment of African and European methods, for combining European and African modes of creative expression... The music in the cities of South Africa is the closest of all to blues."[85]

In the opinion of Joyce Sikakane, in the 1960s Dorkay House survived as a centre of African cultural life only because the apartheid regime concentrated its assaults on progressive political organisations and trade unions. In the 1970s, feeling that they had achieved their purpose the racist authorities turned their guns on cultural organisations, for their activities were in collision with apartheid. "When I set foot at Dorkay House in 1971, it was a hangover from the past cultural heritage."[86]

137

It would be more correct to speak not of a heyday of culture but of a certain measure of cultural development achieved as a result of the efforts to surmount the enormous difficulties stemming from the socio-political and economic inequality of Africans, including of black exponents of culture, in South African society. "The African population is in fact denied the opportunity to enjoy modern culture: almost all public libraries, theatres, concert halls, and other cultural institutions serve whites only," J. B. Marks (Lebadi), Chairman of the South African Communist Party, wrote in 1967.[87]

The conditions under which those who created works of art and tried to make them available to readers or audiences had to work are described by Ezekiel Mphahlele: "I was steering a Syndicate of Artists, which was promoting classical concerts and under the aegis of which I was producing and acting in plays. Most of our players were those who had started off with me at the high school and were teachers, clerks, nurses, messengers, factory workers, but there was the perennial problem of insecurity, and we continually lost members who had to go and live outside Orlando. There was also the problem of transport and we couldn't walk the streets of Orlando at night for fear of assault and killings. We had to do our rehearsals on Sunday afternoons. Our audiences loved scenes from Shakespeare, my adaptations of Dickens and folk tales."[88]

The urban dweller has been and is the principal reader and viewer among the black population, but only a few have a secondary education, in other words, the median cultural level is not high at all. For that reason the authors of short stories, which are the most popular form of literary work, try to meet the tastes and requirements of this reader. These stories were published mainly in the journal *Drum*, which was widely read in the townships. In the journal readers sought and found mostly sentimental love stories or thrillers.

The few literary works that were penned by black authors and won a wide readership in the townships helped to mould the mentality of the educated urban African, meaning, of course, chiefly the urban middle classes and the intellectuals.

In the 1970s, when state and police control and surveillance were tightened in Soweto, more restrictions were placed in the way of the cultural life of its inhabitants.

However, it would be wrong to say that cultural life came to a standstill in Soweto as a result of the stricter censorship and racial segregation. A volume of verse by Oswald Joseph Mtshali under the title *Sounds of a Cowhide Drum* was published in New York in 1971. Some poems by Mtshali were translated into the Russian and published in the volume *African Poetry* brought out in 1973. In South Africa itself this book was warmly received, especially as there it was the first book of verse by an African poet in 20 years.

The works of eight African painters and sculptors were put on exhibition in the Johannesburg Gallery in 1971. A noteworthy phenomenon of Soweto's cultural life of that period was the work of the playwright and producer Gibson Kente. He began his theatrical career in the Union of South African Artists in 1967, subsequently breaking away from it and forming his own commercial theatrical troupe. Kente soon became not only a well-known playwright and producer but also a successful businessman. By the beginning of the 1970s his views had undergone a significant change and elements of African nationalism and radicalism became increasingly distinct in his work. This was seen notably in his plays. He started out with entertaining musicals like *Sikalo* and *Lifa*, which he wrote himself in the musical traditions of *King Kong*, but then he began staging plays with a sharp social message that had a strong political influence on audiences in the townships, particularly on young people. These were plays like *How Long?*, staged in Soweto in December 1973, and *Too Late*, staged in Soweto in February 1975. The ban on the former play in many parts of South Africa prompted large numbers of people to go to Soweto from these parts in order to see the play.

Kente's worsening relations with the authorities led to the bankruptcy of his theatrical enterprise and to his arrest.

The Music, Drama, Arts and Literature Institute, formed in May 1972, continued to function in Soweto. Its General Secretary Z. Mofokeng spoke disapprovingly of the Western actors and musicians touring South Africa, saying that these tours were giving apartheid a boost.[89] In 1977 it was reported that more than 50 writers had gathered in Soweto and united in the Azania[90] Writers' Association.[91]

Some new tendencies were to be observed in the cultural life of the townships in the 1970s. One of these was the Black Conscience Movement that sought insularity from "white" culture and came as a sort of reaction to white racism. Its further development in an apartheid situation may encourage black racism. At the same time, it was fostering the spiritual emancipation and cultural decolonisation of the Africans. The work of the Music, Drama, Arts and Literature Institute was guided predominantly by the Black Conscience ideology. This Institute sponsored culture festivals in different parts of the country and put out a culture information bulletin. The first of its festivals was held in Soweto in March 1973. The Institute's Chairman, Molefi Pheto, formed the Mihloti theatrical troupe which staged the play *Sizwe Banzi Is Dead* in Soweto. Somewhat later, in November 1973, the People's Experimental Theatre staged the play *Shanti*, written by Nthuli Shezi, Vice-President of the Black People's Convention. This political play was highly successful before it was banned by the authorities. *Shanti* was followed by the even more politically barbed American play *Requiem for Brother X*.

The Black Conscience line in the cultural life of the black townships and in the development of South African culture as a whole, expressed in the activities of the Music, Drama, Arts and Literature Institute and the organisations and groups close to it, subsequently led to some constraints on and narrowness of the forms in which culture developed.

Of course, in Soweto cultural life was not limited to the activities of the groups committed to the Black Conscience ideology. The South African Artists Union, which had dominated black cultural life in the 1950s, was disbanded, and its place was taken by the Experimental Theatre Workshop '71, which played a notable role in theatrical life. This troupe staged the satirical play *Crossroads* about the life of a Sowetan township White City Jabavu.

Among the novelists and poets, who enjoyed popularity in Soweto, mention may be made of Wally Mongane Serote, Bassie Head, Miriam Tlali, Sipho Sepamla, and Njabulo Ndebele.

Groups of progressive actors, musicians, and poets sprang

up in many black ghetto-townships throughout the country. Some soon fell apart for various reasons, others seeking commercial success turned exclusively to entertainment, such as the well-known "Harare" musical group (formerly known as "Beaters"), but most helped to awaken the political consciousness of the masses, particularly of young people.

Of the cultural events in the Witwatersrand linked to this trend we should mention the Black Culture Revival Conference and the cycle of lectures under the general heading "Voice of the Black Writer in Africa". The conference, held in April 1980 in the township Thabong, near Welkom, was addressed by, among others, the director of the Isizwe Youth and Culture of Soweto Thabo Ndabeni, who said that "black poetry was aimed at exposing a black's daily problems and frustrations".[92] The poets of this group recited their poems to the accompaniment of African drums.

A cycle of lectures was arranged at the Witwatersrand University in September 1980. Poems were read by Sipho Sepamla, Ezekiel Mphahlele, Ingoapele Madingoane, and Maishe Maponya (the latter two are from Soweto). Heard by a multiracial audience, these poems condemned the system of racial oppression and called for unity among blacks. The purpose of the poets was, as the newspaper *Post* wrote, to tell the other camp how they felt and what they had experienced as blacks living in South Africa.[93]

Another new tendency in African cultural life is the emphasis on traditional elements in art. On the pretext of preserving the ethnic identity of African art the racist regime is enforcing its retribalisation policy and, at the same time, preventing art from harmonising with the present social development level of urban Africans. "Tribal white man," writes the South African poet and civic personality Breyten Breytenbach, "has imposed a way of life on the nation which has reduced culture to folklore, or rather, has denied the progression from folklore to culture. Apartheid, which puts the accent on—and favours—that which distinguishes one group from another, inevitably means the glorification of the banal and the local as opposed to the original and the universal (or even merely national): handicrafts and postcards as opposed to sculpture and painting, the beating of the tomtoms as opposed to the discovery and enjoyment of richer musical forms, inferior journalism as

141

opposed to creative writing."[94]

However, the tendency to return to traditional culture sprang not only from the government's retribalisation policy. To some extent it was due to the Black Conscience Movement's adherence to the principles of African communalism. An attempt to use the traditional *umlinganiso* form of drama was made in the play *uNosilimela*, staged in 1973. But none of this was accepted in Soweto.

Strict censorship disfigures South African culture not only on account of its attempts to reverse development but also because it discourages cultural workers from addressing society's pressing problems. "The true Sowetonian producers and artists," Joyce Sikakane writes, "were limited in depicting the social ills of the community. Their plays lacked any form of rebellion against poverty and oppression. When they did endeavour to portray the truth, the regime's censorship quickly fell on the production."[95] This was the fate of the attempt to make the first African film of Gibson Kente's musical drama *How Long?* in 1976, which depicts the difficulties facing the young African trying to get an education. In 1975 the censorship went so far as to set up a culture department whose control functions included telling black playwrights what to change in their plays and how to make that change. The head of this section, an Afrikaner, wrote a play, entitled *Chaka*, and had it staged.

Official cultural policy forces African languages upon urban blacks: instruction at elementary schools was conducted in these languages; Radio Bantu had educational programmes for schoolchildren; the journal *Bona* was circulated free of charge in schools run by the Bantu education system. Special governmental committees were set up to promote African languages in order to bring them closer to the requirements of the industrialised society. The Afrikaners on these committees modernised the African languages to the extent that parents ceased to understand their children, who were taught these artificial languages in the schools.

In Soweto the language situation, a major element of culture, was extremely complex and contradictory. Most of the permanent residents, chiefly the middle classes, preferred English to Afrikaans. The workers, especially migrant workers, spoke mainly in their native languages among themselves. All rejected Afrikaans but had to learn it to one extent or another as the basic official language of the apartheid system. Naturally, this variegation of language hindered contacts within the African community itself and with the "external" white world, notably in the relations of production.

In the cities ethnic, tribalistic barriers are being surmounted in two directions. The first directon is in the fusion of African languages—the five basic languages spoken in Soweto are merging into two language conglomerates. One is the Nguni language group, which had long ago coupled the Zulu and Xhosa languages. The second—Sotho—conglomerate consists of Sotho, Pedi, and Tswana. The integration of languages does not stop here: words from one conglomerate enter the other, and both use more and more common words borrowed from English or Afrikaans. R. M. Kavanagh notes that there is a tendency towards the formation of a single urban African language.[96]

The second direction in the surmounting of language barriers is the appearance of new languages or, rather, lingua franca and slang performing the function of languages. These take shape on the basis of existing languages. In Soweto there at first appeared a simplified or pidgin, "Sowetan" English, and the *tsotsi-taal.* The latter took shape as the language of the underworld on the basis of Afrikaans with admixtures of African languages. Initially it was used by the lumpen proletariat and the innumerable *tsotsi* gangs operating in the townships. It then spread to students, journalists, and professionals. A new "language"—isiCamtu—appeared in the mid-1970s. It is based on African languages with small admixtures of English and Afrikaans. It is used almost exclusively by young people.

The new languages are mobile, in constant renewal and development, with new words coined in conversation. But the most important thing here is that all these new languages cross and erode ethnic barriers, enabling people to communicate. As Kavanagh says, these languages meet a special need of the black urban population.[97]

Cultural life continues in Soweto despite all the obstacles. In 1983 the number of motion picture theatres increased to three. The Black Theater Malimu, an offshoot of the Theater Malimu in Bloemfontein, was formed in 1981. It was headed by Mogorosi Moraka, a Sowetan playwright. There are plans for opening a school of fine arts, dancing and music, and one more theatre, but for the time being there are no funds for this. Some activity is shown by the African Cultural Organisation, formed in 1975 on the basis of the Johannesburg Festival of Bantu Music, and by the Pelamama Council of Arts, which was set up in May 1981 (the latter received a piece of land in the Mofolo Park for a building of its own).

Apartheid has been unable to halt the cultural development of the urban blacks, nor has there been any significant isolation of African culture. The South African writer Alan Paton points out: "Nor should one overlook the fact that despite the laws and the conventions, and despite the attempt to preserve the separate racial cultures, a great deal of cultural assimilation has already taken place."[98]

In Soweto cultural development follows the pattern of the development of human society, ignoring those who enforce the apartheid policy and sow racial hatred.

Retribalisation—an Instrument of Apartheid

There are survivals of tribalism in the thinking of most urban blacks. De Ridder even believes that the "completely tribally emancipated African is a psychological rarity".[99]

Many keep in contact with relatives in the reservation villages. A survey conducted in Pretoria in 1962 showed that 25 per cent of the blacks who said they were permanent residents of the city were sending money to relatives in rural communities. For various reasons many urban families send their children to stay for long periods with relatives in rural localities. Children often live in the villages until they reach adulthood.

Contacts with relatives in rural communities, where tribalism is still the prevailing way of life and thought, increases the possibilities that tribalism has of influencing the urban dweller. The latter remains in the grip of many tribal customs and beliefs. These include sacrifice to the spirits of ancestors, tribal dances and festivals, witchcraft and fortune-telling. The custom of sacrificing a goat or sheep at funerals is very widespread. This ritual was performed, for instance, at the funeral of Steve Biko, a leader of the Black Conscience Movement in which a large role is played by students.

On the basis of an analysis of fantastic notions held by some 2,500 urban blacks, J. C. de Ridder drew the conclusion that, first, tribalism is still pervasive and, second, belief in witchcraft and magic is still strong.[100] The conventional wisdom on this point is that the strength of tribal loyalty varies from a fierce attachment to mere recognition of tribal origin and the ability to speak the tribal language.[101]

One may argue about the extent tribalism has survived among urban Africans, especially as this category of people is heterogeneous and their socio-psychological status changes constantly. However, it has to be accepted that remnants of tribalist survivals persist in varying degree among most of them. Precisely this is the foundation on which retribalisation is being fostered.

Retribalisation runs counter to detribalisation and adaptation to urban life, delaying the cultural-psychological urbanisation of Africans. In the first place, this process is promoted by the apartheid regime. Moreover, a section of urban blacks, chiefly those who have been least exposed to cultural-psychological urbanisation, tend to revert to individual elements of tribalism and traditionalism; this expresses their reaction to the burdens of life in a modern capitalist city. As early as in the 1950s Monica Hunter wrote of a "resuscitation of traditional forms which were first abandoned by the more educated a hundred years ago, and condemned by the 'school people' as 'pagan' or 'uncivilized'. The change is typified by the use of Xhosa in place of English first names, but appears also in the somewhat self-conscious celebration of traditional rituals."[102] Subsequently there was a growth of the number of marriages involving the payment of bride money. According to official statistics, bride money figured in over 90 per cent of the marriages in Soweto in 1974 (up from 88 per cent in 1963).

Another factor encouraging retribalisation tendencies among urban dwellers consists of the hardships encountered by them in the modern capitalist city, of their disenchantment with the "fruits" of Western civilisation. The negative effects of urbanisation, particularly in the socio-psychological context, are to be seen to some extent in practically every city and every country. But in South Africa the Africans are the hardest hit by these effects on account of apartheid and racial discrimination.

Among the most widespread of the innumerable ills are the falling apart of families and the high crime rate.

Apartheid's denial to Africans of the right to live a settled life in towns and its tolerance of their presence exclusively as labour are what prevent families from holding together in the cities. As a result, there is a disproportionately large number of African men in the towns, and many families have been broken. Helen Suzman, who has been a member of the South African parliament from the Progressive Federal Party, has noted that "in every urban area countless African men and women are living in constant fear of having their family disrupted".[103]

Another cause of distress for Africans living in the cities is the steadily rising crime rate. The rapid spread of juvenile delinquency is particularly alarming. The material insecurity of Africans in the city, unemployment, and appalling housing conditions are compounded by some specific circumstances stemming from apartheid: the most conspicuous of these are the control over the influx of Africans into the cities, the system of passes, the racial discrimination, and the segregation.

No wonder that when they find themselves caught in what for them are destructive urban conditions many Africans tend to look for salvation (or, at least, an alleviation of their lot) in a return to some traditional rituals and customs. An expression of this is the formation of the Makgotla groups—vigilants and traditional tribunals as a defence against the underworld, as we have already noted.

While the Makgotla are a form of active and effective participation in the restoration of traditional elements as counter-balances to the hardships and suffering brought by urban life, belief in magic, witchcraft, and sorcery are survivals of tribalism, passive manifestations of retribalisation. "There is supporting evidence from all parts of the subcontinent that the force of these beliefs has been strengthened by psychological insecurity of those removed from ancestral or other traditional safeguards."[104]

There is thus every ground to believe that certain prerequisites exist for the retribalisation of Africans in South Africa. These are, first, survivals of tribalism and, second, the socio-psychological reaction of urban blacks to the conditions in which they find themselves.

The retribalisation policy of the racist, colonialist regime in South Africa is not something new. The National Party proclaimed the apartheid doctrine after it came to power in 1948. True, apartheid and the accompanying policy had come into practice much earlier, when the socio-economic conditions took shape under which the white exploiting minority found it needed precisely these political instruments in order to pursue its policy.

While in the period of the Boer War and British colonial expansion in the north and east of South Africa in the eighteenth and nineteenth centuries the colonialists saw tribalism merely as an obstacle to their designs, in the early years of the twentieth century the negative attitude to traditional chiefs and the entire system of tribalism changed into its direct opposite. In view of the development of capitalism and the simultaneous growth of African national self-awareness, South Africa's rulers found they needed new methods for implementing the basic principle of colonialist policy, namely, the principle of "divide and rule". Retribalisation proved a new method of this kind. Their attitude to traditionalism and tribalism was formulated in 1929 by Jan C. Smuts, who was the Prime Minister at the time: "If this system breaks down and tribal discipline disappears, native society will be resolved into its human atoms, with possibilities of universal Bolshevism and chaos... Such a breakdown should be prevented at all costs, and everything should be done to maintain in the future the authority which guided native life in the past. We are called ... to take all proper measures which are still possible to restore or preserve the authority of the chiefs and to maintain the bonds of solidarity and discipline which have supported the tribal organization of the natives in the past."[105]

In its election manifesto of 1947 the National Party proclaimed: "The process of detribalization should be arrested."[106] When it came to power this party went further, introducing and implementing a policy of retribalisation.

As a policy, retribalisation was given full rein in the early 1950s as a response of the ruling circles to the steep rise of the rate and scale of African urbanisation. The racist regime saw the rapidly growing black urban population as a real threat to its existence. On account of the growth of their class and national consciousness two basic social groups of the urban population—the proletariat and the middle classes —were becoming the most active force opposed to racial segregation and discrimination. These were the groups that pressed for national liberation and social emancipation. South Africa's racist regime saw the restoration of tribalism as the factor that could undermine the African national unity that had taken shape chiefly in the cities and townships. "The enemy has realised the potency of encouraging tribalism as a means of breaking down unity among the oppressed people," the ANC Youth and Students Section noted in its Declaration.[107] This was also noted by the Communist Govan Mbeki, a scientist prominent in the national liberation movement: "The Nationalist government is deliberately nourishing disunity, attempting to erode the very unity evolved over the years, in order to re-create manageable and weak tribal communities."[108]

This is stated in similarly categorical language by Can Temba: "Somewhere near this point, the authorities decided that the whole process of African urbanization should be repudiated as a policy if not altogether as a fact... And a simple method projected was the retribalization of the people and the re-establishment of the authority of chiefs."[109]

The Bantu Authorities Act No. 68 was enacted in 1951, soon after the National Party with its apartheid doctrine had come to power. This was a major component of the policy of forming "homelands" or Bantustans, pseudo-independent "states" for separate ethnic groups in South Africa. Members of dynastic families obedient and subservient to the white government in Pretoria were put in charge in the Bantustans. This entire action was conceived as part of the general trend towards retribalisation and in keeping with the racist apartheid doctrine. With the adoption of the Bantu Authorities Act "the Nationalists launched a programme of retribalising the African people".[110] The accent in this programme was on retribalising the black urban population. Ethnic separatism and the authority of traditional chiefs were planted not only in the reserves where the Bantustans were created, but also in urban areas where many Africans had become permanent residents and were departing from traditional practices and customs.

South Africa's racist government was employing tactics such as "ethnic zoning" in the townships. This tactics was part of a broader plan for the retribalisation of urban Africans, the implementation of which, the racists count, will facilitate their apartheid policy.

The new townships set up in Soweto in the 1970s were from the outset designated for people belonging to a particular ethnic or language group. Such, for example, were Dlamini, Senoane, Jabulani, Zondi-2, and Zola-2 assigned to the Nguni ethnic group, which includes Zulu, Xhosa, and Swazi. In 1971 there were ten Soweto townships for the Nguni group, six for the Sotho, and one (Chiawelo) for the Venda and the Shangaan. There was neighbourhood and strict ethnic zoning in the old townships in the centre of Soweto. Some of the Soweto townships still have an ethnically mixed population. There were six such townships in 1971. However, the existence of "mixed" townships conflicts with the retribalisation policy. Gradual zoning has been started in such townships. Residents belonging to "foreign" ethnic groups are not expelled, but when a house is vacated (as happens frequently on account of the policy of the racist authorities) the new tenants have to belong to the relevant ethnic group.

Through ethnic zoning the South African government seeks to revive in the black urban population a sense of ethnic oneness with the inhabitants of a given township or neighbourhood. "Ethnic grouping is the natural product of the apartheid policy of the present government... Ethnic grouping is a desperate plan to put a stop to African progress and development ... it is a backward plan aimed at throwing the urban Africans back into their outmoded tribalism. It is a crude plan born of unscrupulous politicians who are desperately trying to fight against the natural course of history."[111] Jordan K. Ngubane writes that the obvious benefit of this tactics to the authorities is that "it makes it so easy in times of crisis to set one group against another and thus keep the Africans from presenting a united front against Afrikaner nationalism".[112]

Ethnic zoning was started in 1955 and it yielded its first

149

"fruits" as early as 1957: on September 15 and 16 of that year there were violent clashes in Dube township between Zulus and Sothos—40 persons lost their lives. A Supreme Court Commission set up to inquire into these bloody clashes offered the following conclusion: "There can to our mind be no doubt that the implementation of the policy of ethnic grouping was one of the causes which led to and facilitated the rioting. The fact that the Basuto were concentrated in a portion of Meadowlands and the Zulus were concentrated in Zondi and the Dube Hostel in the immediate vicinity enabled both sections to gather in force in order to attack one another. It is significant that the rioting did not extend to the Orlando township where ethnic grouping had not yet been implemented."[113] This eloquent admisssion is complemented with the opinion of three traditional Sotho and three traditional Zulu chiefs. They "got the impression" that ethnic grouping was one of the principal factors that led to these clashes.

Ethnic zoning is linked to one more innovation introduced by apartheid—the institution of "tribal ambassadors" in urban areas. The Promotion of Bantu Self-Government Act No. 46 of 1959 allowed the "Bantu territorial authority", i.e., the tribal puppets—the predecessors of the present governments of the Bantustans to appoint, with the consent of the government in Pretoria, their own "ambassadors" (representatives) to urban areas. These "ambassadors" were members of the Bantu Town Councils, the new puppet self-government bodies set up in the townships under the 1959 Act. It is indicative that these "ambassadors" were appointed, not elected members of the councils; this underscored their unpopularity among the people.

Speaking in Phefeni township, Soweto, in 1960, M. de Wet Nel, Minister of Bantu Administration and Development, declared that the main purpose of the 1959 law was "to bring a very close attachment between the tribal chiefs and their subjects in the urban areas".[114] Essentially, this meant subordinating urban Africans to the authority of the tribal chiefs. This was reaffirmed by a Mr. Manyanda, member of the advisory board in New Brighton township, who was quoted as saying that tribal representatives would be appointed who would not only serve on the councils, but would also exercise civil and criminal jurisdiction over African residents in New Brighton.[115] The policy of restoring the authority of traditional tribal rulers is also noted by L. Legwa: "The chiefs were told that their powers were to be increased in the reserves, and extended to the urban areas through the appointment of their representatives or ambassadors in the towns through whom they would control workers of their language-group in each urban area."[116]

By October 1960 as many as 24 "ambassadors" had been appointed in the Witwatersrand. They were assembled once a month for a briefing by this area's Chief Commissioner for Bantu Affairs. Their functions included sorting out housing disputes between fellow-tribesmen and investigating complaints about violations of labour laws and of the application of controls over the influx of Africans to the city; they are supposed to help persons wishing to return permanently to the Bantustans and, lastly, actively influence the work of school councils and youth organisations. They have proved to be unable to exercise any tangible influence on the life of the urban black population and have not justified the hope that they would bring urban Africans under the influence and authority of conservative and unenlightened chiefs of the Bantustans. Nonetheless, this instrument of retribalisation has been preserved and even upgraded by the South African government.

New efforts are being made to "tie" the urban Africans to the Bantustans and subject them to the authority of the chiefs. In 1970 the South African Parliament passed the Bantustan Citizenship Act, which introduced citizenship of ten Bantustans (the ten that had been or were to be set up). This Act (No. 26) applies (correspondingly to "foreigners" in "white" areas) not only to those who were born and live there but also speak the language of the given Bantustan or have relations of kinship with any of the inhabitants, in other words, it applies to practically all urban Africans. While the law was still debated *The Star* of Johannesburg described it as a "curious document" giving blacks the sense of belonging to a Bantustan even if they had never seen it and their parents had come from different tribes.

In theory, acceptance of Bantustan citizenship is not mandatory, but in practice urban Africans have been compelled to this. The Minister of Bantu Administration and

Development M. C. Botha bluntly declared in Parliament that preferential treatment would be given in employment contracts, housing, hospitalisation, and other matters to those Africans who sought a "healthy" relationship with their homelands. He said later that Africans who did not accept homeland citizenship would be "less welcome".[117] In the context of the generally negative attitude of the authorities to Africans in cities, the words "less welcome" could have only one meaning—a hard-line regime making further urban residence practically impossible.

Some firms, in fact, compel their employees to accept Bantustan citizenship. The tone was set by the Department for Bantustan Administration and Development, which obliged all of its black employees to apply for citizenship papers. Reporting this, *The World* cited urban Africans as calling this order "intimidation". One of them, a Soweto resident Khuziwe Ntshona, said it was a gun pressed to the head of urban workers. "It means," she said, the worker "will be compelled to identify himself with a place he does not know. Not everybody was born in a remote place outside Johannesburg. In any event, we are all South Africans."[118]

While the present generation may still resent, protest, or even reject such citizenship at the risk of additional harassment, there is to be no relaxation of the official stand for future generations. In the case of children born to persons permitted to reside in cities, the birth certificates certify their citizenship of a Bantustan. The birth certificate issued to the Reverend Majola, chairman of the Residents' Committee of a Soweto township, upon the birth of his son certifies that the child is a citizen of the Ciskei Bantustan. When this child comes of age he will no longer have a place in the city. Already now he is a "foreigner" in Soweto.

To fragment the black population the South African authorities go so far as to declare holidays for this or that ethnic group; even anniversaries of events of the anti-colonial struggle of the relatively distant past are commemorated. For example, the townships celebrate Moshoeshoe Day—the eighteenth century Sotho ruler who resisted the colonial expansion of both the Boers and the British for a long time. There is also Shaka Day—a famous nineteenth century Zulu chief—it is marked on September 23, as prescribed by the government, although there are no records confirming that he was born on that day.

The system of Bantu education, instituted by a law passed in 1953, is seen by the South African government as a powerful instrument for the retribalisation of the African population generally and of the urban blacks in particular. The substance of this system was spelled out by the then Minister of Native Affairs and subsequently Prime Minister Hendrick F. Verwoerd, who was one of the initiators and obsessed proponents of apartheid. "Native education," he said, "should be controlled in such a way that should be in accord with the policy of the State."[119] He asserted that he would reform the education system, saying that "the natives will be taught from childhood to realise that equality with Europeans is not for them".[120] An official publication stated without mincing words: "The success of apartheid depends, in the first instance, on education."[121]

School education was placed entirely under the control of the central government (it had earlier been the domain of provincial authorities), practically all mission schools were closed and, most significantly, the character of education was changed. Separate education (according to ethnic affiliation) was introduced with the purpose of bringing up "inferior" people in a segregated society who would learn from childhood that "Equality with Europeans is not for them". "The closure of mission schools and the control of all education by the state is meant to realign the process of training the African child and focus his thinking on the things that really endure the totems that give meaning to tribal life."[122]

Urban primary schools were reorganised in 1956 on the ethnic principle. School councils were correspondingly reorganised, wide powers were given to the Bantustan "ambassadors", and instruction was conducted in one of the seven African languages. Syllabuses, particularly those of the primary schools (first seven of the twelve years of secondary education), attended by nearly 87 per cent of all children of school age, were likewise revised. For instance, in the sixth and seventh forms the children studied subjects like tribal affinities and the structure of the life of ethnic groups. This tribalistic indoctrination was conducted on a large scale: for example, of a total of 3.5 million children 518,000 were in the sixth and seventh forms.[123]

"Bantu education meant being taught a tribal identity ... it meant the unquestionable acceptance of the philosophy of apartheid."[124] This assessment is consistent with one given by a person highly competent in matters related to education, Curtis Nkondo, the principal of a Soweto school and chairman of the Soweto Teachers' Committee: "Special syllabuses were drawn up for black children, but the biggest change ... was the rule that for the first six years of primary school, instruction must be in the child's mother tongue. Schools were set up for Zulus, Xhosas, Tswanas, Sothos and the other language groups, emphasising their tribal origins. This is in line with government policy that urban blacks remain citizens of their homelands."[125]

The Bantu education system covered 2.9 million children in 1971 and nearly 5 million in 1982. A close examination of this system clearly shows that it is an instrument for the perpetuation of apartheid. The overwhelming majority of children attend only the primary school, where retribalisation is given special attention: in 1971 primary schools were attended by 95.3 per cent of the black school children (66.4 per cent of the white school children were in primary schools), but only 0.14 per cent were in the senior (fifth) form of the secondary school. True, the proportion of matric students increased in 1982 to 5.7 per cent, but there has been hardly any change in the overall situation. In the case of secondary schools the authorities prefer to have them mainly in the Bantustans, where the conditions for retribalisation are more favourable. In urban areas there is an acute shortage of schools, particularly secondary schools. Soweto, for example, was short of 60 schools in 1969,[126] still, an insufficient number of new schools have soon been opened. When thousands of black children failed to get admittance to schools at the start of the academic year, their families were advised to send them to schools in the Bantustans. Similar advice had been given ten years earlier by the Minister of Bantu Education: "Send your children to your traditional home areas," he said.[127]

The authorities have not confined their retribalisation policy to a reform of school education. In mapping out a university reorganisation programme Hendrick F. Verwoerd declared in 1954: "An increase in the number of institutions for higher education located in urban areas is not desired. Steps will be taken deliberately to keep institutions for higher education, to an increasing extent, away from urban areas, and to establish them as far as possible in the Native Reserves. My Department's policy is that education should stand with both feet in the Reserves and have its roots in the spirit and being of Bantu society."[128] Ethnic universities were opened in 1959: University College of North at Turfloop in the Northern Transvaal and University College of Zululand at Ngoye in Natal. In the case of the Xhosa, by allocating the University College of Fort Hare, which was already in existence at the time, to them, the authorities killed two birds with one stone: they abolished the former multiracial campus, whose existence was a challenge to apartheid, and instituted one more ethnic university.

In these universities even the lay-out and furnishing of the interior premises are essentially tribalistic. However, the teaching staff is mostly white, consisting mainly of Afrikaner proponents of apartheid. In 1967 these three universities had only five black and 53 white teachers; the councils were all-white. In the view of Brian Bunting, "the tribal colleges ... are not universities in the true sense of the word and never will be, no matter how much money is spent on their development. They are not intended to be centres of learning, culture, and education, where the student may acquire access to the treasure-house of world knowledge, but forcing houses for apartheid."[129]

The Bantu education system and the ethnic universities are a major instrument for the retribalisation policy. They do not merely hinder the urbanisation and, with it, the social progress of Africans—they are apartheid's ideological weapon for restoring the old tribal links and lines of development in a new shape palatable for the racist regime.

African youth, chiefly those living in cities and most susceptible to cultural-psychological urbanisation, are the principal target of the retribalisation policy. This policy aims at influencing the mentality of urban blacks, of young people in the first place, at directing their socio-psychological development into the tribal channel and thereby getting them to accept their inequitable status. The white exploiting minority in South Africa believes that this will perpetuate its domination. The American sociologist

Heribert Adam notes that "the enforced ethnocentric structure and indoctrination of South African neotraditionalism--separate living areas, schools, and finally ethnic universities- -pays off for white rule".[130]

To ensure the privileges of the white exploiting minority the racist regime is responding to the growth of African society's cultural-psychological urbanisation with a stiffening of its retribalisation policy, which, along with police terror and mass repressions, is one of its basic weapons. New ethnic differentiations are being forced upon African society at all levels of its organisation and in all areas of its life. While it is itself an extreme form of racial segregation, apartheid is also acquiring the form of ethnic segregation within African community. Essentially speaking, "ethnic apartheid" is no more than an expression of the selfsame colonialist principle of "divide and rule".

[1] Cited in: E. S. Munger, *African Field Reports, 1952-1961*, Struik, Cape Town, 1961, p. 615.

[2] V. I. Lenin, *Collected Works*, Vol. 20, 1977, pp. 29-30.

[3] A. B. Davidson, *South Africa: Formation of Protest Forces, 1870-1924*, Moscow, 1972, p. 119 (in Russian).

[4] Ronald Segal, *Editorial Preface*, Govan Mbeki, *South Africa: Peasants' Revolt*, Penguin Books, London, 1964, pp. 7-8.

[5] Cited in: J. C. de Ridder, *op. cit.*, p. 168.

[6] Ellen Hellmann, *op. cit.*, p. 21.

[7] *A Survey of Race Relations in South Africa (Annual)*, 1971, p. 39.

[8] Cited in: John Kane-Berman, *op. cit.*, p. 95.

[9] *The World*, Johannesburg, March 18, 1961.

[10] Monica Hunter, *op. cit.*, p. 437.

[11] Sheila T. van der Horst, *op. cit.*, p. 98.

[12] Brian Bunting, *op. cit.*, p. 12.

[13] Monica Hunter, *op. cit.*, p. 437.

[14] *The South African Journal of Economics*, Johannesburg, February 4, 1974, pp. 181-182.

[15] *A Survey of Race Relations in South Africa (Annual)*, 1971, p. 39.

[16] Hobart D. Houghton, "Men of Two Worlds", *The South African Journal of Economics*, Johannesburg, April 1960, pp. 178-179.

[17] John Gunther, *op. cit.*, p. 514.

[18] Jan C. Smuts, *Africa and Some World Problems*, Clarendon Press, Oxford, 1930, pp. 99-100.

[19] Ellen Hellmann, *op. cit.*, p. 29.

[20] Allister Sparks, "Portrait of the Non-White Communities", *South Africa Today*, 1968, p. 48.

[21] Ellen Hellmann, *op. cit.*, pp. 14-15.

[22] Francis Wilson, *op. cit.*, pp. 236-239.

[23] Cited in: Hilda Bernstein, *op. cit.*, p. 27.

[24] Joyce Sikakane, *op. cit.*, pp. 45-46.

[25] Ellen Hellmann, *op. cit.*, p. 12.

[26] Laura Longmore, *op. cit.*, p. 17.

[27] Ibid., p. 119.

[28] Ibid.

[29] Monica Hunter, *op. cit.*, p. 480.

[30] Ibid.

[31] *The World*, Johannesburg, May 6, 1961.

[32] A. B. Davidson, *op. cit.*, p. 168.

[33] Martin West, "African Churches in Soweto, Johannesburg", *Urban Man in Southern Africa*. Edited by C. Kliff and W. C. Pendleton, Mambo Press, Gwelo, 1975, p. 19.

[34] Allister Sparks, *op. cit.*, p. 49.

[35] J. C. de Ridder, *op. cit.*, p. 162.

[36] M. Wilson, Archie Mafeje, *Langa: A Study of Social Groups in an African Township*, Oxford University Press, Cape Town, 1963, p. 102.

[37] Joyce Sikakane, *op. cit.*, p. 53.

[38] Allister Sparks, *op. cit.*, p. 49.

[39] *Mayibuye*, Lusaka, No. 8, 1980, p. 3.

[40] Ibid.

[41] *To the Point*, Johannesburg, June 24, 1977, p. 8.

[42] *Rand Daily Mail*, Johannesburg, April 12, 1979.

[43] *South Africa's Urban Blacks: Problems and Challenges*. Edited by G. Marias and R. von der Kooy, University of South Africa, Pretoria, 1978, pp. 117-118.

[44] A. G. Schutte, "A Study of Secret Groups in Soweto", *African Studies*, Johannesburg, Vol. 31, No. 4, 1972, p. 246.

[45] Martin West, *op. cit.*, p. 24.

[46] Ibid., p. 26.

[47] Ibid.

[48] Ibid., p. 34.

[49] Ellen Hellmann, *op. cit.*, p. 11.

[50] B. I. Sharevskaya, *Traditional Beliefs in Tropical Africa and Contemporaneity*, Moscow, 1975, p. 30 (in Russian).

[51] J. C. de Ridder, *op. cit.*, p. 162.

[52] Laura Longmore, *op. cit.*, p. 257.

[53] *Sechaba*, London, October 30, 1985.

[54] J. C. de Ridder, *op. cit.*, p. 160.

[55] Laura Longmore, *op. cit.*, p. 230.

[56] Monica Hunter, *op. cit.*, p. 455.

[57] Ibid., pp. 488, 489, 495.

[58] *The World*, Johannesburg, July 30, 1960.

[59] Ibid., Johannesburg, March 18, 1961.

[60] Ibid., Johannesburg, January 21, 1961.

[61] Monica Hunter, *op. cit.*, p. 462.

[62] Laura Longmore, *op. cit.*, p. 260.

[63] Martin West, *op. cit.*, p. 35.

[64] Laura Longmore, *op. cit.*, p. 259.

[65] Allister Sparks, *op. cit.*, p. 49.

[66] *The Star*, Johannesburg, August 5, 1978.

[67] *The Oxford History of South Africa.* Edited by M. Wilson and L. Thompson, Vol. 2, Oxford University Press, Oxford, 1971, p. 217.

[68] Ellen Hellmann, *op. cit.*, p. 22.

[69] Monica Hunter, *op. cit.*, pp. XIII-XIV.

[70] *The New York Times*, April 15, 1960.

[71] *Rand Daily Mail*, Johannesburg, November 15, 1977.

[72] Baruch Hirson, *op. cit.*, p. 117.

[73] This organisation was formed in Soweto after the 1976 uprising. It is discussed in some detail in Chapter Five.

[74] *Sunday Post*, Johannesburg, November 11, 1979.

[75] Baruch Hirson, *op. cit.*, p. 240.

[76] Laura Longmore, *op. cit.*, p. 111.

[77] *The World*, Johannesburg, August 1, 1961.

[78] Joyce Sikakane, *op. cit.*, p. 53.

[79] Laura Longmore, *op. cit.*, pp. 144-145.

[80] *The UNESCO Courier*, Paris, March 1967, p. 17.

[81] *World Marxist Review*, Prague, No. 9, 1965, p. 57.

[82] Bloke Modisane, *Blame Me on History*, Tomes & Hudson, London, 1963.

[83] Joyce Sikakane, *op. cit.*, p. 74.

[84] Lewis Nkosi, "Les dialogues interdits," *Le UNESCO Courier*, Paris, March 1967, p. 21.

[85] Ibid.

[86] Joyce Sikakane, *op. cit.*, p. 74.

[87] J. B. Marks (Lebadi), *The Great October Revolution and the Liberation Movement in South Africa*, Moscow, 1967, p. 52 (Russian translation).

[88] Ezekiel Mphahlele, *Down Second Avenue*, Faber & Faber, London, 1973, p. 180.

[89] *Sunday Post*, Johannesburg, October 28, 1979.

[90] The name for South Africa used by some African nationalistic organisations.

[91] *Rand Daily Mail*, Johannesburg, May 6, 1977.

[92] *Post*, Johannesburg, April 14, 1980.

[93] Ibid., September 5, 1980.

[94] *The UNESCO Courier*, March 1967, p. 27.

[95] Joyce Sikakane, *op. cit.*, p. 76.

[96] R. M. Kavanagh, *Theatre and Cultural Struggle in South Africa*, Zed Books, London, 1985, p. 41.

[97] Ibid., p. 42.

[98] *The UNESCO Courier*, March 1967, p. 17.

[99] J. C. de Ridder, *op. cit.*, p. 95.

[100] Ibid., p. 162.

[101] *Social Implications of Industrialization and Urbanization in Africa South of Sahara*, UNESCO, Paris, 1956, p. 738.

[102] Monica Hunter, *op. cit.*, p. XVI.

[103] *African Contemporary Records*, 1968-1969, p. 302.

[104] M. J. Herskovits, *op. cit.*, p. 295.

[105] Jan C. Smuts, *op. cit.*, pp. 87-88.

[106] Cited in: *Apartheid: Its Effect on Education, Science, Culture and Information*, UNESCO, Paris, 1972, p. 16.

[107] *Comment*, London, January 3, 1970.

[108] Govan Mbeki, *South Africa: Peasants' Revolt*, Penguin Books, London, 1964, p. 47.

[109] *Africa South in Exile*, London, No. 3, 1961, p. 55.

[110] *The African Communist*, London, No. 66, 1976, p. 23.

[111] *Fighting Talk*, Johannesburg, 1955, p. 8.

[112] Jordan K. Ngubane, *op. cit.*, p. 58.

[113] Cited in: E. S. Munger, *African Field Reports, 1952-1961*, Struik, Cape Town, 1961, p. 615.

[114] *The World*, Johannesburg, December 17, 1960.

[115] Ibid., August 12, 1961.

[116] *The African Communist*, London, No. 11, 1962, p. 35.

[117] *A Survey of Race Relations in South Africa 1976 (Annual)*, Johannesburg, 1977, p. 184.

[118] *The World*, Johannesburg, January 5, 1976.

[119] Muriel Horrell, *Decade of Bantu Education*, South African Institute of Race Relations, Johannesburg, 1964, p. 5.

[120] *African Affairs*, London, April 1958, p. 153.

[121] *The Transkei and the Case for Separate Development* (Series "Reports on the State of South Africa", No. 25), London, 1963, p. 27.

[122] Jordan K. Ngubane, *op. cit.*, pp. 59-60.

[123] *Financial Mail*, Johannesburg, March 10, 1978.

[124] Joyce Sikakane, *op. cit.*, p. 42.

[125] *Sunday Times*, London, October 2, 1977.

[126] *The Star*, Johannesburg, May 17, 1969.

[127] *The World*, Johannesburg, December 17, 1960.

[128] Cited in: Brian Bunting, *The Rise of the South African Reich*, Penguin Books, London, 1964, p. 217.

[129] Ibid., p. 220.

[130] Heribert Adam, *op. cit.*, p. 110.

Chapter Four

REVOLT IN SOWETO

Schoolchildren Protest, Police Open Fire

The revolt in Soweto began on June 16, 1976. At first what was happening looked harmless and caused the authorities no apprehensions. A few thousand schoolchildren gathered to protest a decision by the authorities to introduce the teaching of half of all the subjects at high and secondary schools in the Afrikaans language. Although they were excited, the children were peaceably inclined, the *Rand Daily Mail* correspondent reported.[1] Other reports say they were untroubled, and even merry.[2] But within hours there was firing, people were killed and wounded, and armoured vehicles were racing in the streets. Barricades appeared here and there. Everywhere burned houses and smoke was blanketing the whole of Soweto. Night was turned into day, *The Times* of London wrote.[3]

Speaking in Parliament on the next day the Minister of Police James Kruger declared: "We did not expect something like this to happen."[4] The point is not that the police had overlooked anything or the Minister had not been informed. Soweto had been created by the South African racists as a ghetto for blacks tolerated to live and work in a "white" city. The authorities believed that everything had been done to keep people in fear and submission. That was why Minister Kruger had also been certain that nothing could happen in Soweto that would be dangerous for the apartheid regime. As for the discontent of the students, the latter were no more than schoolchildren of the senior class, which in Soweto is reached by young people aged 19-20 and, over and above that, they had been indoctrinated in a special education system. Since 1953, i.e., for more than 20 years, the Bantu education system had been bringing up young Africans in a spirit of resignation and total subordination to apartheid and the white master. For that reason

Soweto, the Meadowlands township

Centre of "white" Johannesburg

A street in the Pimville township. 1974

A protest meeting in Sophiatown against forced removal to Soweto

"Matchbox" houses in Soweto

A "bachelor" hostel in one of Soweto townships

Black children in "white" Johannesburg

Trade union meeting. The factory, surrounded by barded wire, is out of bounds to union activists

Christian church service

Some Sowetans still believe in sorcery: *a dingaka* practising his witchcraft

Class in a primary school in Soweto

Hector Peterson, the first victim of police bullets on June 16, 1976, the first day of Soweto uprising, carried by his schoolmates

Young Sowetans are determined to continue their struggle

Black policemen get ready to shoot a peaceful demonstration protesting against apartheid

Young Sowetans trying to beat off a police attack

"Hippo" armoured carriers ready to attack Soweto

Reprisals against anti-apartheid fighters

Police and troops beating protesters in Johannesburg demonstrations

Police anti-riot squad prepares for a bloody provocation near the
Mzimhlope hostel (Soweto) in August 1976. A group of policemen
armed with submachine guns (centre and right) are dressed in workers'
overalls

Workers express solidarity with the struggle against apartheid

A striker going through a police cordon during the strike of municipal workers in Johannesburg

A demonstration in support of the African National Congress and other liberation organisations in one of the townships

The faces of angry blacks intent on keeping on their struggle

A police check-point on one of the roads to African townships

"Buffalo" armoured troop carriers in the streets of a township

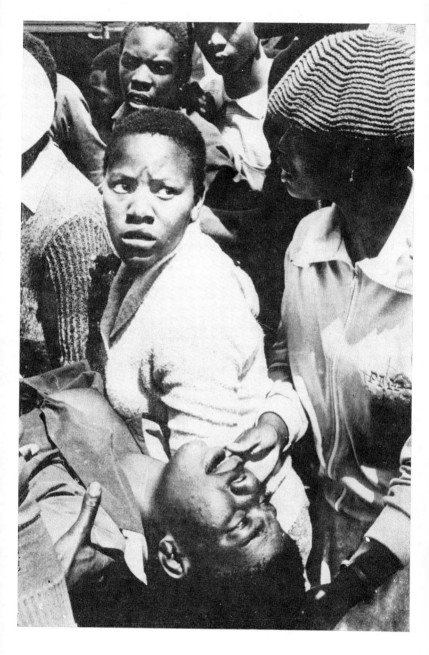

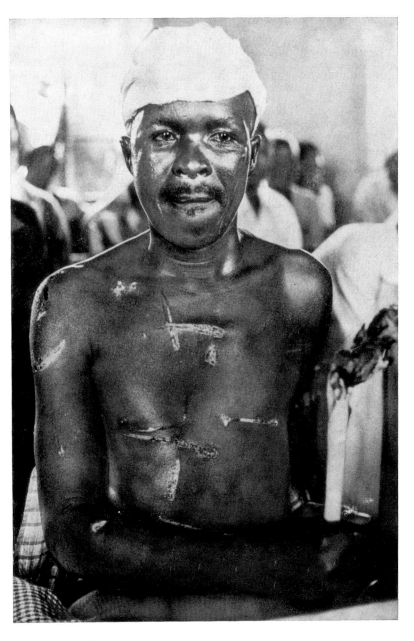

Victims of police terror

Funeral for victims of police terror, which turned into a massive political protest demonstration

Taking an oath to continue the struggle at the tomb of the fallen com-
rade

neither had Minister Kruger grounds for being seriously disturbed even on the morning of June 16 when the first shots rang out in Soweto. Nevertheless, Kruger soon had to abandon his post. He was not forgiven for "not expecting" such a turn of events and was hence charged with not having coped with his job.

The architects of apartheid, who had created Soweto, had miscalculated in hoping that its inhabitants would be submissive: submission was not shown either by the students or by adults. The clash between the young people and the police immediately erupted into an uprising that involved the various social strata of the black population and received the support of other ethnic groups. The first stage of the uprising lasted for several months, up to the beginning of the next year. In subsequent years the forms of the struggle changed, but the struggle itself continued.

Shots were fired and grenades exploded in Soweto in the early 1980s, but as distinct from previous years the police were not the only ones to do the firing. It came also from those who four years earlier had gone to meet police bullets bare-handed in order to protest against the discriminative education system. This time they had firearms, had learned the basics of guerilla street warfare, and had become fighters of Umkhonto we Sizwe (Spear of the Nation), the military wing of the African National Congress. "The Soweto events have opened a new chapter in the history of the revolutionary struggle," it was stated in the report to a plenary meeting of the Central Committee of the South African Communist Party in April 1977.[5]

Thus, it all began on that winter morning in June, well into the academic year. True, in many Soweto schools no classes had been held for several weeks: the authorities were introducing Afrikaans for mathematics and some other subjects, and the students refused to attend classes. The word "Asingeni" ("We Will Not Enter") was painted on the doors of a high secondary school in Phefeni township that had 800 students. Their example was followed by 2,000 students of seven other Soweto schools. Parents and a large number of teachers shared the discontent of students. It was generally held that the introduction of Afrikaans was retarding their children's development.[6] The language used by urban blacks is English not Afrikaans. English is most

11-0343

commonly used in the business and economic life of South African cities and consequently those who study at secondary schools and count on getting a job when they finish do not need Afrikaans. Last but not least is that Afrikaans is a hated language, for it is the language of oppressors. Wilkie Kambule, Principal of the Orlando High School, explained this, saying: "They resent the language because, among other things, they often don't receive good treatment at the hands of Afrikaans officials."[7] Blacks associate Afrikaans with racial discrimination, oppression, and apartheid, and hence its rejection by Sowetans.

An organisation called the South African Students' Movement was formed in Soweto in 1970 on the initiative of the students of three high schools. Its activities included arranging cultural events and various debates, and running a mutual aid fund. Set up legally, it gave high-school students an outlet for airing their grievances and, to some extent, speaking of their involvement in the social affairs and interests of Soweto's adult inhabitants. Of course, the SASM's focus was mainly on school affairs, on affairs related to the Bantu education system. The decision to hold a demonstration on June 16, 1976, to protest against instruction in Afrikaans was adopted at a meeting of representatives of all Soweto schools convened by the SASM branch in the township of Naledi on June 13. An action committee, consisting of two representatives from each school, was formed to organise this demonstration. The SASM General Secretary Tebello Motapanyane was elected to head the committee.

The participants in the forthcoming demonstration began gathering at a high secondary school in Orlando West on the morning of June 16. By 8 a.m. there were about 10,000 pupils (some estimates place the number at nearly 15,000). When the demonstrators, carrying placards bearing words "Down with Afrikaans!", "Afrikaans—Language of Oppressors!", and "Revoke Afrikaans!", were about to march to a stadium where a rally was scheduled a squad of police appeared.

Justice Minister Kruger lied when in the afore-mentioned speech in Parliament he said that the police "fired in self-defence" because "their lives were in danger".[8] There were lies also in the report of the Cillie Commission formed to inquire into the Soweto events in 1976-1977. This report alleges that "the police ... found themselves in a situation of mortal danger".[9]

The police did not even warn the demonstrators to disperse, as they had always done on previous occasions. As soon as they appeared on the scene they attacked the children who had come for a peaceful protest demonstration. This is attested by eyewitnesses.

"I did not hear the police give any order to disperse before they threw teargas canisters into the crowd of singing schoolchildren," wrote a *Rand Daily Mail* reporter who was at the scene.[10] Willie Bokala, another reporter, said he saw a white police officer pick up a stone and hurl it into the crowd. The children in the front rank turned and scattered.[11] Asked whether the police had first fired into the air, the senior police official at Orlando police station said: "No, we fired into the crowd. It's no good firing over their heads."[12] Yet another eyewitness, Victor Dladla, who lived behind the school, where the shooting took place, said: "At about 9.30 a.m. large numbers of schoolchildren came down the road carrying placards. Then a light blue police car carrying five African policemen drove up towards the children. Twice the group of police tried to stop the procession. One policeman then took out his gun and shot a boy who fell. I think he was dead. At that moment the children spread and picked up stones. They started throwing stones at the police. Then the other policemen fired with revolvers at the children and seven more were hit by bullets." This eyewitness account was published in the newspaper under the heading "Shots Before the Stones".[13] Unfortunately, Victor Dladla was not mistaken. The boy was indeed killed. His name was Hector Peterson, and he was only 13. He was the first victim of the unbridled terror that was let loose against the Soweto inhabitants, against young people in the first place, by the police and the special riot squads.

In order to clarify the question of who was responsible for spilling the blood of children in Soweto in the morning of June 16, a question that has been deliberately blurred by the South African authorities, let us recall the evidence of one more eyewitness. Jan Tugwana, a *Rand Daily Mail* reporter, wrote that the first shots were fired on that day in

Soweto while the children began converging on Orlando West. "Two colleagues and I came across two pupils near Mofolo Central and White City Jabavu. It was after 8 a.m. They were carrying placards. One read: '50-50 Afrikaans and Zulu for Vorster'. We stopped our car when we saw another car pull up from the opposite direction. It came from the direction of the Jabulani police station. Inside were three white men and one African. Although they were in plain clothes, I assumed they were policemen. When they saw the placard carriers, one man got out. The pupils separated and bolted. The man ran after the pupil carrying the Vorster placard. He drew a gun and fired two shots in the air. Then he fired another shot in the direction of the pupil, but did not hit him."[14]

After the first shots were fired by the police in Orlando the children who had scattered picked up stones and resumed their procession. Having used up their ammunition, the police retreated to the police station. Sophie Tema, a reporter of *The World*, related that in the first clash she saw a boy of about six or seven years old fall with a bullet wound. "He had a bloody froth on his lips and he seemed to be seriously hurt so I took him to Phefeni clinic, but he was dead when we arrived."[15]

By 10 a.m., angered by the killing of their mates in Orlando, crowds of schoolchildren were scattering throughout Soweto, hurling stones at cars, erecting barricades, and setting fire to administrative buildings, bear halls, and wine stores. Two white officials were killed, one of them in the administrative centre. The office of the manager, the local post office and the local branch of Barclays Bank in Dube were set on fire. *The Sunday Express* reporter recounted that among those who were destroying hated institutions symbolising the rule of the whites differences arose when they got to the library. Some were against setting it on fire, saying: "That's a place that can help our people become educated." Others insisted on burning down the library on the grounds that "it's white property". At first those who wanted to see the library preserved had their way, but it was still burned down at nightfall.[16]

Twenty-one administrative buildings, i.e. the offices of practically all the administrators of townships, were burned in the course of the first day of the Soweto revolt. The

WRAB Chairman Manie Mulder noted on the next day that almost all the Soweto boards were destroyed. "The WRAB offices," he said, "had clearly been the 'prime target'—it represented the white man's property."[17] The offices of puppet Bantu township councils (Jabulani) and schools (Orlando, Diepkloof, Jabulani) were also set on fire. "There could be little doubt that the object of the attacks was to destroy all symbols of state control."[18]

Baruch Hirson, one of the most serious and impartial researchers of these events, gives the following account of the first day of the revolt: "On June 16, the school students stayed firm and threw stones. It was an unequal battle—stones against bullets. Some fled, others fell, but those behind stepped in and closed the ranks. Observers commented on the fact that the youth seemed oblivious of the danger. They kept advancing on the police and pelting them with any object at hand."[19]

The working day was coming to a close and workers began returning home. Hundreds of thousands of workers and junior office employees arrived by train and bus and at once found themselves in the thick of the uprising. A new and powerful force had now joined the embattled schoolchildren. "Earlier in the evening adults returning from work took over the barricades and general lawlessness took hold for a time."[20]

The dispatch from a reporter of the Johannesburg *Financial Mail* quoted words spoken by a motor mechanic on the first day of the uprising: "In our country, the time has come for bursting out. The unrest will continue, there might be a lull, but people are going to get more organised. Those people whose children had been shot in Soweto— they now want to die. Imagine how they felt coming home from work. Their children were killed for no reason."[21]

The working people of Soweto did not merely support their children who had risen in revolt. They joined in the struggle against their own enemy, for their own rights. Their desperation and anger was so deep that on the very first day the uprising spread to the whole of Soweto (and, as the developments of subsequent days and months showed, it extended far beyond Soweto). That morning the police had clearly miscalculated in hoping that a few shots would disperse the unsubmissive demonstrators and restore order in Soweto. Upon realising this, the authorities began sending in large reinforcements to quell the rebellious students. A steady stream of police and riot squads poured into Soweto from 12 a.m. to 10 p.m. These reinforcements came from the whole of the Witwatersrand. By the following morning there were almost a thousand policemen and soldiers in Soweto. They had numerous vehicles at their disposal, including armoured cars called "hippos" by the Africans.

On the second day of the revolt, June 17, fires continued to rage in most of the townships, young people stoned cars driving through Soweto, while the police and riot squads fired at any suspect, chiefly children of school age. "Police vans and armoured cars patrolled the streets, and the crack of FN rifles was heard all day. Shooting was directed at groups of youth in the streets... Often in plain clothes, the police were also seen cruising down the streets in cars, shooting down any child in sight... The police aimed to terrorise and to kill—there were no initial attempts at arrest or detention."[2][2]

On the third day, June 18, there was little change in the situation in Soweto—only more children were killed and wounded and fires were blazing everywhere: in the townships of Zola, Ikwezi, Moletsane, Naledi and Tladi, and administrative buildings, wine stores, and beer halls which were particularly hated by the young people, were on fire. Buses and cars burned on the roads running through Soweto.

The police terror was intensified. The insurgents had nothing but stones to counter the armoured cars, helicopters, and guns with. At about 10 a.m. a large caravan of police vans and armoured carriers escorted the Chairman of the West Rand Administrative Board Manie Mulder, who had personally to view the situation in his "domain". All WRAB-owned cars that had escaped being burned were evacuated from Soweto after this visit. The columns of cars drove past the Orlando police station in the direction of Johannesburg. On that day the authorities began applying court repressions. A large group of court officials escorted by a heavy police guard was brought at first to a rugby field opposite the Orlando police station. From there they were taken in two helicopters to twelve court buildings in various Soweto townships. During the early days of the uprising neither the police nor the authorities realised that the bone of contention was neither Afrikaans language nor the resentment of the students. This misreading of what was taking place and of the in-depth causes of the uprising was mirrored in the above-mentioned apology delivered by the Minister of Police in Parliament.

The Revolt Spreads

While the massive police terror had taken some of the drive off the uprising in Soweto, in other townships around Johannesburg it was only getting under way. Unrest exploded first in Alexandra.

Unlike Soweto, where the first outburst of the revolt lasted for three days from June 16 to 18, in Alexandra fierce battles were fought in the course of one day, June 18. These broke out in the evening of June 17, when details of Bloody Wednesday in Soweto reached the township. The people rose not merely out of a sense of solidarity. They had the same problems, the same sorrows, and the same causes for resentment and rebellion.

Alexandra is a small township, but unlike the Soweto townships it is situated not at a distance from but virtually in Johannesburg itself. It had once been on the city's perimeter, but the now extended city surrounded the township on all sides with white neighbourhoods. The uprising in Soweto did not directly affect the white inhabitants of Johannesburg. They felt that the rising was taking place somewhere far away, beyond the city's perimeter, and that it was the business of the police and the authorities to "restore order" there. But in Alexandra the events took another turn.

In the morning of June 18 the police were shooting not only in the township but in the neighbouring white district of Wynberg where the Hayhoe factory and electronics enterprises were attacked by the insurgents. On that day all factories and offices were closed there and in the neighbouring suburb of Kew, adjoining Alexandra in the south, and many white workers and employees were evacuated. Traffic was halted on the motor road linking Johannesburg with Pretoria and the Jan Smuts airport, the country's main air terminal.

In Alexandra itself there were fires on that day and people marched in the streets carrying placards expressing their protest and anger. One of these read: "Why Are You Killing Children Because of Afrikaans? Amandla!" ("Amandla Ngawethu"--"Power to the People", a rallying cry of the ANC). All over Alexandra the inhabitants, whose only weapons, as in Soweto, were stones, battled with the police, who did not spare their ammunition: in the centre of the township, on 15th Avenue and in Times Square, where most of the shops were located, on Hofmeyer Street and 3rd Avenue, where PUTCO buses were set on fire.

Police reinforcements, including two riot squads, arrived in Alexandra as early as the evening of June 17. But these did not prove to be enough. White "civil defence" units from Sandton (the northern part of Johannesburg) were rushed in. Similar units were alerted in the city's central district and in the Randburg district. "White" Johannesburg was in panic--the authorities now had to think not only of putting down the revolt in the black township but also of protecting the white suburbs around it. "Whites showed signs of panic as the rioting spread further afield," the semi-official *To the Point* noted anxiously. "Unfounded rumours spread, white housewives even began stockpiling food".[23] "For the first time the whites felt the direct impact of the revolt," Baruch Hirson wrote.[24] And this was the principal distinction of the uprising in Alexandra township.

Something that neither the authorities nor the police could have foreseen happened in the very heart of Johannesburg on that day, June 18. A column of students of the University of Witwatersrand marched along Queen Bridge standing over a railway. Several hundreds of white young men and women demonstrated in solidarity with the insurgents of Soweto and Alexandra. They were joined by blacks. The police closed in to "restore peace and order". Batons were used on whites and blacks alike.

The uprising encompassed a huge area around Johannesburg, practically the whole of the Transvaal, and some towns and townships in other provinces. Unrest among Africans, the burning of buildings and cars, and police reprisals were to be observed in Benoni, Nigel, Kagiso, Tembisa, and elsewhere. There were actions against the authorities even in the Bantustans in the north of the Transvaal.

Nor did Pretoria, capital of South Africa and citadel of Afrikaner nationalism and apartheid, escape unscathed. Unrest began in it on June 21. Two townships—Atteridgeville and Mamelodi with respective populations (official) of 65,900 and 103,758[25]—are situated on Pretoria's doorstep. On June 21 the inhabitants of these townships joined the uprising; they were followed by the inhabitants of the townships of Mabopane (population—86,900)[26] and Garankuwa, who, while they live on the territory of the Bantustan of Bophuthatswana, they work in "white" Pretoria.

Approximately the same situation took shape in these townships as in Soweto and Alexandra: school pupils boycotted classes and staged protest and solidarity demonstrations; on the way to these demonstrations they were joined by adult workers; they were fired on by the police; in reply stones were hurled and buildings and buses were set on fire. Smoke from the fires drifted over the townships and dead and wounded lay in the streets.

In the Mamelodi and Mabopane townships the student actions coincided with strikes by workers (1,000) at the Chrysler Park factory and the Klipgat water-purifying plant (170 workers). This heightened the strains activated by the revolt and gave it added strength.

The week beginning on Bloody Wednesday of June 16 saw perhaps the longest and most violent eruption of the rising. Police Minister Kruger announced that in that week 176 persons were killed and 1,139 were wounded.[27] Few people believed these official figures. "The number that died on June 16, or in the days to come, is not known... The police took every step to prevent a full list being compiled. Journalists were warned to keep away from the piles of bodies, on the grounds that it was none of their business! Baragwanath Hospital was closed to the public. Lorries arrived and took away corpses, and many were never accounted for then, or later."[28] Crowds went to the police stations and the morgues in search of missing relatives, parents looked for their children and in most cases found them dead. Some were never found.

The police brutality was evidence of the racist regime's determination to crush by force, to drown in blood the revolt in Soweto and other townships. The police made no effort to disperse demonstrating schoolchildren—they shot to kill. They fired mainly from armoured cars or vans. The broad streets of the Soweto townships and the geometrical siting of the houses made moving targets easy to bring down. "They shot at random and they shot to kill. Any person suspected of being a 'leader' was pursued and shots often found a target. Other youths were considered fair game and if sighted on the streets were instant targets."[29] A great number of children were murdered deliberately. In Mabopane township the police met demonstrating schoolchildren with a curtain of fire on June 21, and 10-year-old George Maboa was the first to be killed.[30] *Rand Daily Mail* photographer Ronnie Kweyi and a Soweto salesman Carl Rabotho saw a policeman firing a pistol at some small boys running across a street in Moroka township.[31]

At the very outset of the uprising Police Minister Kruger took a categorical stand against using rubber bullets to disperse demonstrators, saying that they were not effective enough in the conditions of South Africa. He condoned the use of firearms, declaring that rubber bullets made people "tame to the gun". "Rioters must know," he said, "that when a policeman picked up his rifle the best thing was to get out of the way immediately."[32] His view was that the "moment people in a riotous situation know you have rubber bullets it means, in effect, that you also have rubber guns".[33] The most brutal terror was thus the order of the day and the authorities counted on it to bridle popular discontent.

During the first days of July Soweto buried its dead. Funeral processions moved in the direction of the Doornkop and Avalon cemeteries. Thousands of people joined the relatives and friends of the dead. On the fourth anniversary of the uprising the South African journalist Percy Qoboza was to write: "On Sunday morning I went to Doornkop cemetery. It was very early in the morning. The mist was thick and the wind mild, chilly. Under normal circumstances it could have been a pleasant, warm morning. And yet I found myself shivering. Shivering from looking at all those graves. As I looked at those graves, all or most of them bearing the dates June 16, 17, 18 or 19 beyond, I began to shiver. So many people, so many families, so many friends, so many neighbours. The entire community was affected by the tragedy. I shivered at the legacy of bitterness, hate and deep sense of loss the people are undergoing."[3 4]

The police prohibited the simultaneous burial of the dead, as the Soweto inhabitants had intended (for this reason burials were postponed to July). However, this ban had little effect because the separate funeral processions followed one another, the coffins were lowered into grave one after another, and all this fused into a single, almost uninterrupted demonstration of sorrow and anger.

The funerals of the police victims differed in many ways from customary funerals. Tradition did not permit the presence of young people, according the principal role at funeral ceremonies to married women—relatives of the deceased. All that was now changed: young people marched in the funeral processions playing the leading role. The funerals of the victims of police terror became powerful political demonstrations in which practically the entire population of Soweto participated.

Slogans were chanted, speeches were made, and young people marched with upraised fists. The *Sunday Times* reporter wrote that he was in a police helicopter hovering over a funeral and clearly heard the singing of about 2,000 people who stood around an open grave.[3 5]

In most cases the police were in the vicinity and interfered at the first opportunity. This interference was met with cries of indignation, the proclamation of slogans, and the hurling of stones. The police responded with bullets and on the next day the funerals took place of those who had marched in the processions of the previous day.

This was how those who were found and identified were buried. But many of the dead were taken by the police from the morgues without waiting for them to be identified by relatives and buried without witnesses. The ANC journal *Sechaba* wrote that there were "insistent reports of mass graves and midnight burials in Doornkop and other cemeteries in Soweto".[3 6] Police Major-General W. H. Kotze refused to say how many bodies had been removed in this way. "I'm not going into details about how many children or adults there were," he said, "and nobody's going to tell you. I'm in charge and I'll decide what information is released."[3 7]

Despite the interdictions people gathered in the churches

to pray for the dead. In Jabavu some 250 persons gathered at St. Paul's Anglican Church, where a funeral service was held for Hector Peterson, a 13-year-old schoolboy believed to have been the first victim. Reverend Manas Buthelezi, who conducted the service, told the gathering: "The people who died in the riots have died so that those who live will lead a better life."[38]

Reverend Manas Buthelezi was elected chairman of the Soweto Parents' Association (later renamed the Black Parents' Association) that was formed soon after the outbreak of the revolt. The parents of the schoolchildren killed in the streets of Soweto were not about to stand aloof. The association's immediate concern was to organise the burials of the victims of the rising and help those who could not pay the cost of burying their dead children.

The police gave the new organisation a hostile reception. The very first meeting of the SPA members, scheduled for June 20, was banned, and those who gathered in a church in Orlando West were dispersed by the police who arrived in three lorries.[39] Subsequently, practically all the members of this organisation were harassed by the police.

The first outburst of the revolt was put down. There were raids, arrests, and trials. All the townships of Soweto and other districts of the Witwatersrand were flooded with police. A precarious lull set in. "In Moroka, Jabulani and Orlando...," wrote the journalists who visited these townships on June 26, "the atmosphere was uneasy."[40] Ruins left by the fires and the charred skeletons of burned cars were to be seen everywhere. Of the PUTCO buses alone more than 90 had been burned or damaged. More than 150 buildings, mostly administrative offices, had been razed. The damage inflicted on state property during the first week of the rising was estimated at 25 million pounds sterling.[41]

In early July there were only individual, scattered actions by young people. A calm of sorts was observed: the atmosphere was charged with expectation. Liberation organisations stepped up their public activities. Two "leaflet bombs" were "exploded" on July 8 in a railway station in the centre of Johannesburg. The hundreds of people returning from work found themselves with leaflets in which the African National Congress gave its assessment of the events in Soweto and called for an intensification of the struggle.

172

There was much to disturb the police during these seemingly quiet days. The Institute of Black Studies, which had been set up shortly before the uprising, was planning to hold its first conference in Soweto with the subject "A Black Perspective" on its agenda. This conference was to be attended by leading black intellectuals, including Professor Ezekiel Mphahlele, Professor Herbert Vilakazi, and Mphiwa Mbata, lecturers at the American universities. Fatima Meer of the University of Natal planned to present a report under the heading "25 Years of Apartheid". A wide range of papers were to be presented. Some were politically slanted, and in others the condition of blacks in South Africa was considered from the standpoint of psychology, literature, and even music. "Our conference," said the Institute's director Nimrod Mkele, "is a serious intellectual attempt to assess the position of the black man. We wanted the people of Soweto to feel free to take part."[42]

The Johannesburg police and City Council banned the conference that was due to be held in Dube township in the very centre of Soweto. The acting chief magistrate of Johannesburg Louis Francis said the peace would be seriously endangered by the gathering.[43] The conference was held a day later but its venue was not in Johannesburg or Soweto.

On July 18 the newspapers reported an occurrence that seemed to be no more than a commonplace crime but, in fact, had a political lining and an inner, logical relation to the turbulent events in Soweto. An African employed as a non-resident gardener by a white family in Krugersdorp, north of Johannesburg, shot and killed two white WRAB officials with a pistol he had stolen from his employer, who later said: "All he wanted was living quarters and the right to work to keep his wife and children... when he found jobs, he could not get accommodation, even in a hostel. He was anxious to work... But he was constantly arrested because he did not have the right permit. And he visited the Board's offices regularly to try and straighten things out, but his hands were tied by official tape."[44]

In early July the government employed a tactic designed to quench the student discontent. The instructions prescribing the use of Afrikaans in secondary schools for Africans were invalidated on July 6. Two members of a school council in Meadowlands, dismissed for objecting to the use of Afrikaans in schools, were reinstated on July 18. Two white officials who had been most zealously propagating the use of Afrikaans were removed from Soweto: they were the regional education director and a district inspector. It would seem that the students had made their point and compelled the government to back down. But at that stage of the struggle this small victory satisfied nobody. The young people demanded the dismantling of the entire system of Bantu education, while the involvement of the working masses in the uprising and the brutalising of police repressions led to a broad confrontation between the Africans and the apartheid system as such.

The government's tactic ran aground. On July 26, the day on which students had been ordered to resume classes, the schools remained empty. Fires again blazed up in Soweto in the evening of July 27—flames engulfed another six schools and a youth club. Some 50 schools had been burned or seriously damaged during the last ten days in July in the Transvaal, Natal, and the Orange Free State; in Cape Province the burning of schools began in August. Young people were very eager to study because only a full secondary education opened some opportunities for a more or less bearable life. However, the schools epitomised the discriminative and, hence, hated Bantu education system and were therefore set on fire almost everywhere, especially as they were the most available targets for the students.

The first officially sanctioned meeting of the Urban Bantu Council following the June events was held on August 1. Council members and school principals tried to persuade the students to halt the struggle and return to school. But nothing came of these efforts, either. Even the meeting itself was not properly conducted on account of the stormy protests from the young people assembled for the occasion.

The Urban Bantu Council had earlier had little prestige in Soweto. With the outbreak of the uprising its influence dwindled almost to zero—the Africans simply ceased to notice it. The Soweto Students Representative Council was now in full control of the situation. The Black Parents' Association won growing influence. Disturbed by the fact that the Soweto youth were not ceasing the struggle and, on top of that, were cementing contacts and finding a common language with adults, the police launched a new campaign of arrests. On August 3 they began mass raids of all the townships with the result that there were some violant clashes between the Soweto inhabitants and the police, who used their firearms again. Once more the casualty list was lengthened.

General Political Strikes—Height of the Uprising

The entire population of Soweto spilled out into the streets early in the morning of the next day, August 4. Young people appealed to workers to stay away from work. Most responded, remaining at home. Those who feared to lose their jobs or to be targeted by the police found they simply could not get to Johannesburg. Trains were brought to a standstill by students, who took apart the sections of the railway running through Soweto. Nor was it easy to go by bus on that day; the buses were stoned and many were damaged. The first general strike thus began in Soweto in the course of the uprising.

The central event of that day was a march by 20,000 young people, who formed themselves into a column. They were joined by many of the workers who had stayed away from work. The column grew as it moved through Soweto: new groups of students and workers from outlying townships fell into line with it. The demonstrators planned to go to the central police station on Vorster Square to demand the release of comrades arrested during the uprising. They carried placards: "Release All Detainees!" and "Release Students From Prison!"

This time the police were ready for the demonstration. Police helicopters kept the demonstrators under surveillance as they marched through Soweto. A large police covering detachment reinforced with riot squads on armoured carriers awaited the column in the vicinity of the New Canada Railway Station at the approaches to Johannesburg.

Shots rang out as soon as the head of the column approached the police cordon. From behind the armoured carriers the police fired long blasts[45] at the unarmed students in the front ranks. Three were killed and 15 were seriously wounded by the first salvoes.[46] Swept by the murderous fire from police submachine guns the demonstra-

175

tors retreated to Soweto, where they gave vent to their anger and urge for vengeance. As in June, fires flared up across the whole of Soweto. Everything belonging to the white authorities and associated with apartheid was in flames: administrative buildings, shops, beer halls, and schools. Two houses belonging to black policemen were also burned down.[47]

However, the events of the beginning of August in Soweto were not a repetition of what took place in June. The young people now had the support of the working class. From 60 to 90 per cent of the factory and office workers of various enterprises took part in the general strike staged in early August; most of the industrial facilities and offices in Johannesburg idled on August 4-6. This was due not to the notorious "intimidation" about which the South African press wrote in those days but to "the obvious support that the workers gave the students".[48] This solidarity of the workers with the youth was acknowledged by the *Financial Mail*:[49]. "The events of 4 August inaugurated a new phase in the Revolt of 1976."[50]

Twenty-two persons, all of them Africans, were killed or wounded in Soweto within three days (August 4-6). In the next few days the unrest spread across the country. On August 8 and 9 there was turmoil in Alexandra township, where two persons were killed, in New Brighton township (near Port Elizabeth), Hammanskraal (near Pretoria), and Mafeking, a "white" town on the territory of the Bantustan of Bophuthatswana, where the "parliament" building was burned down. On August 11 there were risings in the townships of Langa, Nyanga, and Guguletu situated on the outskirts of Cape Town. Within only two days 27 persons were killed and more than 100 were wounded there. The actions of the black population around Cape Town were supported by coloureds, despite all the efforts of the racist authorities to divide blacks and coloureds and set them against each other. Clashes with the police took place in the townships around East London on August 17. On August 18 there was further unrest in Port Elizabeth and Uitenhage, where the police killed 10 blacks and wounded more than 20.

A distinctive aspect of all these events was the very active support of the workers for the young people in revolt against the apartheid system. Besides, the sweep of the uprising itself was wider. It was not confined to the Johannesburg-Pretoria area as in June, but spilled over to many industrial areas of Cape Province.

In the meantime, police terror reigned again in Soweto. Many people were arrested, and the police hunted student leaders, particularly members of the Soweto Students Representative Council. On August 11 the Minister of Police James Kruger authorised "indefinite preventive detention". Addressing the conference of the National Party he said: "He [the African.— V.G.] knows his place and, if not, I'll tell him. The blacks always say 'We shall overcome', but I say we shall overcome."[5][1]

In parallel with their counter-assault the police took steps to use reactionary elements within the African community against the students. Acting through the Urban Bantu Council, they formed "Home Guard" groups. A police officer present at a gathering of these "Guards" assured them that they could bear arms and count on backing from the police.[5][2] On the pretext of maintaining law and order in the townships the "Home Guard" made preparations for the physical elimination of defiant students with members of the Black Parents' Association as their prime targets. Winnie Mandela and Dr. Aaron Mathlare had to go to court to draw public attention to the criminal intentions of the Urban Bantu Council and the "Home Guard". The court was informed that at a meeting at the house of T. Makhaya, Chairman of the UBC, Councillor Lucas Shabangu urged that the houses of Winnie Mandela and Aaron Mathlare be attacked, and that the children who tried to prevent workers going to work should be killed.[5][3]

The authorities sought to incite migrant workers against the students. The former were, in fact, peasants who had come to the townships temporarily and were living in the "bachelor" hostels. The students' interests, slogans, and demands for the abolition of the Bantu education system were alien to the migrant workers, who had only one thing in mind—the opportunity to earn money in the city within the time-limit for which they had been recruited. They were generally suspicious of the Soweto youth, for many of them had been victimised by *tsotsi* gangs who were after their weekly pay packets. Living in the isolated hostels, they had little to do with the permanent urban residents; almost all were illiterate, and their class and political consciousness was practically at zero. Hence, there unquestionably was fuel for antagonising them against the insurgent young people and the workers supporting the latter.

Nevertheless, despite the ruthless police terror and the government's tactics of splitting and debilitating insurgent Soweto, the students continued their actions. Preparations for yet another general strike, planned for August 23-25, proceeded energetically and in secrecy in the course of two off-days, August 21 (Saturday) and 22 (Sunday). Leaflets with the words "Azikwelwa madoda!" ("Stay at Home"), signed by the ANC and SSRC, appeared throughout Soweto, in practically every house. The leaflets recalled the massive general strikes of the 1950s and noted the successiveness of the stages of the struggle.

On the first day of the strike, August 23, 80 per cent of the Soweto workers stayed at home.[54] *Rand Daily Mail* noted that the massive stay-away in Soweto involved labour and staff. "The clothing industry reported that all but a few of the 300 factories in the area were closed... In many factories there was a 100 per cent stay-away... Mr. Kruger said workers had stayed away because of pamphlets distributed by the banned African National Congress calling on them to do so, despite the fact that the police had been on hand from 3 a.m. to protect them... The Johannesburg Chamber of Commerce reported yesterday that the extensive stay-away hit industrialists, retailers and insurance companies." Among the causes making the strike effective, the newspaper named the "general politicisation of the estimated 1,250,000 residents in Soweto and identification with a general protest such as withholding labour".[55]

While stoppages of this nature were formerly attributed in the South African press to "intimidation", to "agitators" preventing workers from leaving the townships to go to work, this time there were entirely different pronouncements. "It is not yet clear how much credence can be given to reports that 'intimidation' is the chief cause of the stay-away. Soweto residents point to the fact that no barricades were set up to prevent workers travelling into Johannesburg, as happened two weeks ago. One personnel officer told the *Financial Mail* that 'the biggest percentage of absentees has been among manual labourers. I can't help wondering whether this is not some sort of show of strength, rather than the result of intimidation'."[5][6]

Compared with the strike of early August, the Soweto stay-away at the close of August was indeed a more conscious and effective action of the class struggle. Most of the factory workers and clerical personnel willingly responded to the ANC and SSRC call despite the police terror and the very real danger of losing their jobs and of being evicted to a rural area or a Bantustan. The youth pickets at the Soweto railway stations and the main crossroads had hardly anything to do: they did not have to persuade anybody, much less put pressure on the workers. It was only in the outlying Soweto townships that some groups of people went to work to Johannesburg under heavy police escort. These were mostly migrant workers, but even they were few in number. The reports from most of the hostels were that the lodgers likewise supported the stay-away.

The strike continued into the next day, Tuesday, August 24. However, something extraordinary took place in Soweto in the afternoon of that day: migrant workers living in the Mzimhlope hostel (township of Meadowlands) attacked schoolchildren. However, this attack involved not all who lived there but only the Zulu workers, of whom there were 1,630 in the hostel (10,300 persons were housed in this hostel). Armed with clubs and pangas (knives for cutting sugar-cane) the Zulus roamed the streets of the townships and beat up all children of school age in their way. There were police armoured cars within sight and from time to time they fired not at the Zulus engaged in these outrages but at the children and adult Sowetans supporting them.

The police not only guarded the Zulu migrants but also directed their actions. A *Rand Daily Mail* reporter who managed to make his way into the Mzimhlope hostel wrote: "There I saw a policeman in a camouflage suit, armed with an FN rifle. Through an interpreter, the policeman said: 'You are warned not to continue damaging the houses because they belong to the West Rand Administration Board. If you damage houses, you will force us to take action against you to prevent this. You have been ordered to kill only these troublemakers'."[5][7] The SSRC vice-president

Nkosazana Dlamini subsequently wrote about these events to the journal *Sechaba*: "There is also evidence that the police went to the township hostels and agitated the inmates. There is also evidence that most people who took part in the 'out-riots' were not really hostel dwellers, but disguised policemen, transported to the scene in police cars."[5 8]

On the previous day, August 23, Chief Gatsha Buthelezi of the Bantustan of KwaZulu and leader of the Zulu Inkatha organisation, "called for the creation of vigilante groups", warning the students that they might face a "backlash from responsible elements of the black community".[5 9] Similar inciting statements were made also by senior police officers. Police Major-General Michael Geldenhuys declared: "Agitators who attempt to enforce a work stay-away in Soweto will experience a backlash from law-abiding citizens in the townships." Police Colonel Jan P. Visser was more explicit: "People must go to work and just thrash the children stopping them."[6 0] It is indicative that both Gatsha Buthelezi and General Geldenhuys used one and the same word: "backlash".

The police were able to launch this provocation because of the social and ethnic differences between the permanent Soweto residents and the temporary inmates of the hostels. Nevertheless, it did not spread far. No support was given to the bloody "out-riots" of the Mzimhlope Zulus even by the Zulus living in other Soweto hostels.

On the third day of the strike, August 27, the overwhelming majority of the workers stayed away once again. There was clearly no "backlash". In fact, even Gatsha Buthelezi "dissociated" himself from the provocation, arriving in Soweto on August 28 to conduct his own "inquiry" into what had happened. He charged the police with instigation and with backing the "out-riots" of his fellow-tribesmen.[6 1]

In Soweto the start of September saw steadily mounting pressure being brought to bear on the students: they were urged to return to the schools. This was wanted by the authorities and by parents and school teachers. The SSRC issued a statement addressed to "all residents of Soweto, hostels, Reef and Pretoria". One of the eight points of this statement also urged the schoolchildren to go back to their schools. True, the preceding point demanded that all students and black leaders be released, that the Bantu education be scrapped off, and that apartheid be abolished. As Baruch Hirson points out, this was possibly a tactical move to restore an organisational base for the SSRC.[62] However, in the face of the police terror reigning in Soweto, a return to school by the students would signify their acceptance of defeat. It was unrealistic to expect this, particularly after the successful strikes of August. A few days later the SSRC again spoke of a boycott of classes in the schools and of a boycott of the upcoming exams.

Beginning with June 16, as tension mounted, the confrontation of the Soweto youth and majority of adult residents with the racist authorities grew increasingly more violent. Having spread practically across the entire country, the Soweto revolt gathered strength. The South African government likewise counted more on violence than on reconciliation. This was the only interpretation that could be put on Prime Minister Vorster's speech in Bloemfontein on September 8. He maintained that he would never hold talks on the introduction of the principle of "one man, one vote", i.e., on the universal and equal suffrage. The only way that he knew for governing South Africa was "by the policy and principles of the Nationalist Party". He assured his white audience that law and order would be restored immediately and that if this could not be done by existing methods other steps would be taken. Police Minister Kruger advised that every white had to protect his own property and, if he had to kill in the process, that was justified.[63]

The SSRC decided to conduct another three-day work stay-away in Soweto. The leaflet addressed to "beloved parents" had a special appeal to "our parents in the hostels". It called the workers living in hostels "victims of the notorious migrant labour system" and appealed for a united stand against injustices. "United we stand," it said.[64] On September 5 the SSRC called a series of mass meetings with hostel inmates in order to inform them of the planned strike in advance and enlist their support. A leaflet containing several appeals was circulated in the Soweto townships: to parents—"Cooperate with us!", to workers—"Stay away from work!", and to migrants in hostels—"Do not fight!". Further, it listed the students' objections: "to shooting by the police; to arrests and detentions, to murders in detention and to the cutting down of our parents' wages who have stayed away from work in sympathy with their killed sons and daughters".[65] A special leaflet to taxi-drivers urged them not to transport strike-breakers. Thus, the SSRC took the experience of previous strikes into account and made the appropriate preparations.

On September 13, the first day of the strike, 75-80 per cent of the workers, living mostly in Soweto, did not report for work in the Johannesburg area. A spokesman of the Johannesburg Chamber of Commerce declared that only 2 per cent of the black workers turned up at some factories.[66] Press estimates are that over 175,000 people did not work on that day.[67]

On the first day of the strike there were no serious clashes with the police, as the SSRC had explicitly declared: "We don't want bloodshed." Although beginning from 5.30 a.m. the streets of the Soweto townships, usually filled with people going to work, were deserted, after midday the picture was different. There was an almost holiday atmosphere with people wandering through the streets and boys playing games of soccer.[68]

On the next day, September 14, the situation changed sharply: everywhere the police attacked the strikers, particularly young people. The Sowetans were not found wanting, although the forces were far from being equal. Rails were taken apart and damaged on a sector of the railway running through Soweto. While there were six fatalities on the first day of the strike, 12 persons were killed on the second day. On the third day there were somewhat fewer strikers; on average 60 per cent of the workers stayed away in Johannesburg.

On the whole, the Sowetans successfully staged this strike of solidarity and protest against police terror, thereby paying tribute to the memory of victims of the terror. The situation was more complex in the Alexandra township. Here the workers stayed away on September 14. A powerful police force rushed upon the small population of this township. The police made house-to-house search, ferreting out "agitators" and "instigators", and forcing people out of their homes and compelling them to go to work. Those who expressed any objections were arrested on the spot, pushed into vans, and taken to police stations. More than 800 persons were arrested on the first day—subsequently, many of them were expelled to reserves. These police actions aborted the strike in Alexandra.

When the strike in Soweto was coming to an end the struggle was joined by one more large contingent of the South African proletariat. The workers of the Cape Town industrial area went on strike on September 15. Most of the workers in this area are coloureds. The government evidently hoped that as a result of its policy of apartheid the unity of actions by black and coloured workers had receded into the past. But they miscalculated: a two-day general protest strike against police repressions and the entire apartheid system was a powerful manifestation of the class unity of the workers of Cape Town—both black and coloured—and an expression of their solidarity with the workers of the Transvaal. On the first day, September 15, 75 per cent of the workers stayed away, while 80-85 per cent did not go to work on the next day. Nearly 200,000 coloureds, or about 80 per cent of the Cape Town workforce, were involved. Even migrant workers—those living in the townships of Langa and Nyanga—stayed away from work on those days.

Another general protest strike flared up in the Transvaal a week later. Workers residing in the township of Tembisa (East Rand) initiated the strike on September 20. Many of them had been resettled from the Alexandra township and they had brought with them their militant spirit of resistance, which had always been that township's hallmark. The leaflet urging the Tembisa workers to strike said: "Parent-workers, heed our call and stay away from work like in Soweto and Alexandra. We the Black Society have nothing to lose from staying away from work but our chains! Let our oppressor tremble! ... Our slogan is: Away with Vorster!!! Down with Oppression!!! Power to the People!!!"[6] [9]

The journal *Sechaba* subsequently noted: "The participation of the organised black working class in the general uprisings raised the entire struggle to a new and higher stage. On two occasions, in August and again in September 1976, black workers successfully carried out three-day political general strikes which paralysed industry in the Witwatersrand and in the Cape and seriously shook the confidence of foreign investors in the economic stability of the regime. During the second general political strike in September 1976, called in support of demands for the release of all detainees and an end to massacres of our people, more than 500,000 black workers were on strike in Johannesburg and Cape Town alone."[70]

Hardly had the strike in Tembisa township come to an end than "white" Johannesburg was given yet another jolt: Soweto schoolchildren demonstrated on Eloff Street, in the city's centre, on September 23.

A leaflet that began with the words: "To Town!!! To Eloff!!! To that Exclusive White Paradise!!!", was distributed in Soweto on the eve of that demonstration. The leaflet reminded people of the black demonstration on Adderley Street, the heart of Cape Town. There the "revolutionary demonstrators... brought so much panic to the already frightened whites, that all guns obtainable in the public market were sold out". The leaflet urged: "Let us move forward, Vorster must not delude himself and think that we will stop anywhere short of freedom".

"TO TOWN! TO JOHANNESBURG! TO ELOFF! and surroundings, demonstrate violently your bitterness."

"TO TOWN says the most deprived part of humanity! The Battle Cry will be: VORSTER YOU CAN'T STOP US!"[71]

Of course, the police knew of the planned demonstration and tried to stop the young people who streamed from Soweto to the centre of the city early in the morning. Many were stopped by the police cordons, nevertheless, the demonstration took place. At about 8 a.m. on September 23 some fifteen hundred Soweto schoolchildren, who managed to make their way into the city, gathered at the Central Railway Station. Unfolding their placards, which called for the release of detainees and an end to police repressions, the demonstrators marched along Eloff Street in the central shopping district of Johannesburg. They were instantly joined by black workers in the vicinity, and by white students of Witwatersrand University.

Riot police appeared quickly. This time their main weapons were batons and dogs—they did not venture to use firearms in the heart of the "white" city. Nonetheless, the treatment they meted out was ruthless. Beaten and dogbitten, schoolchildren were bundled into vans and taken to police stations. In the course of the hour and a half that the demonstration and police violence lasted more than 880 persons were arrested. Simultaneously the police conducted raids throughout Soweto and in Alexandra. There they did not hesitate to use firearms.

In October the SSRC and Soweto youth engaged in an anti-alcohol campaign and preparations for a boycott of Christmas festivities. The numerous bottle stores in Soweto and also administrative buildings had been the chief targets of the Sowetans as soon as the revolt broke out. The assertions of the reactionary press that these bottle stores were ravaged by Africans in order to steal liquor proved to be untenable.

Of course, among Soweto's million-strong population and Alexandra's tens of thousands of inhabitants there were many hooligans, alcoholics, and other criminal elements who took advantage of the turbulent events as an opportunity for looting and committing outrages. However, these were rather the exception than the rule. Bottle stores and bars were wrecked and set on fire not for the purpose of getting drunk but for the purpose of eradicating these centres of alcoholism and the accompanying poverty. "Every railway station, and in Soweto you have more than 20 railway stations, had a bottle store. When our parents leave work with their pay, which is very meagre, they immediately buy liquor and then go home without money," said a young Sowetan named Ranwedzi Nenngwekhulu.[72]

At the close of September words reading "Less liquor, more education!", "Away with boozers!", and "No more liquor till next year!" were scrawled on walls in the Soweto townships. On October 31 young people proclaimed a ban on liquor in Soweto. The shebeen owners—their businesses survived the wrecking of government liquor stores—accepted the ban. More, they united in an Association of Shebeen Owners in order to have organised contact and cooperate with the young people.

The drive against alcohol was conducted under slogans expressing sorrow and mourning for the victims of police shootings and solidarity with the detained participants in the revolt. The same slogans were used for the boycott of Christmas shopping and of the Christmas holidays themselves. Agitation to persuade people to refrain from such shopping and join in the boycott of retail outlets run by whites started in October. This could be a signally damaging boycott because in the run-up to Christmas from October to December the urban blacks did most of their shopping estimated at up to 50 per cent of their annual expenditure.

At the end of October the SSRC called for a "period of mourning for the dead" as part of the campaign against alcohol and Christmas celebration. The leaflet that was issued said in part: "All things that we enjoy must be suspended for the sake of our kids who died from police bullets." "No Christmas celebration, shopping, parties, Christmas cards or presents."[73] The shopping boycott was, moreover, a reprisal against companies which docked wages or dismissed workers because they obeyed the call to stay away from work in August and September. At the same time, in a statement for the press the SSRC demanded, among other things, the resignation of the government, the release of all political prisoners, and consultations with black parents with the purpose of achieving a "settlement and peace".

To make the boycott campaign more effective it was decided to stage another strike, this time to last for five days throughout the country. It was scheduled to start on November 2.

Unlike the previous general strike, the November stayaway did not materialise. There were a number of reasons for this. A considerable effort to prevent this strike was made by manufacturers, businessmen, traders, and administrative agencies. On Friday, the day before the scheduled strike, workers of 2,500 companies found in their pay packets a warning signed by the Transvaal Chamber of Industries and printed in three languages: English, Zulu, and Sotho. "You must be strong and come to work," it said, "...listening to the agitators will not improve your position," adding that many blacks were out of work and would be glad to fill any vacancy.[74] This warning had an effect on the workers because after the previous strikes many persons lost their jobs and were expelled to rural localities.

Those who retained their jobs received starvation wages for the duration of strikes. Most of the workers could not afford to lose a week's wages on account of a five-day strike. When the revolt was at its peak (June and August-September) and anger and fury against the police terror was running high, the psychological impulsion was the decisive factor and the workers stayed away from their jobs even if it meant hurtful material privation. But in November the situation was different. Besides, the previous general strikes had not brought any tangible benefit for the workers. This circumstance influenced the Sowetans who were being urged to stay away from work once more.

Thus, when the decision was passed to stage another and longer general political strike all these factors were not taken into account. Nor was the SSRC able to organise a general strike in other parts of the country: it had neither the contacts with nor the necessary influence among the local workers.

Results and Lessons of the Revolt

The drive to boycott shopping and have people abstain from entertainment including the drinking of alcoholic beverages, as a tribute to those who died, was quite successful. In this drive the young people were supported by practically the entire population of Soweto. Many white shopkeepers in Johannesburg, particularly owners of small shops, suffered large losses. The campaign against Christmas celebrations was likewise successful.

Police repressions mounted as the year drew to a close. The police conducted raids regularly, making house-to-house searches and arresting people on the slightest suspicion, especially young people. The courts handed down stereotype sentences: prison terms and flogging. According to data gathered by the South African Institute of Race Relations, in 1976 the courts found 1,281 persons guilty of committing "crimes" during the revolt. Of these 355 were adults and 926 were under the age of 18. All were black, of course. Another 2,915 were held in custody awaiting trial.

Large numbers of young people fled from Soweto. Some, fearing arrest, went to relatives in rural communities, others made their way to the frontier and fled abroad.

Many joined the ANC, underwent military training, and then fought bravely in the Umkhonto we Sizwe units. An ANC leaflet issued to mark Heroes' Day on December 16 called upon young people to join Umkhonto we Sizwe and paid tribute to the struggle waged by them: "To all of you we say: Forward brave fighters! Forward brothers and sisters! Maintain your revolutionary unity and fighting spirit. Together we will raise the struggle to more glorious heights."[75] The following evaluation of the Soweto youth actions in 1976 was given in a report to a plenary meeting of the Central Committee of the South African Communist Party in April 1977: "The inventiveness and ingenuity of the youth, in particular, showed boundless revolutionary imagination. Throughout the period [of the revolt.—V.G.], tactics were varied and new forms of maintaining the pressure were found. At the beginning, the children of Soweto simply faced police bullets and flushed away the tear gas with water, or bravely hurled back the canisters. Later, more sophisticated actions were evolved.

"The youth soon learnt the folly of facing Vorster's terrorists in the open streets in large numbers and they switched to operating in small groups under the cover of darkness. Many police vehicles and 'Hippos' were ambushed and destroyed. Barricades were erected to slow down the enemy and to provide cover in time of attack. Home-made incendiary devices were quickly in evidence. The people also turned their attention to the government collaborators amongst them and to the police informers. The organized destruction of property, which symbolized the racist system of oppression, was carried out by well-planned actions of small organized units."

The report assessed the Soweto revolt's significance: "It made it abundantly clear to the world and the racist regime that our people have reached a stage where they are no longer prepared to behave like sheep led to the slaughterhouse; they are no longer prepared to let other people decide their fate... An indelible mark has been made on the revolutionary and political consciousness of our people by the Soweto events. They raised the people's preparedness and willingness to sacrifice to a higher level, enhancing enormously the striking power of the liberation movement."[76]

According to official (understated) statistics, 575 people, including not more than five whites, were killed in the disturbances of June 16, 1976 through February 28, 1977. In this period 6,000 people were arrested.[77]

"The total number of people who died in the 1976 disturbances," Z. Nkosi writes in *The African Communist*, "will probably never be known. The official figures certainly conceal the truth, because the truth would be bad for morale and for business."[78] The opinion of *Focus*, an information bulletin published by the International Defence and Aid Fund for Southern Africa, is that in all likelihood at least 1,000 people were killed by the police during the 1976 rising.[79]

The Soweto revolt was started by schoolchildren. Headed by the SSRC, they were the initiators and locomotive of most of the subsequent actions and campaigns. However, this was not exclusively a youth rising, much less a revolt of schoolchildren. Their actions, a response to the mandatory use of Afrikaans in the schools and the discriminative Bantu education system, triggered the explosion of anger that had been building up among the urban African population, notably among the proletariat, who were oppressed and subjected to indignities by the ruling white racists.

In Soweto students numbered somewhat more than 168,600, including the 25,600 in secondary schools (March 1975).[80] Altogether, there were over half a million young people under the age of 20 in Soweto. Thus a large proportion of Soweto's youth were young workers and also young jobless. A chronicle of the 1976 events in Soweto indicates that not only schoolchildren but practically all the other young people were involved in the rising.

It would be wrong to say that students of the senior classes, who started the rising, led the young people. They were unable to provide leadership not only because they themselves were inadequately organised. There was certain hostility between them and other young people—young workers and jobless. For most of the Soweto youth the calls, much less orders, issued by school organisations meant nothing. The Soweto youth joined in the struggle because this was essentially a struggle against the system of white minority rule, a struggle against apartheid and racial discrimination, which was consonant with their own interests and aspirations. Anger and outrage united the students and the young workers, inducing them to act jointly. "Some joined the students as fellow victims of apartheid. The cause of anger might have differed, but the anger itself was present in all."[81]

When people speak or write about the 1976 revolt in Soweto they usually focus attention on the first day of the revolt, June 16, i.e., the student protest demonstration and the police gunfire in response. However, the general political strikes of August and September were, of course, the principal landmarks of the rising. "A major high point of the action was the three protest strikes in the six weeks between August and the middle of September," is the view of the South African Communists stated in the report to a plenary meeting of the SACP Central Committee.[82] These strikes were evidence of the black proletariat's mass participation in the revolt. Z.Nkosi writes that it "revealed the class content of national resistance. The initiative was taken by the youth, but became a formidable force when allied with the power of the urban African working class, which rallied to its call... The worker and student alliance was able to rally the forces of the entire community in disciplined mass action."[83] There is no doubt that these were mass actions involving most of the Soweto population.

The students' actions, joined by the other young people of Soweto, erupted into a country-wide rising, with the African proletariat as its backbone. It was supported (in this instance it would be more correct to speak of support rather than participation) by other social strata and groups of the Soweto community. On the third day of the rising Nelson Mandela's wife and leading civil personality Winnie Mandela, resident in Soweto, fully agreed with Eric Abraham, who noted, after interviewing many Sowetans, that "the students have the support of the black population at large and that the base of the confrontation has broadened beyond that of the Afrikaans language issue".[84]

We have cited many facts and eyewitness accounts indicating that support for the direct participants in the rising from almost all strata of the urban black population broadened as the rising itself gained momentum. It was joined even by those who at first failed to understand what was going on or had earlier been provoked into attacking the students, as was the case with the migrant workers of the Mzimhlope hostel. In August and September 1976, when the rising peaked, practically the entire Soweto population was, with rare exceptions, either involved in one form or another or engaged in helping the students.

In Soweto there is a considerable petty-bourgeois stratum and also urban middle classes: the social significance of these groups of the population in the African community is much larger than their numerous proportion of it. Most of these people supported the youth. We have already mentioned the Black Parents' Association (its members include some leading African intellectuals and prominent people from among the petty bourgeoisie), which played a visible role in the Soweto events. Considerable and concrete practical assistance for the students and the striking workers was given by doctors and nurses: in caring for the wounded, they did not merely tend them but hid them from the police. Owners of cars and persons using rental cars likewise helped, especially on the days when bus and railway communication in Soweto came to a halt. "The teachers, nurses, priests, and shopkeepers, and groups of mothers and many others helped in a hundred little ways. They counselled, they tended the injured, they extended credit, or they brought water to douse tear gas."[85] Undertakers took no money for the coffins for victims of police bullets. "During the Soweto events numerous traders, teachers, and other professional groups sided with the people."[86]

Fearing police harassment, some kept their actions and their attitude to the rising to themselves. For that reason many instances of support will remain unknown not only to protect the individuals concerned but also to avoid prematurely revealing some forms and methods of action. The report to the above-mentioned plenary meeting of the SACP Central Committee said: "When the full saga of Soweto can be recorded without concern for security, it will be shown that soon after the initial demonstration, the whole Soweto community became involved in the ferment."[87]

It was thus a rising of practically the entire Soweto population. That not only schoolchildren but also adults were involved is confirmed even by official figures provided by the Johannesburg state pathologist. These figures reveal that of those killed by the police between June 18 and August 18 approximately 50 per cent were over 20 years of age, and 20 per cent were over 30 years of age.[88]

The disturbances spread to most of the country, their main cause being the social and economic conditions in which the urban Africans lived. Widespread poverty, the wretched housing, the constant uncertainty of the future by those who could hardly make ends meet, the racial and social discrimination, and the denial of political rights were what made the Soweto population willing to join in the rising against the apartheid regime. "It seems evident that the underlying causes of the initial riots and the continuing unrest are the poor socio-economic conditions in the townships and the lack of security and deep-seated resentment felt by urban Africans."[89] This coincides with the view of the South African Communist Party that the main cause of the Soweto disturbances was a "growing socio-economic crisis".[90]

Incidentally, the rising clarified an issue that apartheid's apologists sought to confuse, namely the question of whether the Africans had it good or bad. For many weeks and months, beginning in June 1976, the people of Soweto, as of many other cities and townships across South Africa, sacrificed much, even risking their lives, to protest against and show their resentment of the life they were condemned to live under the racist regime.

For its part, the racist regime revealed the brutality and inhumanity of apartheid. According to official data, in the period between June 16 and August 30 alone more than 16,000 rounds of ammunition were fired by police at blacks in Soweto.[91] In this context it would be appropriate to quote Z. Nkosi that "16,000 times in Soweto alone was Vorster's claim that apartheid brings peace given the lie. All over the country it was being proved in action that apartheid opens up only the road to suffering and death."[92]

Not merely the hardships of the urban blacks but the socio-economic crisis underlying their deep-seated frustration explains the cause of the rising. The economic condition of the urban Africans was better and their living standards were higher than in the "white" rural areas and in the Bantustans. Nevertheless, it was the city-dwellers who rose in revolt.

Under white minority rule and apartheid they were more keenly aware of social inequality and of racial discrimination. They suffered more from the knowledge that the racist regime had condemned them to an inferior status. This socio-psychological factor significantly complemented the operation of economic factors, which play the cardinal role in the motivation of human behaviour, particularly in crisis situations.

[1] *Rand Daily Mail*, Johannesburg, June 17, 1976.
[2] Baruch Hirson, *op. cit.*, p. 181.
[3] *The Times*, London, June 17, 1976.
[4] *Rand Daily Mail*, Johannesburg, June 18, 1976.
[5] *The African Communist*, London, No. 70, 1977, p. 30.
[6] *The Star*, Johannesburg, June 19, 1976.
[7] *Rand Daily Mail*, Johannesburg, June 21, 1976.
[8] Ibid., June 18, 1976.
[9] *The Star*, Johannesburg, February 29, 1980.
[10] *Rand Daily Mail*, Johannesburg, June 17, 1976.
[11] Baruch Hirson, *op. cit.*, pp. 181-182.
[12] *The Times*, London, June 17, 1976.
[13] *Rand Daily Mail*, Johannesburg, June 17, 1976.
[14] Ibid.
[15] *The Times*, London, June 17, 1976.
[16] Baruch Hirson, *op. cit.*, p. 182.
[17] *Rand Daily Mail*, Johannesburg, June 18, 1976.
[18] *Sunday Express*, Johannesburg, June 20, 1976.
[19] *Baruch Hirson, op. cit.*, p. 182.
[20] *Rand Daily Mail*, Johannesburg, June 17, 1976.
[21] *Financial Mail*, Johannesburg, June 17, 1976.
[22] Baruch Hirson, *op. cit.*, p. 186.
[23] *To the Point*, Johannesburg, June 25, 1976.
[24] Baruch Hirson, *op. cit.*, p. 186.
[25] *A Survey of Race Relations in South Africa (Annual)*, 1976, p. 192.
[26] Ibid., 1977, p. 420.
[27] *Sunday Times*, London, June 27, 1976.
[28] Baruch Hirson, *op. cit.*, p. 184.
[29] Ibid.
[30] *Rand Daily Mail*, Johannesburg, June 22, 1976.
[31] Ibid., June 19, 1976.
[32] *The Times*, London, June 21, 1976.

[33] *Rand Daily Mail*, Johannesburg, June 21, 1976.
[34] *Daily News*, Durban, June 18, 1980.
[35] *Sunday Times*, Johannesburg, July 4, 1976.
[36] *Sechaba*, London, Vol. 11, 3rd Quarter 1977, p. 5.
[37] *Rand Daily Mail*, Johannesburg, July 9, 1976.
[38] *Sunday Times*, Johannesburg, July 4, 1976.
[39] *Rand Daily Mail*, Johannesburg, June 21, 1976.
[40] *Sunday Express*, Johannesburg, June 27, 1976.
[41] *Sunday Times*, London, June 27, 1976.
[42] *Rand Daily Mail*, Johannesburg, July 14, 1976.
[43] Ibid., July 13, 1976.
[44] *Sunday Express*, Johannesburg, July 18, 1976.
[45] *Daily Telegraph*, London, August 5, 1976.
[46] Baruch Hirson, *op. cit.*, p. 210.
[47] Ibid., p. 211.
[48] Ibid.
[49] *Financial Mail*, Johannesburg, August 12, 1976.
[50] Baruch Hirson, *op. cit.*, p. 211.
[51] Cited in: Ibid., p. 243.
[52] Ibid.
[53] Ibid., p. 198.
[54] *Focus on Political Repression in Southern Africa*, London, No. 6, 1976, p. 2.
[55] *Rand Daily Mail*, Johannesburg, August 24, 1976.
[56] *Financial Mail*, Johannesburg, August 27, 1976.
[57] *Rand Daily Mail*, Johannesburg, August 26, 1976.
[58] *Sechaba*, London, 2nd Quarter 1977, p. 31.
[59] *The Cape Times*, Cape Town, August 10, 1976.
[60] Cited in: Baruch Hirson, *op. cit.*, p. 244.
[61] *Sunday Express*, Johannesburg, August 29, 1976.
[62] Baruch Hirson, *op. cit.*, p. 248.
[63] Ibid.
[64] No Sizwe, *One Azania, One Nation*, Zed Press, London, 1979, pp. 192-193.
[65] Baruch Hirson, *op. cit.*, p. 254.
[66] *Rand Daily Mail*, Johannesburg, September 14, 1976.
[67] *New York Herald Tribune*, September 14, 1976.
[68] *Rand Daily Mail*, Johannesburg, September 14, 1976.
[69] Cited in: Baruch Hirson, *op. cit.*, p. 257.
[70] *Sechaba*, London, 3rd Quarter 1977, p. 3.
[71] Cited in: No Sizwe, *op. cit.*, pp. 195-196.
[72] Cited in: Baruch Hirson, *op. cit.*, p. 265.
[73] *Financial Mail*, Johannesburg, October 29, 1976.
[74] John Kane-Berman, *op. cit.*, p. 116.
[75] Cited in: Baruch Hirson, *op. cit.*, p. 268.
[76] *South African Communists Speak. Documents From the History of the South African Communist Party, 1915-1980*, Inkululeko Publications, London, 1981, pp. 419-420.
[77] *The Star*, Johannesburg, February 29, 1980.
[78] *The African Communist*, London, No. 69, 1977, p. 19.
[79] *Focus on Political Repression in Southern Africa*, London, No. 10, 1977.

[80] *Rand Daily Mail*, Johannesburg, June 18, 1976.
[81] Baruch Hirson, *op. cit.*, p. 194.
[82] *South African Communists Speak...*, p. 423.
[83] *The African Communist*, London, No. 68, 1977, p. 33.
[84] Baruch Hirson, *op. cit.*, p. 193.
[85] Ibid., p. 197.
[86] *The African Communist*, London, No. 70, 1977, p. 41.
[87] *South African Communists Speak...*, p. 423.
[88] *The African Communist*, London, No. 70, 1977, p. 35.
[89] *A Survey of Race Relations in South Africa (Annual)*, 1977, p. 51.
[90] *South African Communists Speak...*, p. 420.
[91] *A Survey of Race Relations in South Africa (Annual)*, 1977, p. 85.
[92] *The African Communist*, London, No. 68, 1977, p. 19.

Chapter Five

THE REVOLT IS SUPPRESSED—THE STRUGGLE CONTINUES. CHRONICLE OF RESISTANCE

1977-1979: Fighting in Soweto

By the close of 1976 the intensity of the uprising had clearly declined. The ruthless, mass repressions had made themselves felt. The thousands of killed and wounded, arrested, or sentenced, with the repressions spearheaded at leaders and the most militant participants in the revolt— this inevitably affected the course of the struggle. The government has already been preparing to celebrate victory. In January 1977 Police Minister Kruger declared in Parliament and then in a long-winded interview for the pro-government journal *To the Point* that the worst was now over and that "as far as the security position is concerned, it is better now than at any time during the last year".[1] But he was wrong again.

Suppressed and still, or rather, smoldering, Soweto began to stir again, to muster strength for a resumption of the struggle. As a matter of fact, the struggle never ceased. Explosions continued to shake Soweto. On December 6, 1976, a bomb exploded in the Carlton Centre in Johannesburg. A day later there was a powerful explosion in a house in Soweto. The police reported that a cache of explosives had gone off. On the same day, yet another mine was blown up—this time on the railway track. On January 17, 1977, a bomb was detonated in a hostel in Krugersdorp.

Mass actions and demonstrations by the working people and students in Soweto began in March 1977 and continued on a growing scale throughout the rest of the year. On March 28 there was a demonstration to commemorate Heroes' Week. On April 27 the Sowetans marched in protest of the announced rent rise. In both instances there were violent clashes with the police: many of the demonstrators were wounded and 84 were arrested. A rally was planned for May 22 at the Jabulani stadium to protest against the

government's decision to create the Bantustan of Bophuthatswana, but it was banned by the police. Students continued their actions at many Sowetan schools.

In June 1977, i.e., a year after the revolt broke out, the
SSRC and the senior high-school students headed by it were
in fact the masters of the situation in Soweto despite the
police terror, when it seemed that the white supervisors
from the West Rand Administration Board should have been
in control.

Clear proof of this seemingly debatable assertion was
what happened to the Urban Bantu Council. This puppet
body and its "Mayor" David Thebehali had never had any
influence. Nonetheless, the government relied on it, hoping
that by giving it more powers it would create the semblance
of concessions and thereby side-step deciding the paramount issue—the abolition of apartheid and giving blacks
political rights. Moreover, it hoped that this perk in the
shape of "self-government" and "authority" in the Soweto
community would draw to the Urban Bantu Council the
support of some sections of the African bourgeoisie and
urban middle classes and thus split the united resistance to
apartheid. Thus, despite its total impotence, the UBC was
a potential threat to the liberation forces.

The Soweto Students Representative Council was determined to force the total dismantling of the UBC. From the
outset of the uprising the UBC offices and councillors were
a target of the students. The struggle against the UBC was
now more organised and diversified. Members of the SSRC
had effective talks with the councillors, including the
"Mayor" David Thebehali and the "Deputy-Mayor" Richard
Maponya. "At the beginning of June, Soweto's 'Mayor',
David Thebehali, was waylaid by a carload of students and
taken to a meeting for a 'man-to-man' talk. Until then,
Thebehali had defended the UBC system with all his might...
But he emerged from that meeting a changed man. In the
afternoon he resigned from the UBC, taking the majority of
the councillors with him. 'I think the time has come for the
old guard to give way to the youth,' he declared."[2]

Developments later showed that in this "gracious" gesture of the apartheid regime's servitor there was everything
except sincerity. Before a year passed Thebehali was
"mayor" again, this time his title was Chairman of the Com-

197

munity Council, a new variant of the puppet self-government body. Nevertheless, in mid-1977 Thebehali meekly submitted to the SSRC's demand, realising that he was faced with a force to be reckoned with.

What happened to Richard Maponya, a wealthy businessman, followed roughly the same pattern. He was taken to the high school in Orlando West and "spoken to". According to *Time* magazine, Maponya did not reveal the details of this "talk", which lasted about an hour. Student representatives later said that Maponya was threatened with a boycott against his store and, vaguely, perhaps worse.[3]

The purpose of the "talks" with the councillors was not only to put an end to the UBC once and for all. They were part of a broader campaign against collaborators and abettors of the hated regime and against traitors among the blacks. While formerly there was a mixed feeling of fear and respect for the West Rand Administration Board police and even police informers in the urban black community—they were feared and, at the same time, envied as having made their way in life—the attitude towards them changed completely after 1976. They were no longer feared. More, they were killed—not indiscriminately, but only in cases where they had been particularly brutal. An indicative case occurred in Dobsonville in early March 1977 when some 500 students wrecked a WRAB office. Among the police who tried to prevent this attack, particular zeal was shown by one Zondi. This cost him dear: a group of students immediately went to his house, located in a neighbouring township, and set it on fire with bottles of inflammable liquid.

Attacks on black policemen and their homes subsequently became customary in Soweto. A police sergeant named Chapi, who played a major role in putting down the revolt of 1976, was killed in Soweto in June 1978.[4]

Time correspondent William McWhirter reported that in mid-1977 there were fewer post-midnight police raids in Soweto and fewer peremptory demands by police for blacks to show their passbooks. The students headed by the SSRC "were, in fact, the dominant, virtually unrivaled political power within Soweto". McWhirter made another important point: noting that the tactics of the students were to assert their strength in the Soweto community rather than to intimidate anybody, he wrote, that "they have definitely succeeded in winning support from the whole community".[5]

There have been many instances when the stand of the SSRC determined the actions of organisations or professional groups in Soweto. Take the following. When a group of doctors collected money and organised a mobile dispensary with the intention of sending it to rural areas, the SSRC demanded that it should remain in Soweto where it was needed more at the time. The doctors acquiesced.

The strength of the SSRC's influence in Soweto was clearly seen on the anniversary of the revolt. Even football clubs, which are extremely popular in Soweto, responded to its call for an abstention from spectator sports. As in previous cases, the SSRC's injunctions were carried out and backed even by people like shebeen owners and Soweto's numerous pirate taxi drivers. An indicative acknowledgement was printed by the journal *To the Point*: "Such allegiance is being given not only to the students themselves or to particular leaders, but also for what they stand for."[6]

The resistance in Soweto rose to a high pitch on anniversaries of the June revolt when schoolchildren, the first victims of the police terror, were shot and killed. Preparations were made by the two opposing sides: the Sowetans and the racist authorities.

On the eve of the first anniversary the SSRC circulated a leaflet calling for a work stay-away on June 16 and for memorial services in the churches. Leaflets issued by the ANC also appeared everywhere. One of these said: "PEOPLE OF SOUTH AFRICA remember Soweto, remember the June massacres, the murder of our children, the brutal torture of prisoners, the assassinations by the police!

"We call upon you: STRIKE! STRIKE! STRIKE! June 16 to June 18 stay at home—do not go to work—strike in honour of our brave children and youth—strike for freedom!...

"The stirring revolutionary events which started in Soweto and spread throughout the country shook white South Africa to its foundations. WE MUST CONTINUE THE STRUGGLE!"[7]

For their part the police started their assaults with a hunt for student leaders: on June 12 they arrested 20 SSRC members, on June 14 they attacked a student meeting at the Orlando High School, which was still the main centre of resistance, and arrested another eight persons. On June 15 they set up road-blocks on all roads leading to Soweto, to New Canada in the first place, checking identities, searching, and detaining all suspects, mainly youths. Leaflets put out by the police, warning against strikes, were distributed.

At this juncture there took place an event that neither side foresaw but which seriously alarmed "white" Johannesburg. On June 13, in the city's centre three Africans armed with submachine guns and hand grenades opened fire when they were spotted by the police. Two whites were killed, and two others were wounded.

Then came June 16, the first anniversary of Bloody Wednesday. High-school students of Orlando, Orlando West, Senoane, and Meadowlands—a total of more than 3,000—stayed away from classes. Many workers responded to the strike appeal and stayed at home. Two bombs were set off on railway tracks running through Soweto. People gathered in the churches to pay tribute to the memory of victims.

Meanwhile, the police launched operations to suppress resistance. Firearms and tear-gas canisters were used in many Soweto townships, even against congregations in churches. Nine persons were killed or wounded in Soweto on that day. There were approximately similar developments in other black townships: in Nyanga and Guguletu near Cape Town, and in Mamelodi near Pretoria. In the township of KwaNobuhle near Uitenhage ten persons were killed and 32 were wounded in the course of two days (June 16 and 17). A section of the railway track in Durban was blown up.

The authorities replied with police terror and further repressions that mounted steadily during that year. In January, summing up police operations for 1976, Police Minister Kruger announced that there would be 52 trials involving 386 persons under the Terrorism Act.[8] According to far from complete estimates of the South African Institute of Race Relations (the police flatly refused to provide such information) the number of persons arrested in 1977 increased continuously: 471 by March 25, 662 by September 30, and 714 by November 30. As before, a particularly large number of young people were taken into custody. In mid-August there were police raids in Soweto high schools. Students were truncheon-whipped, dogs were set upon them, and teachers also had to bear much. The police arrested 175 persons in a single day.[9]

The struggle against the discriminative Bantu education system began to gather momentum once again. As early as in June teachers and members of school boards that controlled the ethnically grouped schools began to resign in protest against that system. Mass resignations by teachers, that led to the practical abolition of the ethnic school boards, took place in many instances as a result of influence exercised by the SSRC. To illustrate: members of the Zulu West School Board that administered the schools in the Jabulani, Zola, and Emdeni areas resigned after negotiations with the SSRC.[10] The entire Meadowlands Zulu School Board resigned after getting an ultimatum from the SSRC. By mid-September 450 teachers had refused to work in the Bantu education system. It was expected that this figure would reach 600 (of a total of 750 teachers working in 40 senior high schools and secondary schools in Soweto) by the end of the month.[11]

Simultaneously, more and more students stayed away from classes. Of the 27,000 students of these schools, only 300 registered for classes. More than 4,000 primary school teachers also declared that they could not accept the discriminative education system but would continue classes because it would be unreasonable to let 143,000 small children idle in the streets.[12]

In almost all, including primary, schools classes ceased in October 1977. All the 170,000 students boycotted classes as a protest against the Bantu education system. This was reported by the newspaper *The Star*, whose reporters went to Soweto schools at the time and found them empty.[13] Students and teachers began returning to the schools only in January and February 1978.

The disintegration of the UBC left a sort of administrative vacuum in Soweto. The authorities immediately began laying the ground for a new puppet self-government, the community councils, for whose formation the relative act was soon passed by the South African parliament. The elite of the Soweto community, including the merchant bourgeoisie and intellectuals, likewise became active in an effort to fill that vacuum. Nthato Motlana, a doctor by profession and a member of the Black Parents' Association, was the most enterprising among them. He headed a provisional committee that was subsequently called the Soweto Committee of Ten after the initial number of its members.

The Committee of Ten rejected the government's project for setting up community councils and proposed its own plan for turning Soweto into a normally functioning city with an autonomous self-government: the whites were to turn their powers over to Africans. This was a manifestation of opposition on the part of that section of the urban middle classes, notably professionals, which, while rejecting apartheid and white minority rule, sought to find, on the crest of the rising tide of national liberation struggles, a form of resistance to the racist regime acceptable to itself. The essentially opportunist stance of the urban middle classes was nonetheless more progressive than the attitude taken by the corrupt top echelon of the merchant bourgeoisie and the "chiefs" in the Bantustans. Moreover, this active opposition to the government by a section of the urban middle classes undermined the government's plan to lure these classes to its side and thereby undercut the long-established ANC-led front of struggle against racism and apartheid.

The philosophical views and political persuasions of the members of the Committee of Ten represented diverse shades of black nationalism. As a young man Nthato Motlana was Secretary of the ANC Youth League and had cooperated with Nelson Mandela. In reply to a call from the Black Peoples Convention to Sowetans to form a civic body representative of every black man's aspirations, Motlana declared that all organisations battling for civil power in Soweto were entertaining wrong hopes and were dreaming. He said that people should be interested in occupying the parliament where all laws were made.[14] In October 1977 he said that "South Africa will be Azania in ten years" (in other words, delivered from white minority rule) and that his philosophy was "one man one vote".[15]

A few words about other members of the Committee of Ten who in subsequent years were to play a significant part in Soweto's life.

Tom Monthata, a school teacher—he believes that the

black man's basic nature is communalistic and God-fearing and hopes that the people will use their opportunities and capabilities to administer their affairs by themselves.[16]

Leonard Mosala, a factory worker, who later became a trade union functionary (African Chemical Workers Union), said he regretted his participation in the UBC and described himself as a black nationalist.[17]

Mrs. Ellen Khuzwayo, the only woman of the Committee of Ten, declared: "We are paid low wages and have been given the type of education that makes us hewers of wood and drawers of water. Blacks are entitled to the rights, opportunities, and privileges that people anywhere in the world receive. Some of us will struggle for this until our dying days."[18]

Reverend Mashawabada Mayathula (died in 1980) helped to form the South African Students' Organisation, was the first president of the Black Peoples Convention (founded in 1971). He was imprisoned for addressing a rally in 1974 to celebrate the victory of FRELIMO in Mozambique. He was nicknamed "Castro" in recognition of his services in the struggle against apartheid. In the last years of his life he was also the president of the African Independent Churches Association. An ANC Statement on Mayathula's death, signed by the ANC General Secretary Alfred Nzo, calls him a "great son of our country, and a close comrade-in-arms... a dedicated fighter for freedom, national independence, and peace".[19] Other members of the Committee of Ten were R. Ramokgopa, T. Mazibuko, V. L. Kraai, D. Lolwane, and L. M. Mathabathe. All were prominent and influential in the Soweto community.

In October 1977 the racist government undertook another police counter-offensive in order to crush the resurgence of resistance by practically all strata of the Soweto population that started in mid-1977. This time the main targets were the public organisations opposed to the racist regime and leading intellectuals, who supported the anti-apartheid struggle in one way or another. The Internal Security Act was invoked to arrest all the members of the Committee of Ten (they were held in custody for more than a year) and some other persons, including whites. The same act was invoked to ban 18 public organisations: Black Peoples Convention, Black Parents' Association, South

African Students' Organisation, South African Students' Movement, Soweto Students Representative Council, and some women's, youth, and educational organisations—and also a religious organisation called the Christian Institute. Police Minister Kruger declared that the ANC had infiltrated all these organisations and that its members were planning a people's war to liberate the blacks.[20]

The World, the most widely read newspaper among the blacks in Soweto and the whole of the Witwatersrand, was likewise banned. As early as 1973 it had a circulation of 110,000 copies.[21] Its circulation unquestionably increased in subsequent years. Speaking on television in October 1977 in an effort to justify this ban, Kruger declared that *The World* had a large circulation in the black areas where there was intimidation, unrest, and constant confrontation with the police. He told viewers (most of whom were whites, of course) of the seditious "home education" scheme published in *The World* in 1976 when the rising in Soweto was at its height. One lesson was about Lenin and power, in which a comparison was drawn between the situation before and after the October Revolution, noting: "Before the Russian revolution the peasants had very little land; afterwards the peasants were given more land. Before the revolution the employers took all the profits; afterwards the workers owned the factories." Kruger said that this lesson implied that the revolution in South Africa was not over yet.[22]

Towards the close of 1977 Soweto again held its breath in the face of mass arrests, bans, and other repressions. There was fear and tormenting presentiment even in Dube, where the heads of many families were not at home at Christmas—they were in prison.

In spite of this the resistance continued. The Soweto Action Committee called for the observance of a period of mourning over the Christmas holidays: "We cannot afford to be merry when our leaders, brothers and sisters are in jail."[23] This Committee published the Soweto Unity Pledge that embraced many of the social, political, and educational problems worrying the Soweto community. After the wave of police repressions in October, when practically all legal African public organisations were banned, this was the first attempt to give people a general political orientation and set out the objectives that had to be achieved, for instance, "the defence of freedom of speech, association, and movement" and "to restore and preserve our land for which our ancestors and our children have paid the price of death, exile, and imprisonment".[24]

Explosions and gunfire were heard more and more often in the cities and townships. After the November explosion in the Carlton Centre, a powerful bomb was detonated in the Central Police Station in Germiston. This explosion, which destroyed the station, was heard within a radius of 10 miles.[25] Two days later, another powerful bomb went off near the Benoni railway station, damaging 14 cars parked in the vicinity. A large explosive was discovered in the big chain store O. K. Bazaars in Roodepoort shortly before it was to go off. There was panic in many large stores and the police searched all shoppers, looking into their bags for bombs. The Police Minister told all shoppers and restaurant-goers to look closely at all unusual or suspicious objects.[26] General Gert Prinsloo, Commissioner of Police, said that terrorist organisations had declared war on South Africa, and the explosion 'at the Carlton Centre was just "part of their strategy to break down the nation's morale".[27] Newspapers were full of hysterical stories about "city terrorism" and urged vigilance.

Thus ended 1977, the second year of the Soweto rising, for what took place in that year was a continuation and development of the outburst of anger in Soweto in 1976.

The beginning of 1978 saw further explosions, fires, and shooting in Johannesburg and the whole of South Africa. The armed struggle grew increasingly more intense. February was a particularly disturbing month. The chance discovery of a time-bomb on February 14 in the 22-storey Bosman Building next to the Trust Bank Office in Bree Street brought the centre of Johannesburg into public focus once again. Had it detonated it would have brought down the entire building. Ten days later a police station in Daveyton (East Rand) was badly damaged by a powerful explosion. Bombs exploded in other towns and townships, for example, in Port Elizabeth in March.

The police went all out to prevent the growth of the armed struggle. In the early hours of April 1, a huge operation to comb Soweto, Alexandra, and other townships around Johannesburg was mounted jointly by the police and the army. All seven roads leading to Soweto were blocked. Troops armed with bayoneted rifles stopped cars, pointing their guns at the people in them while the police searched for weapons and explosives. This, Colonel Gert Slabbert told reporters, was simultaneously an exercise in cooperation between the police and the army.[28]

This was a disquieting situation for "white" Johannesburg. The figures for white emigration are a compelling indication of the state of mind of South Africa's white population. In 1978 emigration exceeded immigration for the first time in 18 years (20,686 people emigrated, and 18,669 persons entered the country); compared with 1975 the number of immigrants diminished by more than 50 per cent, while the number of departures doubled.[29]

On the eve of the second anniversary of the Soweto revolt the police again carried out massive raids, arresting over 1,000 persons in Soweto and other townships near Johannesburg within only a few days.[30] Soweto found itself in what in fact amounted to a state of siege when large numbers of heavily armed police appeared in a so-called crime prevention operation. But, regardless of the police cordons, people went to Rockville on June 16 to attend a memorial service in the Regina Mundi Church. The assembly of some 7,000 people was addressed by Bishop Desmond Tutu, who said that the black people would get their freedom and it would be freedom for everybody, including whites.[31] The congregation was then addressed by Nthato Motlana, who was released from prison in March after having been in detention for five months. He compared the National Party's racist regime, that was thinking in terms of centuries of domination, with the Nazi Reich that boasted it would last a thousand years.[32]

In the Regina Mundi Church memorial services went on for two days, Saturday and Sunday. The thousands who attended them heard people speak of racial oppression and freedom. For two days heavily armed police were posted around the church. Time and again there were short but violent clashes, shots were fired, and clouds of tear gas drifted along the ground. There were even larger memorial rallies in Diepkloof, where nearly 20,000 people gathered. There, too, Nthato Motlana was one of the main speakers. "The services also demonstrated the support the leaders of

206

the banned African National Congress have among Soweto youth... their songs were about Mandela, Sisulu, Mbeki."[33]

The situation of a day in September taken in its stride by the Soweto community was described by police Major Gerrit Viljoen: "There was a total chaos in Soweto that day. The mood was so hostile that even children of two and three years old were waving fists in the black power salute."[34] On that day the local police had to call for reinforcements from Pretoria.

On December 7, 1978, yet another explosion shook Soweto. This time the Community Council building was blown up.

The onset of 1979 was marked by mines blowing up railway tracks linking the Soweto townships with Johannesburg: in January—between the stations at Mzimhlope and New Canada; in April—between Kliptown and Nancefield. Acts of this kind had become customary and surprised nobody: neither the people of Soweto, who accepted them as almost the normal run of things, nor the police, who already expected new sabotage on the railways. But what took place in the township of Moroka on May 3 was unusual and unexpected, at least for the government and the police.

The police station in Moroka was attacked on that day. It was not merely a bomb or a grenade explosion as was the case in Jabulani, Germiston or Daveyton. In the darkness of night the police station came under a hail of submachine gun fire and grenades from three ANC fighters. One policeman was killed, five were wounded. The attackers suffered no losses. Having scattered ANC leaflets they were gone. On the next day the newspapers reported that the attackers caught the police unawares, that the police were unable to fire a single shot in reply, and that the reinforcements that were called out combed the area in search of the "terrorists" but caught nobody.[35]

After this attack the police added guards and were on constant alert. But these supplementary precautions proved to be unavailing.

On November 2 a small group of fighters attacked another police station in Soweto. This time in Orlando and in broad daylight. This developed into a battle in the real sense, even though it lasted only a few minutes. The attackers directed their fire at the station itself and at police

207

cars parked nearby. Policemen rushed out of the buildings and returned the fire with pistols but were cut down by submachine gun fire. Two were killed and two were wounded. At the same time, at another end of the police station's courtyard one of the attackers threw several hand grenades that landed near barracks in which were about 60 off-duty policemen. They panicked: some sought the shelter of trees outside the station territory, but most hid under beds in the barracks in fear.[36]

This Orlando police station was used as a headquarters from which the bloodthirsty police operations against the students were directed in June 1976. The attack was thus an act of retribution.

As in Moroka, the attackers did their work and disappeared, "dissolving" among the people of Soweto. The thorough searches and raids conducted throughout Soweto and other townships around Johannesburg yielded nothing. The atmosphere in the townships was clearly not conducive for the police searches. A senior police officer grumbled that "it is difficult to operate in an area like this. Soweto is so easy to hide in."[37]

Staff members of the Terrorism Research Centre (the fact that an institution of this sort was set up in South Africa was also a sign of the times) said the attacks on police stations "should be seen in the context of attacks on black policemen, since collectively they seemed to signal a bid to break the morale of the black policemen and thereby discourage blacks from serving in the police force".[38] Since of the police force's total strength of 35,000 (1979) almost 16,000 were black, one can see why the government was worried about the morale of its flunkeys. Even more disturbing for the government were the symptoms of the black policemen's unreliability. It was learned that former policemen, who had gone over to the side of the freedom fighters and joined the ANC, had taken part in the attack on the Moroka police station.[39]

In June 1979, as in previous years, the Soweto community honoured the memory of those who died in the 1976 revolt. Once more thousands filled the Regina Mundi Church and once again there were speeches denouncing not only the police terror but apartheid as a policy, the bantustanisation policy in particular.[40] There were similar rallies at this time in many other townships: Alexandra, Atteridgeville, Mamelodi, KwaThema, Tembisa, Kagiso. On June 16 shops were closed in Soweto for two hours as a token of mourning; all sports, entertainment, and spectacles were called off. A new organisation, the Congress of South African Students, took part in the memorial rallies in Soweto.

The Terrorism Research Centre estimated that 110 explosive devices, incendiary shells, and hand grenades were used in 91 armed clashes (called "incidents") in the period from the beginning of 1977 to June 15, 1979, i.e. before the battle in Orlando, which took place in November.[41] Possibly to show that his subordinates were acting effectively the new Police Minister Louis le Grange, who replaced Kruger, succumbed to the temptation to engage in similar computations. He declared that in a two-year period the police had confiscated 1,076 detonators, 175 firearms, 34,000 cartridges, and 376 hand grenades.[42] From the evidence of three years of political trials (1976-1979), a young Johannesburg lawyer named Glen Moss drew the conclusion that the "guerrilla and terrorist conflict in South Africa has grown into a low-intensity civil war". He declared: "It can no longer be seen as a temporary phenomenon. Instead the evidence points to the conflicts now being a built-in part of the structure of our society. Only a thorough restructuring of society can remove its causes."[43]

1980: Explosions and Strikes Shake Johannesburg

In early February there were three funerals at Soweto's Diepkloof cemetery—on the 2nd, 6th, and 9th. The deceased were three former pupils of the Madibane high school in Diepkloof. This was the township where they had lived: Humphrey Makhubo and Wilfred Madela in Zone No. 1 and Stephen Mafako in Zone No. 3. Following the murderous repressions of June 1976 all three fled from South Africa, joined the ANC and, after a period of military training, returned home with arms in hand. On January 25, 1980, they seized the Folkskas Bank in Silverton (Pretoria), and sent the government the ultimatum that they would release their hostages in return for the release of

Nelson Mandela. Riot police stormed the besieged buildings, killing the three fighters and several hostages.

The funerals of the three young Sowetans were in fact massive political demonstrations. At the first funeral there were only 600 mourners, for there had been no time to notify people in the other Soweto townships, but some days later nearly 2,500 people attended the second funeral and when the third took place there came 10,000 mourners.[44] There were placards with demands, cries of "Amandla", and freedom songs were heard. Also, people could be heard saying, "He was not a terrorist but a hero... So, we can show our enemies that we respect our dead", many blacks regarded the three men as "heroes who died for their freedom".[45] The police tried to disperse the mourners with tear gas. In reply they got a hail of stones.

Investigative reporters asked Sowetans what they thought about the seizure of the bank and hostages in Silverton and about the deceased "terrorists". Of the 504 persons questioned by them 73 per cent expressed positive feelings about the killed, and of these 38 per cent (191 persons) called them heroes.[46]

Early in the morning of February 13 the inmates of the Mzimhlope hostel on the northern fringe of Soweto and passengers in the train running through this area carrying workers to Johannesburg witnessed an extraordinary police operation. About 500 police, including a special detachment from Pretoria, a riot squad, and security forces were combing abandoned pits and mine dumps located between a football field in Orlando and the New Canada railway station. With submachine guns and dogs, they moved in an unbroken chain, wearing camouflage uniforms and having two-way radio communication with their command. They were looking for "terrorists", who allegedly had a cache of arms and explosives there. The outcome of this massive operation, which began at 2 a.m. and ended at 10 a.m., was the arrest of some homeless tramps who had been sleeping in the abandoned pits.

The police futilely tried to find guerrillas. And on April 4, 1980, they themselves were "found" by guerrillas in what the South African newspapers called the biggest ANC operation since the appearance of guerrillas. This was the first time the guerrillas used a rocket-propelled grenade.[47]

One more police station was attacked, this time in a "white" area called Booysens in the southernmost part of Johannesburg. Driving to the building in two cars the guerrillas fired rocket-propelled grenades, threw several hand grenades, and scattered leaflets demanding the release of Nelson Mandela and Walter Sisulu, following which they escaped unharmed in the direction of Soweto.

This attack had a shattering psychological effect. Whites were frozen with shock. This time the regime's bulwark and custodian of law and order had been attacked not in some distant place but in a "white" area only a mile away from the city's centre. One resident of Booysens living near the police station probably put in words what was felt on that day by many people in Johannesburg: "I heard this terrible explosion which shook the whole house... I was scared to death and went to hide in the back of the house with my husband."[48]

Hardly had Johannesburg recovered from the shock of Booysens than another event took place. Close to midnight on June 1 people living in the southern districts of Johannesburg were awakened by distant explosions. They saw the glow of a fire on the horizon. This was from the fuel reservoirs of an oil-from-coal plant and a refinery close to the town of Sasolburg. Pillars of flame rose to a height of almost a kilometre, and could be seen 80 kilometres away. A special ANC statement said these were massive, daring raids by units of Umkhonto we Sizwe.[49] Eight fuel tanks were destroyed worth almost six million rand. That same night mines were discovered in the building of the US Fluor, a company building oil-refineries.

Media comments were that these were "successful... bombings of the key oil-from-coal Sasol plants. The shock registered by whites reveals how little they know of the lessons of history: that more repression normally stimulates ever more effective insurgency methods."[50] "These 'armed propaganda' actions dramatically shattered any remaining illusions of invincibility that the enemy harboured. On the other hand, they injected a new sense of confidence and inspiration into the masses."[51]

Nor was there tranquility in Soweto itself. Rallies acclaiming the victory of the people of Zimbabwe, which won liberation from colonialist and racist oppression, were held there in March and April. Two youth organisations, the Congress of South African Students and the Azanian Students Organisation, called a rally in solidarity with the people of Zimbabwe at the Sefikeng Church Hall in Meadowlands. A crowd of more than 300 people were told: "Yesterday was Mozambique and Angola and now that Zimbabwe was free, tomorrow it would be Namibia and South Africa."[5][2] In mid-April there were several more rallies sponsored not only by youth organisations but also by the Committee of Ten, the South African Council of Churches, the Writers Association of South Africa, and the Black Lawyers Association. Rallies saluting the liberation of Zimbabwe took place in Dube, Alexandra, and more remote townships: Tembisa, Sebokeng, and Sharpeville. Bishop Desmond Tutu of the South African Council of Churches, to which all the Christian denominations and organisations are affiliated with the exception of the Roman Catholic and Dutch Reformed, said in his sermon that he was filled with joy and that "we should not lag too far behind". The Congress of South African Students issued a statement declaring: "Africa is in a process of revolution. And now that Zimbabwe, so near to us, is undergoing revolution we hope and trust that it will serve to oil the process of change in our country."[5][3]

Soweto was preparing to mark the fourth anniversary of the 1976 revolt. As usual, there was to be a mass rally in the Regina Mundi Church on June 16. There were to be speakers from the Committee of Ten and the Black Lawyers Association. On the next day there were to be rallies in the same location sponsored by COSAS and the Azanian Students Organisation: not only young people were invited but also "parents, workers and all black progressive organisations".[5][4] Similar rallies were planned in other townships and cities. The organisers appealed even to pirate taxi drivers to reduce their rates for that day and provide some of their cars to transport people to the venues of the rallies. These were the plans and intentions.

But two days before the anniversary the government had announced that all meetings of more that ten persons would be banned and that the police would take harsh measures to disperse unauthorised gatherings. "In their own way the elaborate police precautions will commemorate the significance of Soweto. They demonstrate how afraid the rulers are of their helots."[5 5]

Nevertheless, about 300 people turned up in the square in front of the Regina Mundi Church. They were surrounded by the police, who used tear gas and then attacked them with dogs and batons. The tear gas reached even the foreign journalists who had come for on-spot accounts. In the afternoon, when people again gathered near the church, the police used more modern weapons: a riot control van and tear-gas guns mounted on the roofs of cars.

"We may not have the legal right to gather at Regina Mundi and all the other places we intended going to," the *Post* newspaper wrote in an editorial, evidently, expressing the feelings and sentiments of its African readers, "but you will never succeed—try as you might—to obliterate the real significance of June 16. It is something that is ... engraved in our hearts and minds. June 16 is the day of our people... They will not forget... We will never allow this country to forget."[5 6]

Nor did the government intend to forget Soweto. More, it initiated long-term measures, preparing for the inevitable battles in the future. Construction was started of a new prison. The old Johannesburg prison, known as the Fort, clearly could not accommodate all prisoners, whose numbers were increasing steadily. Besides, it was situated in the very centre of the city, on Hospital Hill—this was not very convenient for the white inhabitants. The new prison is much larger (it can hold 4,000 prisoners) and its location is more "convenient", right by Soweto, near Diepkloof township.

A new building is added to the existing police station in Protea, a new outlying Soweto township, thus forming a complex of several three-storey buildings in which riot and security police are quartered; it has the relevant technical facilities and depots. Incidentally, the riot police are armed with an innovation, the quirt, a type of riding whip described as "more desirable than other forms of batons because it did not break bones".[5 7]

The 21st Battalion of the South African Armed Forces, stationed at Lenz, near Soweto, was activated and given a larger range of action. Actually, this unit was a boot camp for security police recruits from among blacks. In 1974, when this base began to function, it trained only 11 men.

In 1980 there were 500 blacks in the 21st Battalion. The six months' training course was for frontier guards, but these men could be used also in nearby Soweto.

There was more ferment in Johannesburg at the close of July and early August 1980. This time the blow was struck by the black African proletariat. More than 500 workers downed tools at the Orlando Power Station on July 24 demanding a higher wage for unskilled workers (from 33 to 58 rand a week). In reply the City Council's chief engineer Wessel Barnard told the strikers: "I want you to be back at work within 30 minutes or else I will be left with no option but to repatriate all migrant workers and dismiss the rest."[58] But this did not frighten the workers. Their demands were supported by the Black Municipal Workers' Union, formed two months earlier and uniting two-thirds of the total of about 15,000 workers employed in the various services of the Johannesburg City Council. The other workers belonged to the Union of Johannesburg Municipal Workers, which had been set up by the city authorities.

Responding to a call from the BMWU the workers of other enterprises and public utilities pledged support for the workers of the Orlando Power Station. Transport workers, another 800 electricians of the Van Beek Compound in Doornfontein, and workers of the Kelwin Power Station in Isando stayed away on the next day. Ambulance drivers and other health service workers declared they were prepared to strike, but the trade unions urged them carry on working so that sick people would not suffer. These were not only solidarity strikes—the workers made common demands: higher wages and recognition for the BMWU.

Three thousand workers, mainly of the Selby, Norwood, and Nancefield compounds went on strike on July 28. On the next day the strike was joined by more than 10,000 workers of practically all the municipal utilities: engineering, power, gas, and transport; work was stopped by garbage collectors, and workers in the markets, parks, libraries, and the city's fiscal authority.[59] The city transport functioned with long interruptions. On many buses an armed policeman stood beside the driver. Mountains of garbage piled up in the streets, and public lavatories were closed. "It is the biggest strike to hit a single employer [the City Council.— V.G.] in South African history," the media noted.[60]

Johannesburg's Mayor Carel Venter sounded the alarm at the outset of the strike: "We are all very concerned. It has become a political issue now."[6][1]

The Cabinet of Ministers held an emergency meeting to hear the Labour Minister Fanie Botha and consider the situation. It was decided to reject the demands and suppress the strike, which had paralysed life in Johannesburg almost entirely. There were massive layoffs, and the dismissed were at once evicted from hostels and compounds. Labour recruiters were promptly sent to the Bantustan of Venda. The "ambassadors" of the Bantustans of Venda, Transkei, and Bophuthatswana were told to admonish the strikers. But it was the police who were relied upon to suppress the strike by force.

Police vans filled with arrested trade unionists and strikers raced through the city's streets. In some places there were violent clashes between the workers and the police. A particularly tense atmosphere reigned in the Selby Compound (on West Street), which had become the main centre of the resistance. Delegations from other compounds and columns of workers even from other districts of the city came here; at rallies and meetings the workers discussed their grievances. At the gates of this compound there were frequent short but fierce collisions between the workers and the police.

One of these collisions occurred in the morning of July 29, when workers from other compounds arrived in Selby. Baton-swinging police tried to prevent them from entering the compound. The workers used stones and the police retreated. On the next day the media reported that the "confrontation of police, management, and striking municipal workers at the West Street compound showed complete solidarity of the workers".[6][2] After long, turbulent and fruitless talks the management tried to persuade some 3,000 workers, who had come to Selby from other places, to leave in the buses specially chartered for them.

But the workers did not succumb either to arguments or intimidation. They fought their way through the police cordon, marched out of the compound gates, but did not board the buses. They ignored the savage police dogs pulling at their leashes and the barrels of machine guns aimed at them. Their opponents were frightened much more. Municipal officials who tried to persuade workers to return to work, it was reported in the media, "addressed the gathered crowd—ringed by the menacing barrels of police guns". Noting the total unanimity among the strikers, *The Star* wrote: "This seemed to indicate the start of a more determined stand by the workers."[63] On June 31 the same paper wrote anxiously about the City Council's ineffective attempts to come to terms with the workers and end the "mass stoppage of essential services in Johannesburg", adding that the strike "must be settled quickly for strikes are dangerous things in South Africa today. They tend to touch off boycotts, sympathy strikes, confrontations with the police."[64]

The strike was indeed broken that day, July 31. Large numbers of police surrounded the Selby Compound and "filtered out" all the strikers gathered there, separating more than 1,200 of them, forcing them into waiting buses, and taking them to the empty Deep City Compound in the city's southern outskirt. The workers were kept there all night without food, in anti-sanitary conditions, and on the next day again forced into buses at gun point and taken to the Bantustans of Venda, Bophuthatswana, Transkei, and Gazankulu.

Concurrently, the police arrested the entire leadership of the Black Municipal Workers Union, including its president Joseph Mavi. They were charged with violating the Sabotage Act, a charge that could carry the death sentence.

Meanwhile, the authorities continued their efforts to split the trade union movement. They announced that they would "register" (in other words, recognise) the conciliatory Union of Johannesburg Municipal Workers, whose members had not participated in the strike.

The eight-day strike of 10,000 Johannesburg workers was thus broken. Many of them were migrant workers, i.e., regarded as less advanced contingent of the working class. Nevertheless, they stood their ground against their class enemy. Here a large role was played by the trade union, which proved able to organise and lead the workers. But a similarly significant circumstance was that the atmosphere which had reigned in the Johannesburg industrial area in the course of a decade and especially after the Soweto revolt influenced the African proletariat, fueling its class

216

consciousness. The struggle was joined by workers who had never been committed before.

More than 1,300 strikers were laid off, and of these nearly 1,000 were deported to the homelands. This condemned their families to extreme poverty. But the defeat of the strike harboured the seeds of further anger and further explosions. This was noted with alarm by observers from among the most prescient representatives of the ruling camp. "Oh, yes," they said, "the strike has been broken. Whatever it is, the price is surely too high. Johannesburg built a reservoir of bitterness for the country this week."[65] There were other, even more worried voices. Robert Lambert, a lecturer in industrial sociology of the University of Natal, declared that the deportation of striking black workers to the homelands would raise the level of frustration there and turn the homelands into fruitful catchment areas for the banned African National Congress. The possible alternatives of this deportation of workers who had been "unionised and politicised by their role in the short but intensive strike," Lambert warned, was first, "that they would try to organise the workers in these territories into trade unions. The second was that they would be unable to do so, but their presence would raise the level of frustration and thereby the number of potential recruits to insurgency."[66] Sam Moss, a member of the Johannesburg City Council, criticised the Council's actions, declaring that the "strike last month was the first of many rounds in a 'war of attrition'. 'The strikers have lost the first round, but the final battle will not be won by the Council'."[67]

Three months later the South African newspaper reported that up to 15 per cent of the deported workers returned to Johannesburg despite the ban on them, and the City Council had to reinstate them in their jobs.[68]

The Rent War

Meanwhile, a fresh crisis was brewing in Soweto. This time the focus was on one of the most urgent issues that directly concerned every family—the question of rent. This was a long-standing and painful problem: small pay and exhorbitant rent for a matchbox house.

In 1979 David Thebehali, who had been made "Mayor" of Soweto for another term, announced that rents would be increased by 87.8 per cent, from 19.50 to 36.62 rand a month.[69] The actual rent was 5 rand, the rest of the sum consisting of various payments for communal services, administrative expenses, the school tax, and so on. It was this latter part of the rent that was to be raised to 31.62 rand. The payments for administrative expenses, consisting of almost one-third of the entire sum, were to be increased from 5.93 to 10.41 rand.[70] This money went mostly into the upkeep of the West Rand Administration Board, the apparatus that controlled the life of blacks in Soweto and other West Rand townships. The WRAB offices were, it will be recalled, one of the main targets of black anger during the 1976 revolt and almost all were burned down. The WRAB personnel includes white officials (mostly fiercely racist Afrikaners) and black policemen, who were hated and called "black shirts"; in 1975 the WRAB had a personnel of almost 10,000.[71]

Thus, one-third of the rent was in fact used for the maintenance of the racist apparatus of control and compulsion, and it was this component of the rent that was to increase most. Moreover, it was learned that the administration agencies, including the WRAB, deducted large sums—up to 40,000 rand annually—from their revenue for the South African Bureau of Racial Affairs.[72] This organisation conducts research and publicises the results in an effort to justify apartheid in South Africa. Its chairman, Carel Boshoff, is also the head of the Afrikaner Broederbond, a secret racist organisation. Thus, by raising rents the authorities intended to compel blacks to pay more to their direct oppressors.

Moreover, they hoped that the higher rents would "patch up the holes" made in the budget by the intensified struggle against apartheid. These "holes" were made, in particular, by the sharp decline of revenue from the sale of alcoholic beverages in Soweto: from 38 million to 22 million rand.[73]

The puppet self-government agencies in Soweto tried to vindicate the higher rents with the argument that the money was needed for modernising the townships, and even sought to benefit from the Africans' sense of national pride and their striving for independence. All these subterfuges were exposed by the Sowetans themselves. Their attitude to the planned rents increase was articulated by the chairman of the Committee of Ten Nthato Motlana: "The people of Soweto cannot afford it. What will solve the situation is that the government should inject more money into the development of Soweto. They created the area, they must pay for the maintenance."[74]

In August 1979, when the plans to raise rents were announced, a mass, unrelenting campaign of resistance to these plans commenced in Soweto. The first mass rally took place in Soweto two days after the rents announcement was made. "Masses of residents threatened in great unison that they would start a shanty town by putting shacks up and leave their houses empty if the increases were not halted," the *Post* wrote on the same day. There and then, at the rally some 4,000 persons signed a petition urging the authorities to prohibit rent increases "unless they wanted to see an ugly situation erupting in the townships".[75] There were similar rallies in all the Soweto townships. The protest campaign was led by the Committee of Ten. At a rally in Orlando its chairman Nthato Motlana urged the WRAB to pull out of Soweto because it was spending public money to maintain an inflated personnel of white officials.[76]

On September 23 the Committee of Ten announced the formation of a new organisation, the Soweto Civic Association. Nthato Motlana said that the SCA would handle matters related to the day-to-day needs of the Soweto inhabitants and that it would have a branch in every township. The SCA planned to increase its membership to 100,000 and later set up branches in other inner-city districts across the country.

This new organisation's attitude to the apartheid regime was defined in declarations calling for an end to racism, the establishment of a unitary state based on the "one man one vote" principle, the dismantling of community councils and the bantustanisation policy, and the dissolution of the discriminative education system for blacks.[77] It was thus obvious that the SCA intended to act outside and despite the structure of administration over urban blacks established by the government. The SCA announced its rejection of apartheid. "The powder keg that is Soweto will continue to rumble and might explode," Nthato Motlana said in one of his speeches. "There is only one thing that will satisfy blacks and that is the dismantling of apartheid. The policy of separate development is a fraud and a dishonest man-oeuvre which should be dismantled."[7] [8]

Under pressure from the people the Community Council and the authorities, while not generally abandoning their idea of increasing rents, had to postpone the first phase of the increase (by one-third) scheduled for September 1, 1979. For a while the issue of rent increases lost its acuteness. But in March 1980 the rent war resumed its momentum.

The Soweto Community Council began a new drive to persuade the inhabitants of the townships that there was no alternative to raising rents. Once again these attempts were firmly repulsed. At a rally held in the township of Emdeni to consider this problem three members of the Community Council were called traitors and renegades. It was unani-mously decided that nobody would pay rents under the new tariff.

A meeting held in the Lutheran Church in Zone No. 9 of Meadowlands was addressed by Nthato Motlana, who denounced the rents increase. Through the SCA and the growing number of township civic associations (by April 1980 their number had risen to ten) the Committee of Ten undertook to organise and lead the rent war. Rallies were planned in all the Soweto townships. Wherever these were held the people decided not to pay the higher rent.

The principal battles of this "war" began in July 1980 when Soweto's "Mayor" David Thebehali announced that rents would, after all, be increased by only 75.2 per cent instead of by 87.8 per cent as was planned. The first phase of the increase was scheduled for August 1, 1980, and the third, and last, for February 1981. Thebehali believed that this would yield an additional revenue of 5 million rand.

The *Post* newspaper commented on this official decision in editorial and noted: "Escalating costs and a continuing inflationary spiral make nonsense of all this talk of a stable economy. Added to that is the frightening rise in unemploy-ment figures among blacks. There are indeed many factors that make us completely against any added incumbrance on a population that is already groaning under incredible economic pressure. Our main argument is that places like

Soweto are not of our making. Community councillors, who were simply too eager to jump the bandwagon of an unsupportable system, will now willy-nilly have to carry the can."[79]

On August 1, the date set for the first rent increase, the tension in Soweto rose to white heat. The authorities announced that those who failed to pay the rent would be made to surrender the keys to their houses.

The SCA and its township branches, which in September numbered 18, reinforced their resistance campaign. They were supported by other public organisations, one of which was the Azanian Peoples Organisation. A leaflet printed in English, Zulu, and Sotho stated that unemployment had reached a staggering level and that the cost of living had become unbearable. This leaflet urged the people of Soweto not to pay the new rents.[80] The people were told by the SCA that in the event they were threatened with eviction and judicial harassment they should go to their township SCA branch where they would be provided with defence counsels. In order to make such suits legal the SCA filed an application with the Supreme Court, naming as respondents the Minister of Cooperation and Development, the West Rand Administration Board, the Soweto Community Council, and the Administrator of the Transvaal, i.e., the officials and agencies charged with exercising control over Soweto. Moreover, it was planned to appeal against the actions of the Community Council and thereby compel it to annul the rent increase.

There was a large protest rally on August 24. While at the outset of the rent war such rallies were usually attended by 100-200 people, this time nearly 2,000 people crowded into the Anglican Church in the township of Phefeni. Two of the resolutions passed at that rally stated that "the Soweto Civic Association led by the Committee of Ten is our leadership, and we, the house, advise any resident to join it" and "the people of Soweto, led by the SCA, should not pay increased rents".[81] These resolutions and the fact that Nthato Motlana, who chaired the rally, was lifted shoulders high by people who sang his praises show that the SCA had at that stage become the leading organisation in Soweto and its chairman Nthato Motlana, the city's leading personality. This resulted from the SCA having set up a ramified network of branches and having headed the resistance to the upcoming rent increases.

Protest rallies took place one after another, with more and more people attending them and the speeches becoming ever sharper. In most cases the discussion of the rent problem developed into a discussion of political issues, and the rallies themselves ended with the proclamation of political slogans and the singing of freedom songs. Addressing one such rally in the township of Klipspruit, Nthato Motlana said: "Some people say we shouldn't bother ourselves with civic matters as there is no liberation through civic matters. Every journey begins with the first step. We have to start somewhere. Presently we are living in Soweto just because somebody decided for us. We travel in crowded trains, live in 4-roomed houses and our children can't decide which schools they want to attend. These are the basic needs of every human being, the right to decide on one's own."[82] In another speech he declared that parents would no longer stand aloof and watch their children shot.[83] Leonard Mosala, also of the Committee of Ten, said that the rents battle would determine the future of the Soweto people. "Our battle," he declared, "is a total and final liberation of the black man. People in the country had to unite in order to win their struggle against oppression."[84]

Workers and junior office employees became the main protest and resistance force in the rent war in Soweto. Women, who bore most of the burden of concern for the family budget, were particularly active. The struggle was supported also by the trade unions. The Johannesburg branch of the Black Allied Workers Union said that "the bulk of the people of Soweto merely manage to live from hand to mouth. Intellectuals would say they live below the minimum poverty datum line. We simply say they earn low wages and it is difficult to see how they can pay high rents unless, of course, their earnings are accordingly adjusted."[85]

The rent war reached its peak in October 1980. This was prompted by two circumstances. The first was the announcement that in most of the Soweto townships the rent increase would enter its second phase on October 1 (in Diepkloof and Meadowlands an approximately similar increase was set for November 1). The second was the visit to Soweto by the Minister of Cooperation and Development Piet Koornhof.

At the start of the year it was announced that there would be celebrations to mark the 75th anniversary of Soweto. There were angry protests as soon as this announcement was made. The chairman of the Diepkloof Civic Association told a 300-strong audience: "Soweto is not worth celebrating as it has brought about the continual harassment and humiliation of blacks ever since its existence. The various Soweto community councils have R25,000 to spend on a pleasure festival when they ought to divide the money amongst widows and pensioners."[86] This was the "festival" scheduled for mid-October that Minister Koornhof planned to attend. He was to be conferred with the Freedom of Soweto by "Mayor" David Thebehali.

On the day before this visit the SCA, the Federation of South African Women, and some other organisations called upon the people of Soweto to mark the visit of the Minister on October 15 with a general strike. Already angry at the rent increases and quite ready to explode, people willingly responded to this call, especially as a strike would express their protest against the rent increases as well.

Many of those who for one reason or another decided to go to work found they were unable to do so. Two powerful explosions shook the ground that morning near the Dube railway station. These blew up a section of the main railway and badly damaged the signal system. Trains that daily transported up to 150,000 workers were halted for several hours. The media later reported that another eight explosive devises that failed to detonate were found—the first explosion had damaged the wires linking them.[87]

Such was the beginning of the "festival" commemorating Soweto's 75th anniversary. The atmosphere was charged to bursting point long before the Koornhof visit. Thousands of people streamed to the Community Council's offices in Jabulani where the Minister was expected. More than 6,000 people gathered, chanting slogans, singing freedom songs, and raising clenched fists. Facing them were the police reinforced with riot squads and security agents. Both sides awaited the Minister: one to voice protest and anger, the other to muffle that voice.

Unexpectedly, instead of a convoy of cars everybody saw

223

a military helicopter coming in to land. This change in the "festival" arrangements was made because of apprehensions for the safety of the Minister, who feared to drive through the seething Soweto townships. He had boarded a helicopter at the last minute.

As the Minister came down from the helicopter he was met with angry shouts. "There were no cheering crowds or welcoming crowds, only angry residents, some of them absent from work to demonstrate their rejection of the farce."[88] After quickly escorting Koornhof into the building, where the "Mayor" was awaiting the distinguished guest, the police fell upon the demonstrators, using batons and tear gas. They even brought up an armoured car with a gas spraying installation mounted on it.

The treatment handed out to women was particularly brutal. At the call of their Federation about 500 women gathered in a separate group in order to hand a statement to Thebehali. This statement said in part: "We, the women of Soweto, hereby reject the leadership of David Thebehali and the Community Councils. We also reject vehemently the increased rents which aids racist organisations like SABRA. We have no citizenship in the land of our birth, and therefore reject the honorary citizenship conferred on Dr. Koornhof."[89] Time and again the police dispersed the women with batons, but they returned again and again. This went on for nearly seven hours.

Meanwhile, the ceremony of conferring honorary Soweto citizenship proceeded in the Community Council building. However, tear gas penetrated the building. It was reported on the next day that "several of the black councillors and their wives wept quietly into their handkerchiefs while Dr. Koornhof spoke".[90]

Such was the "festival" of Soweto's 75th anniversary that turned into an explosion of anger and indignation on the part of the people of this African ghetto. Once more people picked up stones—the tested "weapon of the proletariat"—to hurl them at cars. PUTCO buses were a special target—33 were damaged in a single day. Many people were savagely beaten by the police, many others suffered from the tear gas. Those arrested were charged under the Riotous Assemblies Act. Piet Koornhof could congratulate himself on yet another "achievement" of the police: one person was killed and one other received a bullet wound. As though rounding off the events of that October in Soweto, on the 30th there were another two explosions, this time in Diepkloof. Two grenades were thrown into the WRAB office.

The authorities got what they wanted despite the stormy protests in Soweto: a three-phased increase of rents, an operation that was completed in early 1981. But the rent war did not end. The people of Soweto continued their resistance—many simply refused to pay their rents and had the support of the civic association and other public organisations. The SCA tried to get the Supreme Court to annul the rent increases, but to no avail. The main weapon of the authorities was the eviction threat to those who refused to pay. The people of Soweto had to yield.

The "war" was resumed at the close of 1981 when the WRAB announced that there would be a further rent increase, this time by 8 rand. Once again there were protest rallies and these heard angry speeches from representatives of diverse organisations, including a speech from Nthato Motlana. The police replied with further raids, arresting those who were in arrears with their rent and threatening them with eviction. Once again Soweto had to succumb.

In this rent war only one of the sides won repeatedly— the government represented in Soweto by the WRAB. The forces were unequal, of course, but with every new "victory" there was more anger in Soweto, more hardly restrainable resentment of what the authorities were doing. It is indicative that when it became known that rents were to be raised by another 20 rand the Transvaal Chambers of Commerce and Industries, which united the leading businessmen in the area, warned the government that there would be a painful backlash. In their view this could trigger "serious disturbances doing enormous damage not only to Soweto but to the economy of South Africa".[9] [1]

As well as discontent, a striving to protect their interests and join forces grew in the townships. The rent problem worried not only the people of Soweto. There was opposition to the rent increase in practically all townships. Noting the intensification of the rent war in 1982, ANC monthly *Mayibuye*, circulating illegally among blacks in South Africa, wrote: "They are relying on our lack of national cohesion on the rents issue... We must unite our forces and meet to decide on common action throughout the country."⁹ ²

The ANC Heads the Struggle

It would take too much space to list all the daring attacks by Umkhonto we Sizwe fighters, who blew up railway tracks and power stations, and attacked police stations and administration offices. Combat operations by patriots in South Africa had become a day-to-day reality. Nevertheless, each year brought something new, raising the struggle to a higher level. The year 1981 was no exception.

The attack on Voortrekkerhoogte, the principal military base situated on the southwestern outskirts of Pretoria, staggered the government and the entire white population. In the night of August 12-13, 1981, this most prestigious military base and symbol of the racist regime's military strength was attacked with rockets. It was later learned that the rockets were fired from a heavy-calibre launcher sited some three miles away from the target. The knowledge that the Umkhonto we Sizwe fighters had such a powerful weapon threw the military and the police into confusion. The newspapers wrote with alarm that this was the largest rocket-launcher of its kind, that it fired missiles weighing 77 kilos and had a range of nearly 11 kilometres. The implication was that no place in South Africa was secure.

The ANC President Oliver Tambo characterised this operation as "an expression of our determination to intensify our struggle; to take the offensive on all fronts... The attack on Voortrekkerhoogte is an indication of the capacity we have reached within the country to deliver heavy and effective blows, including particularly blows against the military set-up."⁹ ³

Immediately after this missile attack the police began a search for the attackers. All nearby roads were blocked and the entire region of Pretoria and Johannesburg was cordoned off. The search was exceptionally intensive in Soweto. But this was a futile exercise. As the English newspaper *Guardian* noted: "The townships offer fleeing insurgents a chance of merging with local people and hiding until the intensity of the search eases."⁹ ⁴

Events of a spectacular nature also in political terms occurred two months before the attack on the Voortrekker-hoogte base.

The apartheid regime planned pompous celebrations to mark the 20th anniversary of the republic. It wanted to involve the largest possible number of Africans in order to make them believe that the racist regime was a benefit to them and there was no sense in fighting apartheid. However, nothing came of this. More, a boycott of Republic Day was announced not only by blacks but by most of the Indians and coloureds and even many whites. "Millions of South Africans—either individually or as members of more than 55 organisations representing all races—have pledged to ignore the 20th anniversary celebrations of the republic. Hostility directed against the celebrations has revolved around the apartheid system—pass laws, homeland policies, the stripping of blacks of South African citizenship, the Group Areas Act, and unequal education systems—at mass rallies countrywide."[95]

Republic Day was boycotted by political parties, churches, trade unions, universities, women's and youth organisations, and even some township community councils (Alberton, Evaton, Vaal, Mamelodi, Atteridgeville, and Daveyton). In Soweto the boycott was joined by the Committee of Ten and by the Alexandra Liaison Committee. The Soweto Community Council was alone in deciding to mark the anniversary of its masters.

On Republic Day the people of Soweto held a protest rally against the "republic". At the Methodist Church Centre in Jabavu people pledged to bring about revolutionary change in the country and support the liberation movements "that must ultimately rid South Africa of white rule and the oppression perpetuated upon the majority of the country's people". Placards held by participants in this rally bore the words: "No apartheid republic", "We will fight side by side throughout our lives until we have won our liberation", and "Forward to a People's Republic". The people heard sermons in which not a word was spoken about humility and submission. One of the priests declared that neither the army, nor the police with their modern weapons, nor massive raids would stop the freedom struggle. "They cannot stop the revolution that will liberate the people of South Africa," he said in conclusion.[96] The rally began and ended with revolutionary songs and the chanting of freedom slogans. This time the police, sitting in four vans in the square in front of the church, did not venture to disperse the rally. Similar rallies and demonstrations took place in many cities across the country.

During these days there were no explosions in Soweto. But in Durban a powerful explosion damaged the Defence Force recruiting office. This "salute" was even heard on the city's outskirts.

The blacks had their own anniversaries, which they felt they had to commemorate. First and foremost, this was, as in previous years, the day to remember the victims of June 16, 1976—the fifth anniversary of the Soweto revolt. As before, the authorities and the police tried to prevent demonstrations and rallies. But these took place in spite of everything.

As in previous years, Sowetans gathered for the commemoration services in the Regina Mundi Church, which the newspaper *Sowetan* aptly called the "Mecca" of mass political gatherings. Nearly 10,000 people filled the church and the area around it, but the commemoration services were aborted. The police threw tear-gas canisters into the church, and the choking and blinded people ran out in panic. Furniture in the church was damaged in the rush. After this incident the church authorities wrote to the sponsoring organisations asking them to refrain from holding such gatherings. This letter stated in part: "It is futile to make an urgent appeal to the Minister of Police to impose a ban on the use of tear gas during commemoration services. The police have their reasons for using it."[9] [7]

On June 16, 1981, a general strike, now an established tradition, was staged in Soweto. More than half the workers stayed at home on that day. There was a particularly large number of strikers in the townships of Pimville and Klipspruit. There was no attendance at schools, shops were closed, and leaflets were distributed everywhere. An ANC statement on the occasion of the fifth anniversary of the Soweto uprising said: "Since 1976 the people's determination has not been smothered. In fact, the survivors of Soweto have matured into the national liberation movement and the people's army, Umkhonto we Sizwe, and they are responding in a fitting manner to the reactionary violence of the Pretoria regime."[9][8]

A column of demonstrators with the black-green-gold ANC flag carried in its front rank marched through the township Alexandra on June 21. The police tore the flag from the hands of the demonstrators but failed to disperse, the demonstration or disrupt the rallies that were held in the churches for lack of other premises. Again the people demanded the release of Nelson Mandela and all other political prisoners, and proclaimed slogans of resistance and struggle. One of the speakers, Bishop Desmond Tutu, declared: "We have come to rededicate ourselves to the struggle. We are the victims of the most vicious system since Nazism."[9][9]

Leaflets with the last words written by the South African patriot Solomon Mahlangu were distributed at a commemoration service in Soweto township of Emdeni. "My blood will nourish the tree of freedom. Tell my people that I love them and that they must continue the struggle. A luta continua," he wrote to his mother before he was hanged on April 6, 1979. One after another, the speakers denounced apartheid. The people sang freedom songs and chanted the ANC call, "Amandla!".

In August the judicial bodies committed fresh outrages: the Pretoria Supreme Court passed the death sentence on ANC members Anthony Tsotsobe, Johannes Shabangu, and David Moise. These young men, who had grown up in townships in the Transvaal, were charged with innumerable "terrorist" acts, including the explosion at an oil-refinery near Sasolburg and the attack on a police station in Booysens. As the sentence was passed they heard it with calm and courage. Then they broke into a song with the words: "*Abafana bombkhonto balwelizwe*" ("The boys of Umkhonto are fighting for their land"). In the courtroom there were some 200 people and these answered with the song *Somlandela* ("We Shall Follow Your Lead"). After this there was a protest demonstration, joined by whites, in the square in front of the court building. There were some arrests. All of this was reported in the newspaper *Sowetan*. It was obvious that far from intimidating people judicial reprisals of this nature were bringing more people into the struggle.

In December 1981 Sowetans gathered at the Avalon

Cemetery to unveil a monument on the grave of a Soweto schoolboy, who was the first of the police victims on June 16, 1976. The words on the stone read: "Zolile Hector Peterson. Deeply mourned by his parents, sisters, and a nation that remembers. Time is on the side of the oppressed today. Truth is on the side of the oppressed today." A clenched fist, the symbol of resistance, was engraved over these words.

In *Embers of Soweto* a South African poet and patriot, who writes under the pen name of A. N. C. Kumalo, vividly describes the spirit of Soweto:

> *Out of the crucible*
> *Warrior army of new age*
> *Despising gas, batons, bullets,*
> *Defying centuries of slavery,*
> *Advancing without care on armoured cars*
> *Striking metal with clenched fists,*
> *Warrior cry "Amandla!"*
> *Rising in every throat.*
>
> . . . .
> *Winging with the incandescent embers*
> *Warrior cry whirls and*
> *Soars with collapsing child,*
> *Ignites triumphant Freedom's gun.*

As the year drew to a close there were several more attacks on offices personifying apartheid. In Orlando West Uncle Tom's Hall, where rents were usually collected, was burnt down. Also in Orlando, the court building was blown up. "Mayor" David Thebehali escaped vengeance by a miracle: a grenade exploded near his car.

In the years that passed since the Soweto uprising the ANC had gained in stature and influence. This was due in part to its clear-cut programme, the Freedom Charter, and to the actions of Umkhonto we Sizwe fighters, despite the fact that in the preceding 20 years the ANC had functioned in the strictest secrecy, which gave it very limited opportunities for political work and public relations among the population. The ANC built up its strength and received growing support from the people.

In August 1981 *The Star* conducted a selective poll to

learn the attitude of the blacks as well as the Indians and coloureds to the various African political parties and their leaders. Some 700 persons were questioned in three of the country's largest cities: Johannesburg, Cape Town, and Durban. They were asked what party they would vote for if parliamentary elections were now held? Forty per cent said they would vote for the ANC. In Johannesburg 47 per cent favoured the ANC. Nelson Mandela was, as could have been expected, named as the most popular leader: he got a poll rating of 76 per cent.[100] As a party, the ANC got the highest rating among all categories of those respondents: skilled workers, unskilled labourers, intellectuals and urban middle classes, all age categories and all ethnic groups. It is symbolic that more Zulus favoured the ANC than the Inkatha Zulu organisation.

In Soweto, as everywhere else, the ANC and Nelson Mandela were found to have the widest support. Even Nthato Motlana, whom 70 per cent of Sowetans wanted to see holding the office of mayor of Soweto, owed his prestige to his efforts to have good relations with ANC members; he missed no opportunity to remind people that he had once been an ANC activist. Nevertheless, as Motlana himself conceded, his influence and authority as a moderate leader was in decline. "People," he said, "are fast becoming disillusioned with the leadership of those who say peaceful change is still possible. We live within the system and are part and parcel of it. We become despised because of our links with it. The only people who appear to buck the system are the African National Congress."[101]

The level of public consciousness in Soweto has also undergone a change. Right after the 1976 revolt some people were inclined to consider the students as the main force of the struggle. But life was correcting the assessments of the social significance of this or that stratum or group. Those who participated in the revolt were now giving a different assessment of their role in the common struggle. "Today we realise that our struggle must be based on the working classes, not on intellectuals."[102] One of the students, son of a factory worker, said: "The Matanzimas and the Sebes [puppet rulers of Bantustans.—V.G.] taught us it was not a black-white thing, it was not only whites exploiting and oppressing us. We looked for an explanation

and found it in a class analysis of society." An indication
of this change among young people was their adaptation of
the old ANC song *We Will Follow Luthuli*. The names
now sung in place of Luthuli's were those of Tambo, Mandela, Joe Slovo, Marx, and Lenin.[103] Many of the young
people who took part in the Soweto revolt were joining the
South African Communist Party and looking for and finding answers to their questions in Marxism-Leninism.

On January 8, 1982, the African National Congress
marked its 70th anniversary "at a pitch of power, influence,
and prestige higher than ever before in its history. It has
established itself without doubt as the effective leader of
the struggle of the oppressed people for liberation, and the
importance of its role in shaping the destiny of our country is acknowledged by friend and foe alike."[104] Indeed,
during the anniversary there were eloquent acknowledge-
ments. The *Sunday Tribune* wrote: "... in fact the country
is experiencing a powerful black political revival, central
to which appears to be growing support for the policies
laid out in the Freedom Charter."[105] *The Star* noted:
"Mr. Mandela is still regarded by a majority of blacks as
their leader. And the ANC has become an increasingly
effective revolutionary force with considerable international
recognition and support."[106] Earlier, this same newspaper
had pointed out that the ANC not only enjoyed growing
support from socialist countries and front-line states but
was getting it also where support counted most—"on the
home front".[107]

[1] *To the Point*, Johannesburg, January 28, 1977.
[2] Ibid., June 24, 1977.
[3] *Time*, New York, June 27, 1977, p. 29.
[4] *Citizen*, Johannesburg, June 27, 1978.
[5] *Time*, New York, June 27, 1977, pp. 28, 29.
[6] *To the Point*, Johannesburg, June 24, 1977.
[7] *Sechaba*, London, 4th Quarter 1977, p. 3.
[8] *To the Point*, Johannesburg, January 28, 1977.
[9] *Rand Daily Mail*, Johannesburg, August 17, 1977.
[10] Ibid., July 13, 1977.
[11] *Financial Mail*, Johannesburg, September 23, 1977.
[12] Ibid.

[13] *The Star*, Johannesburg, October 21, 1977.

[14] *The World*, Johannesburg, June 8, 1977.

[15] *Sunday Times*, Johannesburg, October 16, 1977.

[16] *The World*, Johannesburg, August 9, 1977.

[17] Ibid., August 11, 1977.

[18] Ibid., August 12, 1977.

[19] *Weekly News Briefings*, London, No. 38, 1980.

[20] *Rand Daily Mail*, Johannesburg, October 20, 1977.

[21] *Financial Mail*, Johannesburg, August 17, 1973.

[22] *Citizen*, Johannesburg, October 24, 1977. In: *Weekly News Briefings*, Issue No. 43, 1977.

[23] *Rand Daily Mail*, Johannesburg, December 19, 1977.

[24] Ibid.

[25] *Citizen*, Johannesburg, December 7, 1977.

[26] Ibid., November 25, 1977.

[27] Ibid., November 26, 1977.

[28] *Rand Daily Mail*, Johannesburg, April 1, 1978.

[29] *The Star*, Johannesburg, December 4, 1979.

[30] *Rand Daily Mail*, Johannesburg, June 13, 1978.

[31] Ibid., June 19, 1978.

[32] Ibid.

[33] Ibid., June 20, 1978.

[34] Ibid., October 5, 1978.

[35] *The Star*, Johannesburg, June 4-5, 1979.

[36] Ibid., November 3, 1979.

[37] *Sunday Express*, Johannesburg, November 4, 1979.

[38] *Rand Daily Mail*, Johannesburg, November 3, 1979.

[39] *Natal Mercury*, Pietermaritzburg, June 28, 1979.

[40] *Rand Daily Mail*, Johannesburg, June 18, 1979.

[41] *Post*, Johannesburg, March 15, 1979.

[42] *Sunday Times*, Johannesburg, January 27, 1980.

[43] Ibid., June 17, 1979.

[44] *Rand Daily Mail*, Johannesburg, February 7, 1980; *Sunday Times*, Johannesburg, February 10, 1980.

[45] *Rand Daily Mail*, Johannesburg, February 12, 1980.

[46] *Daily News*, Durban, February 22, 1980.

[47] *Sunday Post*, Johannesburg, April 6, 1980.

[48] *Citizen*, Johannesburg, April 7, 1980.

[49] *Weekly News Briefings*, London, No. 22, 1980, p. 1.

[50] *The Times*, London, June 16, 1980.

[51] *The African Communist*, London, No. 83, 1980, p. 31.

[52] *Sunday Post*, Johannesburg, March 9, 1980.

[53] *Post*, Johannesburg, April 17, 1980.

[54] Ibid., June 12, 1980.

[55] *The Times*, London, June 16, 1980.

[56] *Post*, Johannesburg, June 16, 1980.

[57] *The Cape Times*, Cape Town, July 17, 1980.

[58] *Post*, Johannesburg, July 25, 1980.

[59] *The Star*, Johannesburg, July 30, 1980.

[60] *Rand Daily Mail*, Johannesburg, July 30, 1980.

[61] *Sunday Times*, Johannesburg, July 27, 1980.

[62] *The Star*, Johannesburg, July 30, 1980.

[63] Ibid.
[64] Ibid., July 31, 1980.
[65] *Rand Daily Mail*, Johannesburg, August 3, 1980.
[66] Ibid., August 8, 1980.
[67] Ibid., August 15, 1980.
[68] *The Star*, Johannesburg, October 16, 1980.
[69] *Rand Daily Mail*, Johannesburg, October 16, 1980.
[70] Ibid., August 10, 1979.
[71] Alan Brooks, Jeremy Brickhill, *op. cit.*, p. 175.
[72] *Sunday Times*, Johannesburg, October 15, 1980.
[73] *Mayibuye*, Lusaka, No. 5, 1980, p. 6.
[74] *Post*, Johannesburg, March 17, 1980.
[75] Ibid., August 13, 1979.
[76] Ibid., August 20, 1979.
[77] *The Star*, Johannesburg, September 24, 1979.
[78] *Post*, Johannesburg, October 5, 1979.
[79] Ibid., July 7, 1980.
[80] Ibid., August 28, 1980.
[81] Ibid., August 25, 1980.
[82] Ibid., September 29, 1980.
[83] Ibid., October 13, 1980.
[84] Ibid., September 29, 1980.
[85] Ibid., September 19, 1980.
[86] Ibid., April 21, 1980.
[87] Ibid., October 17, 1980.
[88] Ibid., October 16, 1980.
[89] Ibid., October 20, 1980.
[90] *Daily News*, Durban, October 16, 1980.
[91] *Weekly News Briefings*, London, No. 36, 1981, p. 11.
[92] *Mayibuye*, Lusaka, No. 5, 1982, p. 5.
[93] Ibid., No. 9, 1981, p. 1.
[94] *Guardian*, London, August 14, 1981.
[95] *The Star*, Johannesburg, May 28, 1981.
[96] *Weekly News Briefings*, London, No. 23, 1981, p. 4.
[97] Ibid., No. 26, 1981, p. 5.
[98] Ibid., No. 24, 1981, p. 1.
[99] Ibid., No. 26, 1981, p. 5.
[100] *The Star*, Johannesburg, September 23, 1981.
[101] *Weekly News Briefings*, London, No. 3, 1982, p. 1.
[102] Ibid., p. 2.
[103] Ibid.
[104] *The African Communist*, London, No. 88, 1982, p. 9.
[105] *Weekly News Briefings*, London, No. 3, 1982, p. 1.
[106] *The Star*, Johannesburg, January 9, 1982.
[107] Ibid., January 7, 1982.

Chapter Six

RESISTANCE AT A NEW STAGE

The Situation in Soweto and Other Black Townships

It was 1984, eight years after the uprising began in Soweto. What had changed in this span of time? Were the Sowetans living a better and calmer life? Were they now happy? The reply could only be in the negative as was borne out by the events of 1984-1986.

Greater Soweto occupies a territory of 8,200 hectares, and includes Dobsonville. Administratively it consists of three parts: Soweto proper, Diepmeadow (comprising Diepkloof and Meadowlands, hence the name), and Dobsonville. Accordingly, there are three administrative bodies: township councils, whose functions are spelled out in the 1982 Black Local Authorities Act, No. 102. Under the new law the powers of these councils have been extended and the WRAB is now, ostensibly, the executor of their will, their agent. However, real power remains in the hands of the WRAB. Its officials are among the personnel of the councils. Besides, the councillors themselves are at the beck and call of the Minister in Pretoria, who may simply disband a council objectionable to the government.

The declarations about the powers of township councils having been extended are no more than demagoguery. But the government had its own calculations, namely, to shift the responsibility for the calamitous situation in the ghettotownships from the actual master to his servitors and, in addition, to make the latter answerable for maintaining "law and order". Moreover, the Pretoria regime is planning, at some point in the future, to replace the present administration boards with "regional development boards" that will take over with no change in the former's functions.

Generally speaking, in Pretoria they have a penchant for renaming their institutions, giving this out as the apartheid regime's evolution in the direction of moderation. For example, the former Bantu Administration Department, which had jurisdiction over the WRAB and other administration boards, is now called the Department of Cooperation and Development, while the Department of Police and Prisons has been given the more euphonic name of Department of Law and Order. But a change of signboard does not change the nature of apartheid's institutions or of the system itself. As a matter of fact, not only the names of ministries and departments are changed. Under instruction from the government, Africans in South Africa were named "natives", "non-Europeans", "Bantu", and "blacks". The change in name was made by white officials without asking the Africans for their opinion.

But let us return to Soweto[1]. New houses are being built, and more townships are springing up around Soweto. But the housing situation remains critical: in 1983 Soweto was short of 35,000 houses, and with each succeeding year the shortage increased by 4,000. Of the total of 105,000 houses in 1983 only 18,648 were owned by those living in them, while the remaining 83 per cent are occupied by tenants and an unaccountable number of persons renting a corner or a bed. Only somewhat above 5,000 houses belong to their tenants under a 99-year leasehold scheme.[2]

Rents are rising steadily. In 1985 the rent for a four-room house averaged 80 rand, but already then the WRAB chairman began talking of increasing it to 120 rand. About one-third of the houses have electricity, and the network of telephones has been significantly enlarged. The large Blackchain Centre was built near the Baragwanath hospital. The Small Business Development Corporation is promoting the growth of the number of industrial workshops in Soweto. The African Bank, an apartheid operation set up in 1975 specially for black businessmen, is expanding its operations.

The number of schools in Soweto has increased to 365, and these now have a body of 216,000 students. Primary schools remain ethnically divided, and in the first four years instruction is conducted in one of the African languages. Then, at the choice of parents, instruction is conducted in English or Afrikaans. Afrikaans is no longer obligatory, and most choose to study in English.

There have thus been some changes for the better in the infrastructure of the Greater Soweto townships. But has life become better in this "best" of South Africa's ghetto-townships? The statistics produced by repeated surveys of the economic condition of Sowetans indicate that in Soweto life has not improved. In 1984 up to 40 per cent of Sowetans lived below the poverty line, while more than half (51.6 per cent) were jobless.[3] This is a median figure. The situation in individual Soweto townships is even worse: 48 per cent live below the poverty line in Moroka, 52 per cent in Phiri, and 60 per cent in Jabavu.[4] The wage rises won by workers at great cost are quickly nullified by the escalating inflation, the increases in rents and train and bus fares, and the growing prices of food and clothes.

In 1983 Sowetans were polled on their own assessment of their everyday life.[5] One poll was taken among people who had come for purchases in the supermarket in Diepkloof, i.e., among not the poorest. It was found that housing remains the basic problem: 78 of the 108 respondents said there was not enough of it, it was inferior, and the rents were constantly rising.

Most people in Soweto try to give their children an education to help them climb out of poverty. For Sowetans education is thus one of the most vital and pressing problems. It would be appropriate to recall at this point that the protest against the discriminative education system was the spark that kindled the 1976 revolt. Since then the Bantu education system has been dismantled, the ministry concerned has been renamed, and the government has spoken much of innovations and improvements in school education. But what is the actual situation? How do the Sowetans themselves evaluate the present state of education? Only 42 (of the same 108) said that there were some improvements, 14 replied that nothing had changed, and 44 declared that things had grown worse.

Of course, different people have different opinions and judgments about everyday matters and about socio-political issues. But the vast majority of those polled (81 persons) reiterated their negative attitude to the bantustanisation policy and said there should be a single parliament to which representatives of all South Africans would be elected.

Elections to township councils were held in November and December 1983 in Soweto, Diepmeadow, and Dobsonville, i.e., throughout the whole of Greater Soweto as in many other South African ghetto-townships. The 1982 Black Local Authorities Act enlarged the number of people eligible to take part in the election of township puppets: the age qualification was lowered (to 18) and migrant contract workers were given voting rights. It was calculated that this would considerably increase the number of voters (in 1978, it will be recalled, less than 6 per cent of the "legal" residents voted in Soweto) and the new councils would acquire at least the semblance of support from the inhabitants of the townships. But these hopes never came true. At the elections in 29 townships, located mainly in the Transvaal, only 21 per cent of the voters went to the polls (compared with 30 per cent in 1978). Fewer people came to vote for the puppet councillors in Diepmeadow and Dobsonville. True, their number increased somewhat in Soweto itself, up to 10.7 per cent, but this was in no way evidence of a growth of Sowetan support for the local self-government bodies. Besides, the number of people in the election lists in Soweto was just above 262,000; the actual number is, as we have already noted, much larger. Official data about the number of people voting at these elections were far from the reality and did not show the actual state of affairs. For instance, it was announced that 36.6 per cent (the highest figure) of the voters went to the polls in Kagiso. But it turned out that this was a bloated figure. In the election lists there were only 18,300 of the 34,000 persons eligible to vote, and only 1,016 (or 3 per cent) cast their votes.[6] Thus, the majority of Sowetans, as the people in the other townships, refused to place their confidence in the puppet councillors.

Nonetheless, the new councillors were considered elected. In Soweto the Sofasonke Party, headed by Ephraim Tshabalala, won the majority, and the former "Mayor" David Thebehali had to step down. The victor owed his success to unvarnished deceit: he promised that monthly rents would be reduced from 40 to 17 rand, which was, of course, not done.

In addition to the Sofasonke Party, the contenders were, as before, the All Nations Party, the Makgotla Party, the Masingafi Party, the Federal Party, and the Chiavelo Residents' Protection Party. After long vacillation and manoeuvres the Inkatha, headed by Gatsha Buthelezi, did not venture to take part in the elections, evidently fearing that if it joined the company of apartheid's puppets it would lose its positions in Soweto.

The people of the Greater Soweto townships quite manifestly preferred other political and public organisations, those that were resolutely opposed to the racist apartheid regime. Shortly before the elections to the township councils, *The Star* published the results of its poll in Soweto on the attitude of residents to various organisations and their leaders. This poll involved 571 persons. As might have been expected, the leader of the African National Congress Nelson Mandela, who by that time had spent 20 years in prison, was given the highest popularity rating (82 per cent). Of the organisations that should be represented in the South African Parliament the ANC had the largest backing (34 per cent) despite being under a ban for over 20 years and, consequently, denied unhindered access to the people. Nevertheless, it was shown that the ANC was the most popular party among the African population. The Pan-Africanist Congress got an approval rating of only 3 per cent, which put it at the bottom of the list. The Inkatha Party found itself in roughly the same predicament, getting a 6 per cent rating: this is not only a legal organisation but enjoys practically undisguised support from the government. As for Gatsha Buthelezi, he set a record of unpopularity, the ratings putting him behind the former "Mayor" David Thebehali, who was patently a servitor of the regime. Many (59 per cent) said they would have voted for Nthato Motlana, president of the Soweto Civic Association. Such were the real socio-political sentiments in Soweto.[7]

Sowetans showed their attitude to the puppet self-government bodies not only by staying away from the elections but also by more determined actions. Shortly before the elections the houses of the "Mayor" of Diepmeadow and the "Vice-Mayor" of Soweto were set on fire. But this was only the overture. Leaflets headed "Why Bombings on Councillors?" appeared on a day in February 1984 at all railway stations, i.e., the busiest places in Soweto. These demanded that all Soweto councillors resign by the end of the week, declaring that 90 per cent of the people of Soweto had rejected their leadership and the councils' entrenched apartheid. This was a serious and unequivocal warning.

Upon the expiry of this ultimatum petrol bombs were thrown into the houses of many councillors and other menials of the regime. Fires broke out in Soweto, Diepmeadow, and Dobsonville. Soweto's "Mayor" Ephraim Tshabalala was made a special target: his house, dry-cleaning factory, and fish and chips shop were bombed. During the first seven months of 1984 there were 12 attacks on houses of councillors despite the round-the-clock police protection, the police cars circling these houses, and the additional fire-fighting devices. All this took place prior to September 1984 when a new and more powerful wave of popular resistance arose.

Meanwhile, life went on in Soweto. Rents were increased once more, this time by 5 rand, although before the elections it was promised that they would be reduced. Water rates rose by 2.15 rand. At the same time, there was a 10 per cent increase in the general sales tax, hurting mainly poor people who were already hard hit by the unceasing rise of price for prime necessities. The condition of the people deteriorated, while the new "Mayor" was devising plans for Soweto's development. As a first step it was intended to build a fence around the whole of Soweto with tall gates where a toll of 5-10 cents would have to be paid for each car. Then he announced that he intended to build a 150-million-rand casino in Soweto, a 21-storey hotel, and 400 new beer halls—and even a Disneyland in Dlamini. While "comforting" the Soweto homeless and hungry with such plans, Tshabalala did not forget himself: he decided to build a new residence for himself at a cost of 400,000 rand, which he planned to call the "White House". Such was the president of a party committed to total self-sacrifice: the name Sofasonke means "we shall die together (for the common cause)". The people of Soweto remembered a statement made by Tshabalala in 1965, when he said that "apartheid is a blessing for Africans". He most probably had himself and his ilk in mind. Before the year 1984 ran out this avaricious manipulator had to step down in favour of another leader of the same party, Edward Kunene. "E. T.'s" resignation brought no essential changes for the people. The explanation was a simple one: a rival faction had taken over the leadership of the Sofasonke Party.

The vast majority of Sowetans gave their support not to the "parties" that had adjusted to the apartheid system but to organisations that were championing the interests of working people and opposing apartheid. The civic associations affiliated to the Soweto Civic Association remained the most popular of the legally functioning organisations. In 1984, the SCA Executive, consisting of eight persons in addition to president Nthato Motlana, was renewed with persons having closer links to the working people in Soweto. The new members were Frank Chikane, Ike Mogase, Amos Masondo, Pat Lephanya, Nat Ramogopa, Vusi Khanyile, and Alfred Khasago. The civic associations owed their growing prestige to the fact that in their policy they indeed expressed the interests of the people in their townships. A logical outcome of this was the SCA's incorporation in the United Democratic Front.

The anger of most of the country's population over the attempts to reform apartheid instead of eradicating it led to the decision to form a people's front of resistance to these attempts. In this way the United Democratic Front was born in December 1983. Its central purpose was to unite the efforts to defeat the Constitution Bill and the three Koornhof Bills. The former provided for the establishment of a three-chamber parliament, in which, in addition to whites, there would be representatives from the Indians and coloureds, with the whites retaining their dominant role. The government hoped that this wooing of coloureds and Indians would divert them from participating in the general struggle against apartheid. As for blacks they continued to be denied political rights. The three Koornhof Bills defined the further destiny of the black urban population in "white" areas, including Soweto. These were the Black Local Authorities Bill (later passed as Act No. 102), the Orderly Movement and Settlement of Black Persons Bill, and the Black Community Development Bill.

Albertina Sisulu, who resides in Soweto, was elected one of the two UDF presidents. Moreover, she was elected to head the UDF Transvaal organisation. The first UDF Executive included Frank Chikane, one of the leaders of the SCA. Evidence of the rapid rise of the UDF's prestige and influence was that two months after it had been formed it was joined by 530 organisations with a membership of nearly two million.

Such was the political situation just before the new upsurge of the movement of resistance to the apartheid regime. It must be added that in 1983 and in 1984, as was the case formerly, bombs and grenades were exploded in the apartheid system's institutions and important economic installations, and there were shoot-outs with the police. These shoot-outs involved fighters of the People's Army, Umkhonto we Sizwe.

In March 1983 a senior staff member of Pretoria University's Institute for Strategic Studies declared that there was "nothing extraordinary" about these blasts, that they had become a regular feature of life in South Africa. An explosion in the Supreme Court building in Pietermaritzburg was described as "customary". But soon there was an "uncustomary" explosion. A car filled with dynamite was exploded at the building of the operational headquarters of the South African Air Force and the Department of Military Intelligence in the centre of Pretoria on May 20. Twenty persons were killed and over 200 wounded. "Good God! This is war!" exclaimed one of the surviving servicemen. "That explosion shook the public," an official in Pretoria later said. By the "public" he meant the white population, of course. The Africans were jubilant. "The boys have finally struck where it hurts most," a newsman was told by the mother of two young men who left the country in order to return as trained fighters and join in the liberation struggle.[8] The ANC put out a statement saying that "this operation, like others before it, was planned and executed by units of our People's Army—based and operating within South Africa".[9]

In August a bomb was detonated in the so-called "Consulate" of the Bantustan of Ciskei in a Carlton Centre highrise building in the heart of Johannesburg. Then another was exploded in the Ciskei "embassy" in Pretoria. Bombs seriously damaged power substations, plunging into darkness large parts of white-populated Randburg and Sandton, the northern suburbs of Johannesburg. Towards the end of the year there were explosions in the buildings of the ministries of Foreign Affairs, of Cooperation and Development (one of the principal agencies of the apartheid system), Internal Affairs, and other government institutions. Explosions and shots reverberated in Soweto and other townships. There the main targets were police stations.

In South Africa it has now become a tradition to commemorate the Soweto revolt of June 16, honour the memory of those who died, and demonstrate determination to continue the struggle. This date was commemorated also in 1983. At least 20 rallies were held in the industrial areas of the Transvaal. At one of them, in the Regina Mundi Church in Rockville (Soweto), the ANC flag was raised. The main speaker, Bishop Desmond Tutu, spoke of the need for uniting all the forces opposed to apartheid and called upon his listeners to dedicate themselves to the struggle for the freedom of their country, South Africa. At another meeting, in Coronationville (Johannesburg), one of the speakers said that it was common knowledge that the survivors of the 1976 unrest had swelled the ranks of the military wing of the ANC and the hands which held stones now held submachine guns and rocket-propelled grenades.[10] As usual, the police beat and dispersed the people, arresting some of them.

On the next year, too, continuing the tradition, thousands of people gathered in the Regina Mundi Church. They were addressed again by Nthato Motlana, Albertina Sisulu, and Frank Chikane, who called for unity in the liberation struggle.

Such then was the situation in Soweto and Johannesburg on the eve of the new tide of unrest at the close of 1984.

It all began on September 4 in the Vaal Triangle—the cities of Vereeniging, Sasolburg, and Vanderbijlpark—a large industrial area south of Johannesburg. Driven to desperation by economic oppression and denial of political rights, the inhabitants of Sebokeng, Sharpeville, Evaton, Lekoa, and Boipatong rose in revolt. The drop that exhausted their patience was the rent increase by almost 6 rand. Workers refused to go to work, schoolchildren stayed away from classes, and protest demonstrations got under way. The angry inhabitants attacked councillors and police—several persons were killed. More than 60 houses, mostly belonging to councillors or the administration board, and many cars and buses were set on fire. Large contingents of police and army units were sent to the scene. More than 30 persons died in these townships on the first day of the disturbances.

The struggle was joined by the inhabitants of the East Rand townships situated to the east of Johannesburg. Unrest flared up in the townships of Tembisa, Wattville, Vosloorus, and Daveyton. "Nor was the revolt confined to the Vaal Triangle. In every province of South Africa, in every main centre, the flames of revolt were lit and soared ever higher into the air."[1]

The people of Soweto did not remain uninvolved, either. Barricades appeared in the streets of the Soweto townships, shooting broke out, and fires were lit less than a week after the unrest had erupted in the Vaal Triangle. In Moroka, Molapo, Rockville, Central West Jabavu, and Mofolo there were clashes with the police, while clouds of tear gas and the smoke of fires clothed the streets. Reinforced police units patrolled the streets of the townships and army helicopters hovered constantly overhead. The Baragwanath hospital was filled with wounded. Bongani Khumalo, leader of the Transvaal division of the Congress of South African Students, was among the many who died during these first days.

Meanwhile, the Release Mandela Committee organised a one-day strike of workers residing in Soweto. Leaflets urging Sowetans "to stay away in unity, cooperation, and understanding", appeared in all the townships.

The government tried to crush the spreading resistance by sending army units to the townships, for in many cases the police proved to be helpless. On October 7 troops of the South African Army entered Soweto, and on October 23 Sebokeng was occupied by 7,000 policemen and soldiers. But the stepped-up repressions and the use of the army against the people did not quell the unrest. On the contrary, they intensified it. Alan Boesak, patron of the United Democratic Front, declared at the close of October that Pretoria's deployment of troops in black townships to curb unrest showed the government could no longer contain the growing tide of opposition to its policies. "The regime cannot now control the situation and still does not know how to respond to the legitimate demands of the disenfranchised majority."[1][2]

Much of note occurred in 1984, but the most significant event was the general political strike of November 5 and 6 in the Transvaal. The workers acted together with students who refused to attend classes on these two days.

This strike owed its success to the thorough preparations. The Transvaal Stay-away Committee, set up for the purpose, consisted of representatives of more than 30 organisations, including the UDF, AZAPO, COSAS, the Transvaal Indian Congress, and the Release Mandela Committee, and 15 trade unions. Thami Mavi, president of the Soweto UDF branch, was elected to head the committee. The ANC appeal, issued on the eve of the strike, said: "We call on you, our people, to go on the offensive... The two-day work boycott must be a success... This is a demonstration of the unity of all forces fighting against the hated system of apartheid, a demonstration of the maturity of our political consciousness."[13] The Stay-away Committee distributed 400,000 leaflets and 5,000 placards listing the working people's demands. These included the stopping of rent and bus fare increases, the release of all detainees and political prisoners, the withdrawal of the police and army from the townships, the resignation of community councillors, and the withdrawal of unfair taxation. These demands met the vital interests of all residents of ghetto-townships, including Sowetans. So there was a huge response to the call for a general strike.

On the first day 90 per cent of the workers in the Vaal Triangle and 85 per cent in East Rand stayed away from work. In Soweto the percentage was lower, 66, but even this signified that most of the workers went on strike and supported the demands formulated by the Stay-away Committee.

As on many occasions in the past, Gatsha Buthelezi played a divisive role. But, as Thami Mavi pointed out, the stay-away showed that the people were supporting not Buthelezi's Inkatha but the trade unions, the community organisations, and the students associations, i.e., those who were leading them in the struggle. The Stay-away Committee estimated that in the townships, where its leaflets and posters were distributed, the stay-away rate was from 75 to 95 per cent. Thus, more than a million people took part in the strike, bringing the entire industry and business life in the Transvaal to a standstill for two days.

The strikers' demands were not met by the government. However, the strike of November 1984 was a major moral and political triumph that influenced the further course of the liberation struggle. In the view of political personalities, reported in *The Star*, the political results of this strike were the following:

—unity was achieved among a considerable section of the population of the townships in the industrial heart of South Africa. The workers, middle class businessmen, adults, and students closed ranks;

—the first steps towards joint actions were taken by township community organisations and trade unions;

—there had been a transition from rhetoric to concrete, largely disciplined, actions;

—the people had shown they had seen for themselves the real face of the government and that it was a farce to say Pretoria was committed to change.[14]

Professor Edward Webster of the University of Witwatersrand, who analysed 18 general strikes that had taken place since May 1950, said that this was the most successful stayaway in the 35 years, that it had been used as a political weapon.[15] Speaking of the situation in November after the general strike, the Minister of Law and Order Louis le Grange said that the present riots in the townships were more serious than the 1976 riots as they involved more adults.

Until March 1985 there was relative calm in Soweto and the other Transvaal townships. But this was a very uneasy calm. The police repressions continued, the townships were patrolled by soldiers in armoured cars, and from time to time there were fires and shooting. According to official data for the period from September 1984 to March 1985, the repressions led to the arrest of about 10,000 people, the death of 216 blacks and one white, and the wounding of 736 blacks and 15 whites. Four black policemen and five councillors were killed and 181 policemen were wounded. Attacks were registered on 109 councillors, and the houses of 66 of them were burned down; 147 councillors resigned under pressure from the people; in some townships fear led entire councils to resign as a body; 516 cars and 1,080 buses were destroyed. The material damage was estimated at 40 million rand.[16]

On March 21, 1985, exactly on the 25th anniversary of the Sharpeville massacre, the entire country was shaken by the news of a mass shooting of Africans near the town of Uitenhage.

En route to the funeral of a police victim in a neighbouring township, several hundred residents, including many women and children, of the township of Langa found their way barred by a Casspir armoured troop carrier, from which police opened fire without warning. According to official figures, 20 persons were killed. Democratic organisations believed that the actual number of killed was 43. Many more people were wounded.

This killing of Langa residents topped the terror against the black population of South Africa that had reigned almost without a break since 1984. Three weeks after the shooting nearly 80,000 people filled the stadium in the township of KwaNobuhle, which was where demonstrators were headed on March 21. They came to the funeral of the police victims of that day. The coffins, draped in ANC flags, stood in the centre of this huge gathering. Police and troops in armoured cars were deployed around the township, but at that moment they did not venture to interfere. The funeral became a mass political protest demonstration. The people sang freedom songs and chanted slogans honouring Nelson Mandela, Oliver Tambo, and Umkhonto we Sizwe. Leaders of mass democratic organisations addressed the rally, calling for unity and an intensification of the struggle.

In 1985 there were several mass funerals, attended by tens of thousands of people, which turned into political demonstrations. In July tens of thousands of residents of the townships of KwaThema and Duduza in East Rand attended the funerals of victims of police terror. Somewhat later 40,000 people attended the burial of four resistance activists in the small township of Cradock in the eastern part of Cape Province. At the funeral they raised the ANC flag and a banner with the inscription "South African Communist Party". In December more than 50,000 people came to the funeral of 12 police victims in the township of Mamelodi near Pretoria. On that day all activity ceased in Pretoria, for all the black workers refused to work and went to the funeral.

At this time there were no mass funerals in Soweto. But there, too, the protest movement continued to gain momentum. As in East Rand, in the Soweto townships the main targets of attack were councillors and the police. To remove them from the townships in one way or another would have meant making the townships ungovernable for the apartheid regime. Precisely this aim was defined in a document adopted by the ANC Second National Consultative Conference in June 1985: "The masses of our people have been and are engaged in a struggle of historic importance directed at making apartheid unworkable and the country ungovernable."[17]

By that time Ephraim Tshabalala had been stripped of the office of "Mayor" but continued to be regarded as one of the apartheid regime's principal servitors and, consequently, a target of the anger of Sowetans. Little wonder that his houses and businesses were attacked again and again. Some of his operations were destroyed by fire in April 1985: a cinema, a restaurant, a dry-cleaning factory, and a shop in Mofolo. The houses of many councillors, including that of the new "Mayor" Edward Kunene, were also attacked. Kunene had inflamed passions in Soweto with his cynical remark about homeless people who had built shacks for themselves in Protea-North. He said that squatting was a crime and that Protea-North squatters must either sleep in the open veld or go back to their homelands. Commenting on this statement UDF Executive Committee member Popo Molefe said that Kunene "had shown himself to be an apartheid tool in the hands of Minister Gerrit Viljoen. He is clearly part of the apartheid struggle to deny our people freedom of movement and citizenship rights."[18]

Black policemen were also singled out as targets. Petrol bombs were thrown into their houses. In just one small township, Duduza in East Rand, the houses of 36 policemen were destroyed by fire. In the period beginning in September 1984 and ending in September 1985 protestors burned and destroyed the houses of nearly 400 black policemen across the country.

The struggle increasingly spilled over also into "white" Johannesburg. At two gold mines in the Transvaal, one run by the Anglo-American Corporation and the other by the Anglo-Vaal Company, all involved workers were dismissed as soon as they went on strike: 14,000 at one mine and 3,000 at the other. But this time there was a fightback in a quarter the mine-owners never expected. Their head-

248

quarters in the centre of Johannesburg was fire-bombed. "The two bomb blasts that went off in the heart of Johannesburg's financial world," the newspaper *Sowetan* editorialised on the next day, "will send back waves throughout the country and right across the world... The bomb blasts have not only put the plight of mine-workers on the map, but they must certainly shake South Africa's leaders."[19] Just over a month later another bomb blast went off in the centre of Johannesburg, this time in the 50-storey high-rise in the Carlton Centre. The bomb exploded on the 15th floor in the offices of a state-run chemical and explosives concern.

On the next, 9th, anniversary of the Soweto uprising Sowetans again gathered in the Regina Mundi Church to pay tribute to the memory of the victims. Bishop Desmond Tutu spoke, saying: "Apartheid is totally and wholly evil... President Botha did not tell the truth when he claimed that white South Africans also carried passes. If you can show me just one white person who has a reference book, then my name is Ronald Reagan."[20] The SCA president Nthato Motlana moved a resolution condemning South Africa's aggression and terror against neighbouring countries and demanding the immediate release of all political prisoners. The rally heard speeches from leaders of trade unions and youth organisations and sang songs honouring ANC leaders.

On July 21, 1985, the government declared a state of emergency in the country's main industrial areas—the Witwatersrand, Vaal, and the eastern part of Cape Province. In October the state of emergency was extended to the western part of Cape Province, including Cape Town. Although the state of emergency was proclaimed in only particular areas, the police acted throughout the country, letting no law to constrain them. Altogether, more than nine million people, including the population of the Transkei Bantustan, found themselves affected by the emergency. Naturally, among them were the people of the Soweto townships.

These measures were recognition by the government that it had failed to crush the people's resistance that intensified in September 1984 and was continuing to grow. The former measures proved to be ineffective, and new, harsher measures were inaugurated.

What came of the state of emergency? Did it bring peace

and tranquility and justify the government's hopes of suppressing the popular unrest? No, it did not. The following statistics characterise the new situation. By December, i.e., in 15 weeks since the state of emergency was proclaimed, 5,875 persons had been arrested (over 7,000 were taken into custody since September 1984) and almost 500 persons lost their lives (over 1,000 since September). In just November nearly 100 persons were killed in the ghetto-townships. In Soweto the proclamation of a state of emergency likewise led to a steep rise in the number of victims and to an intensification, not a weakening, of the struggle. In the year before the state of emergency was proclaimed in Soweto nine persons died, but after the emergency was introduced 48 persons lost their lives during the first five months.

The repressive machine struck mainly at leaders and activists of the UDF and the COSAS; the latter organisation was banned and 500 of its members were arrested during the first few days of the emergency. In the first month the police arrested 34 UDF leaders, mostly in areas to which the state of emergency was not extended. Generally, of the persons detained by the police during this time at least 86 per cent were UDF members.

A few days after the state of emergency had been proclaimed cabinet ministers Chris Heunis and Gerrit Viljoen arrived in Soweto to discuss security problems with the Soweto City Council, i.e., with the apartheid system's puppets. For two hours they heard the councillors voicing their appreciation for the government's action, which had allowed law and order agencies to function more effectively. The following weeks in Soweto showed what this appreciation boiled down to. On August 15 the state of emergency in Soweto was augmented with a curfew from 10 p.m. to 4 a.m.

Adults were arrested if they were found in the streets, but children were arrested for staying at home during the day. Schoolchildren boycotted classes in response to the police repressions. They demanded the release of their fellow-students from prisons and police station cells. Police and soldiers kept combing the townships, going into every house and pushing out children of school age. They were bundled into vans and armoured troop carriers and taken to police stations. The lengths of these repressions were seen, in particular, in Diepkloof and the White City Jabavu. In August an armoured troop carrier drove to a school in Diepkloof's No. 3 Zone and the police packed more than 50 children, aged from 7 to 10, into it, seizing them during playtime. On another day in the same month 800 children were detained by the police. Of these, some of whom were under age seven, 300 were held in a Moroka police station all night. Many were beaten.

In one operation, in which they dispersed and beat students near the Moletsane high school, police threw tear-gas canisters into the Entokozweni Early Learning Centre, in which there were some 150 toddlers aged from six months to two years.

Brigadier Jan Coetzee, the senior police officer in Soweto, declared: "The raids in Soweto were conducted by security forces and were aimed at all pupils outside school premises during school hours. We are going to bring the school situation in Soweto back to normal."[21] But these "normalisation" measures produced results contrary to what the government expected. By early October the number of schoolchildren staying away from school had risen to 100,000. Another 55 schools were left empty in October.

The hardening of the repressions, of the mass police terror, and the virtual military occupation of the black townships fueled more discontent and anger than ever in almost all sections of South African society. Church leaders became increasingly more militant in their opposition to apartheid. A group of 400 Christian leaders from 47 denominations called upon Christians to stay away from work for one day as a protest against the apartheid regime's repressive policies. October 9 was declared a national day of prayer-work stay-away. Church leaders appealed to President Pieter W. Botha to lift the state of emergency, withdraw the security forces out of the townships, release all political prisoners and detainees, begin negotiations with the actual leaders of all the groups of the population, unify the education system in the country, and put an end to the institutionalised discrimination. All these grievances reflected the interests of the masses and that explained the wide response for a day of prayer-work stay-away.

At least 50 per cent of the Sowetan workers did not report for work on October 9. On that day the factories in

Johannesburg were empty and, as in November 1984, business came to a standstill. The same situation prevailed in other parts of the country. Mass prayer meetings were held in the churches on that day: speakers bitterly denounced the apartheid system and declared their solidarity with its victims.

Nor did women—the mothers of children who had fallen victim to the repressions or could become victims at any moment—stand aloof from the general resistance movement. A call demanding the withdrawal of troops came from the Khotso House in Johannesburg at the close of September. This call was made by black and white mothers at a conference on "Troops in the Townships—A Mother's Perspective". Appealing to white women, a black mother urged: "March on Soweto and take your young sons—and their guns—out of our townships." Another said: "As we talk here, a child may be dying in Soweto. It is time that we, as mothers, took some form of action."[22] Some days later a group of 19 white women from Johannesburg and three black women from Soweto appeared in front of the Moroka police station in the centre of Soweto carrying posters with the words: "End Apartheid" and "Make Love Not War". They came to demand the immediate withdrawal of troops from the townships. Before the police arrested all of them, a representative of this group of mothers made a statement to the press: "We are here in solidarity with the women of the townships of South Africa. Black and white youths are being brutalised by the conflict in our society— a conflict born of apartheid. The harassment, assault, and detention of children must stop."[23] There was no time to say more, for the police were already pushing the women into vans.

In mid-October, shortly before this took place, Soweto and a tiny house in Diepkloof, where a woman named Pauline Mamike Moloise was weeping in inconsolable grief, held the attention of the whole world. Her son, Benjamin Malesela Moloise—an upholsterer by trade and a fighter by persuasion—was wrongly sentenced and spent two years in a death cell. The international campaign to save his life acquired a high pitch when it was learned that his execution was set for October 18. On the day before the execution Pauline Moloise was allowed to see her son. He told her: "Mummy, I want you to know something—I did not kill Selepe [the police informer executed by an Umkhonto we Sizwe squad of fighters.—V. G.]. I was involved with the ANC and know who killed Selepe, and I do not regret my involvement. Tell the people that the struggle must continue." Benjamin Moloise gave his mother his last, still untitled, poem, which had the words:

> I am proud to be what I am.
> The storm of oppression will be followed
>   by the rain of my blood.
> I am proud to give my life, my one solitary life.

"To our people," a statement of the ANC National Executive Committee said, "we say that the murder of Benjamin Moloise must become the signal for ever greater blows against the enemy in every corner of our land. Those who are leading him to his death must feel the blows of our anger and be deafened by the cry of 'Mayihlome!' (To Arms!)"[24]

The heroes and martyrs who gave their life for freedom will never be forgotten by their people. The time will come when monuments are dedicated to them and towns of a free and democratic South Africa are named after them. Meanwhile, monuments are erected only on their graves. But even this is not easy to do in the face of racist practices. For example, after executing three patriots—ANC members Jerry Semano Mosololi, Thelle Simon Mogoerane, and Marcus Thabo Motaung—the police tried to bury them secretly in unnamed graves. People revering the memory of their heroes found the graves of these victims of terror in the Mamelodi Cemetery, and in 1984 the markers with four-digit numbers on these graves were replaced with tombstones with the names of the fighters, who fell in the struggle against the apartheid regime.

To this day the Ministry of Prisons, now hypocritically named the Ministry of Law and Order, is hiding from the South African people the remains of yet another courageous patriot and fighter for the freedom of South Africa, the Communist Bram Fischer, who died in 1975 while serving a life sentence.

In East Cape, near the "white" town of Beaufort West there is a small location for blacks—some 600 hovels in which 6,000 persons live. This would seem to be one of the hundreds of unnoticeable and unknown small townships in South Africa. Yet it entered the history of the liberation struggle, and it did so under a new name—KwaMadlenkosi.

Tshaka Kratshi Madlenkosi was the leader of a youth organisation heading the resistance movement in the township. He was killed by police, evidently in the belief that this would intimidate the township's inhabitants and break their resistance. But they were wrong. The people gave their township the fallen hero's name and turned it into a "liberated zone" with their own administration. True, they did not hold out for long. After calling out reinforcements the police took the township by storm. People were killed and wounded as the sides exchanged fire. The white racists restored their authority and practices in the insurgent township of KwaMadlenkosi. But it had been free for a short span of time. As a matter of fact, during this time the township acquired one more hero. A youth climbed on a roof and with a homemade catapult hit an army helicopter with a stone, forcing it to land. October 18 was named "Helicopter Day" in honour of this small victory.

In Soweto parks were named after Nelson Mandela, Oliver Tambo, and Walter Sisulu. Lately, a spontaneous movement started in the townships around Johannesburg: people began clearing foul-smelling dumping grounds and refuse-filled streets and planting trees, bushes, and flowers. This was done mostly by young people of the Soweto Youth Congress. But the authorities viewed even this as a threat to the regime. In Pimville security forces uprooted trees and flowers looking for bombs. In another township, Central Western Jabavu, police and troops dispersed people who had come for the opening of the Oliver Tambo Park. The Nelson Mandela and Steve Biko parks in Mohlakeng near Randfontein were destroyed before they could be opened—the busts of Nelson Mandela and Steve Biko placed there were smashed. But these actions of the police only angered the young people, and parks with "seditious" names appeared in the Soweto townships and in many others, including Mamelodi, Atteridgeville, and Witbank.

Of course, the appearance of new names was not the most important thing in the life of the ghetto-townships, but it was evidence of significant changes, of shoots of something new. Of far greater importance was the appearance in 1985 of new, people's government bodies in the course of the struggle against the apartheid regime. New liberated zones and street committees emerged in some townships in East Cape—in the Port Elizabeth, Cradock, and Queenstown areas. The street committees were elected at general meetings of the inhabitants of the townships concerned. These bodies were making their first steps. They began collecting rent—the people preferred to pay it to them rather than to the puppet councils. They determined the date of work stay-aways and boycotts, and organised the funerals of victims of police terror, turning them into political demonstrations. Lastly, they performed judicial functions. In Atteridgeville, for example, they set up 12 people's courts and a higher appeal court, which they called the Advice Office. These courts handled cases involving charges of collaborationism with the racist authorities as well as civil cases. In Alexandra there were as many as 18 street committees by the end of January 1986, and their number was to be increased to 44 in accordance with the number of streets in the township. People's courts were also set up there.

It was planned that the formation of people's government bodies would be preceded by the abolition of community and township councils and the expulsion of councillors and police from the townships. This is exactly what took place in some townships. In one case—in the township of Sebokeng—all the councillors headed by the mayor fled to a heavily guarded camp with a tall barbed-wire fence around it.

By mid-1985, of 38 township "self-government" bodies set up in accordance with the new law, only five were functioning normally. Eight councils resigned in a body. In the period from September 1984 to June 1985 a total of 240 councillors, including 27 mayors, turned in their resignations. Despite its renovation by the apartheid regime, the self-government system was obviously falling apart.

In the insurgent townships the police failed not only to protect the councillors from the people's anger and ensure the functioning of the township councils, but were in some cases forced to save themselves by fleeing. This was seen in the townships of Duduza and Daveyton in East

Rand, where the houses of 17 policemen were set on fire in June 1985. Fearing for their lives, the custodians of "law and order" fled from these townships. Countrywide, 29 policemen were killed and 82 were wounded in the riots in 1985. And yet only 20-30 years ago, black policemen enjoyed a measure of esteem in the townships; they were envied and nobody dared to raise a hand against them. But now, in Soweto and other townships, police came under fire and were killed, and it is noteworthy that their attackers usually disappeared with the captured weapons.

The attacks on police and members of township councils meekly taking orders from the authorities were carried out in accordance with the ANC tactics of making the apartheid unworkable and the country ungovernable.

At the close of 1985 and in the early months of 1986 resignations began coming not only from councillors but also from policemen. True, there have not been many cases of policemen giving up their jobs, but in each such case there was a strong political and psychological backlash. *The Cape Times* ran a front-page photo of police Constable Thomas Makhubela, of Atteridgeville, publicly burning his uniform. He said he could no longer tolerate being labelled a "killer" and "sell-out". A UDF spokesman noted that this was a sign that "black cops now realise that apartheid is evil". Another policeman of the same township declared that he had not only resigned in response to a call by political organisations but would be active in the struggle for the liberation of black people.

The insurgency caused real panic among South Africa's rulers. General Bert Wandrag, chief of South Africa's crack counter-insurgency, was quoted as saying that "the objective is to create so-called liberated areas in the black townships, from where the terrifying war can be spread to the cities and white suburbs to bring about the downfall of the government".[25]

The closing months of 1985 and the early months of 1986 brought Johannesburg further bomb blasts, again in the centre of the city, in places that hurt the apartheid system most. On November 1, when the entire centre of the city was filled with police and troops, a bomb exploded in the Institute of Bankers in Franwell House on the corner of Eloff and President Streets. In early March 1986 an explosion shook the building housing the Vehicle Staff—Police Headquarters in John Vorster Square, destroying three floors.

In the townships there was a new mood. This was felt especially where the struggle had made visible break-throughs—in the area around Cape Town and Port Elizabeth and in East Rand and West Rand.

White residents of Cape Town found that blacks were no longer afraid of the police or troops. One of them related: "I saw a girl walk right up to a Casspir (armoured car), spit at it, and then turn round and calmly walk away."[2 6]

"Now all the people are asking: where do we get guns and ammuniton," a reporter was told in the township of Athlone. "People who have had a taste of revolution are not in the minority any more."[2 7]

Upon learning the sentence passed on her son on a charge of "threatening the security of the state", a 72-year-old Sowetan woman said: "I'm very proud of my son. It is people like him who will liberate us."[2 8]

A reporter of *The Star*, who visited Tsakane, a typical South African township, on May 14, 1985, filed the following story:

"The last white suburban house vanishes from view about 10 km before the bleak aspect of Tsakane township presents itself, confirmation that this is a separated world... Two Casspirs dart across an intersection and disappear. The ochre and blue Methodist Church is crowded, 500 people where 250 could more comfortably fit. People balance on window-sills. Posters say: 'Kill apartheid not detainees' and 'Army and police out of townships'. Outside ... the crowd swells and swells... Fierce oratory gives way to the soft lament of a hymn. Names of heroes—Mandela, Tambo—are woven into the tapestry of song and prayer...

"Suddenly a single bell in the church tower begins a slow, spaced toll and an intense silence falls upon the crowd, by now at least 20,000 strong... The coffin is borne from the church, one white flower upon it, and the procession begins: along Xhosa Street, right into Ndabezitha Street, and two kilometres down the slow slope to the cemetery.

"The security vehicles betray a flicker of presence... The discipline is uncanny... The singing ebbs and flows and, every now and then, a section of the crowd breaks into a chanting jog... The graveside service is quickly over and muted mourners begin to plod home.

"This, everyone knows, is the moment when trouble comes... Casspirs and Hippos emerge from sidestreets to show themselves to the thousands on Ndabezitha Street. They forge a way through the walkers. Anger ripples. To the crowd this is provocation, insult... 'Why do they treat us like dogs?' asks a woman who has casually fallen into step with me. And, like an echo of other voices, she asks another question: 'Why do they hate us? Fear perhaps?' She professes to misread the question. 'Yes, they should be afraid of us.' She is middle-aged and she was fired last week from her job as a supermarket cashier after four years of service.

"Bitterness goes as quickly as it came. Yes, she has a home of her own in Tsakane, three children. Yes, the oldest is boycotting school. No, she is not worried about what lack of education will do to his future. He will get his education when the great day of freedom dawns. To her, it is just around the corner. Or, at least, a real possibility in her lifetime. It is a theme oft-repeated. These people, going home, are plainly no dispirited mass. They walk and talk as if the day of political destiny is at hand. There seems a sense of purpose, of mission, even of hope. Tomorrow, freedom!".[29]

Such was the scene found by a reporter in a typical township on a usual day in 1985.

The Six-Day War in Alexandra

A rising broke out in the township of Alexandra on February 15, 1986. The South African press called it a "Six-Day War". Within these few days 80 persons were killed and nearly 300 wounded in the violent clashes.

The cause was, for those days, quite a trivial one—a police attack on people returning from a funeral. But this time the blacks resisted, and the police called in troops, triggering greater anger. A regime of military occupation was actually established in Alex. The roots, the in-depth causes of this rising were in the living conditions in that ghetto-township: poverty, unbearably crowded housing, police harassment, and arbitrary expulsion, in other words, everything to which apartheid condemns blacks in South Africa.

The township's self-government bodies headed by Sam Buti had become a puppet of the apartheid regime. It saw its function basically in building up its own police force, its own mini-army, allocating money for it that could be used for building homes to be let for a moderate rent. Deploying of additional repressive forces in the township instead of improving housing conditions gave rise to a new wave of indignation. An indication of the people's anger was that Sam Buti's house was damaged on two occasions by explosions, even before the February events took place.

The growth of the resistance in Alexandra was fostered by the fairly high level of the organisation and politicisation of its inhabitants. In addition to the Alexandra Civic Association and the Alexandra Residents' Association, which had been in existence for some years, embryos of people's government—street committees—appeared in the township. These saw the Alexandra Action Committee as their umbrella authority. They performed many, including judicial, functions but their main task was to "conscientise" people, to arouse their political awareness. They achieved much in this area since they were set up, and this undoubtedly influenced the developments in February and in subsequent months.

As soon as columns of armoured troop carriers and police appeared in Alexandra, the people took retaliatory steps. Barricades were built everywhere, and stones and petrol bombs were used in the fighting. These were thrown not only at the police and the armoured troop carriers. Industrial enterprises in the nearby white suburbs of Johannesburg were attacked. Several policemen were killed or wounded in the collisions.

Rallies and demonstrations were held throughout the township to protest against the police terror. The main demands were: the immediate withdrawal of the security forces from the township, the release of all the people detained during these days, and the lifting of the state of emergency. Young people marched in the streets chanting: "Mandela, our leader" and "Down with Botha and his reforms".

Sam Buti fled from the township, finding refuge in the affluent white suburb of Sandton. Not only councillors but all of the township's policemen, the entire mini-army, fled with him. One policeman told a reporter: "We are leaving this place. We see we have no future here."[30] With their families, the policemen and councillors hid in two churches in the neighbouring "white" suburb.

Nor did the white authorities feel they were in control in Alexandra. They were able to reappear in the townships only on armoured troop carriers and only in the main streets. They did not venture to drive into the narrow side-streets or move about in the township on foot. The situation in those days was controlled by insurgents (they called themselves "comrades") and the committees set up by them. Their representatives, activists of the resistance, went from house to house, urging the people to join more resolutely in the struggle.

One of the activists, making a gesture with his arm to indicate an industrialised sector of northern Johannesburg, told a reporter: "Look, everybody who works here lives in Alex. When we have conscientised them, then at a word from us, we can stop all these factories with a strike or cripple the shops with a consumer boycott." The reporter then offered some conclusions of his own: "When white South Africa established the ghetto townships, it did so partly for security reasons. The townships could be quickly sealed off by the security forces and access to them easily controlled. Now the comrades are trying to stand that strategy on its head, turning the townships into bases for the revolutionary struggle."[31]

The "Six-Day War" in Alexandra ended, but the resistance continued in other forms. In early March Alex's inhabitants buried their dead. Sixty thousand people came to the funeral meeting at a stadium in the centre of the township. Seventeen coffins draped in ANC's black, green and gold colours stood in the middle. The dead (the youngest was only 12) were given the highest honours—they were called fighters of Umkhonto we Sizwe. Many flags were unfurled: among them were the flags of the ANC and the UDF, and even a red flag with the hammer and sickle and the words: "Workers of all countries, unite!" A Freedom Charter banner said: "The people shall govern." The speeches were interrupted with cries of "Viva Mandela, Viva Kathrada, Viva Tambo" and freedom songs. A UDF leader Frank Chikane said a war was taking place "between the apartheid forces and the oppressed majority".[32] The people were powerfully impressed by the speech of Albertina Sisulu. She appealed to the mothers of white soldiers to stop the government from sending military forces to kill black children. "We as mothers—black and white—should be fighting together more and more. What happens to black children will happen to white children... Today there is no peace in South Africa, but the government says there is. Why then are soldiers roaming the streets of our townships killing the children."[33] Mike Beea, chairman of the Alexandra Civic Association, drew acclaim when he rejected the option of "going cap in hand to a government which is killing our children" and proclaimed instead: "We shall defeat the system. We shall govern in our country."[34]

The funeral of another group of victims of police terror took place ten days later. The police did not venture to ban the first funeral: the situation in the township had been much too tense, and, besides, even with the termination of the "Six-Day War" the balance of strength was not in favour of the authorities. This time the police decided to prevent mass funerals and to enforce this decision they resorted to the dirtiest methods. At first, they obstructed the identification of the bodies, and then 11 of the 13 bodies that were to be buried simply disappeared from the morgue.

However, neither subterfuges nor outright violence enabled the authorities to restore their position in the insurgent township. There was a lull in the struggle, the shooting died down, but the people did not submit.

In mid-March, the government repealed the state of emergency evidently having realised that there was no sense in it. This, too, was a victory that encouraged the people to fight on.

After the state of emergency was lifted in Alexandra, many activists of the resistance returned home from prison. This was marked by a general meeting of two youth organisations in the township: the Alexandra Youth Congress (uniting schoolchildren) and the Alexandra Students' Congress (uniting high-school senior students). A decision passed by this meeting called upon all students to join the youth organisations and upon adults to join the Civic Association; it said that there had to be strict discipline and that no action should be taken without first getting the consent of the leadership. The vandalism that had taken place in the township during the riots was condemned. One of the speakers stressed the significance of discipline in the resistance movement. "We can see the situation is volatile," he said. "Tsotsi elements are hijacking our efforts when they demand that parents give food and money. But they speak without a mandate from the comrades. Here in Alexandra we have committees—Ayco, Asco, and the Civic Association (also affiliated to the UDF). Only they have the mandate of the people." The organising secretary of Ayco, Patric Banda, who conducted the meeting, said: "The people shall govern. The time has come for us to learn to govern ourselves. Alexandra police station is no longer functioning, and people say 'go and see the comrades'."[3 5]

The apartheid regime had no intention of backing down. This held true in Alexandra as well. It had recourse to further, more subtle and sinister tactics.

Groups of balaclava-clad men appeared in Alexandra in the night of April 22-23, 1986. Some said they were police, and others—political activists. They beat up and killed activists and leaders of the resistance, and set their houses on fire. This was a night of counter-revolutionary terror unleashed by reactionary and conservative elements with police support.

On the next day, in response to the attempts of the people to resist the gangs of killers, armoured troop carriers entered the township. In order to block their progress burned cars were piled up to form barricades. In some streets people dug traps, camouflaging them with tarpaulins. These people were mainly adults, providing evidence that there was universal participation in the resistance. By building barricades and digging trenches, they aimed to prevent the armoured troop carriers from patrolling the streets, thereby holding up their progress.

Again there was shooting in the township, people were killed or wounded, and clouds of smoke and tear gas filled the streets.

Practically the entire population of the township, more than 50,000 people, went to the stadium for the protest rally. The terrorist actions of apartheid's agents were unanimously denounced and it was decided to form "self-defence units to protect ourselves from the agents of the system". On the day after the night of terror and murder not a single worker went to work and not a single student went to school—all were at the rally and guarded their township against a new incursion by the army and police.

Following the rally, 10,000 people marched along one of the streets. Their way was barred by a column of armoured carriers with 200 armed policemen and soldiers. The two sides were separated only by a barricade of burning tyres. Then followed something totally unexpected: it was not the demonstrators that hastened to disperse as guns were pointed at them, but the policemen and soldiers turned back. A lone fighter, armed with a submachine gun, stood his ground. The first burst of fire struck down a white police constable. For nearly an hour this unknown fighter held the police and troops at bay and then disappeared, dissolving among the thousands of the township's inhabitants.

At about 4 a.m. on the next day a group of policemen led by a lieutenant tried to force their way into a house but were driven off with fire from submachine guns.

At this juncture the last three councillors in Alexandra and the "Mayor" Sam Buti resigned. The township council had exercised no real authority in the township since February but now it ceased to exist formally.

Despite the military presence and the police terror real authority in Alexandra increasingly passed into the hands of the people's representatives. The youth organisations and the Civic Association first formed the Alexandra Action Committee with Moses Mayekiso, a prominent trade unionist from COSATU, as its chairman, and then representatives of the four organisations formed the Residents' Joint Committee, which became the people's governing body in the township. After the puppet council disintegrated, a Special Administrator, Jacobus Burger, was appointed, but he was ignored entirely in Alexandra.

As it set about restoring law and order in the township, curbing the criminal *tsotsis*, and forming self-defence units, the new people's power decided on beginning a rent boycott and a boycott of shops owned by whites. The boycott included shops run by blacks charged with collaborating with the apartheid regime. The special boycott committee issued a statement listing demands, among which were: the withdrawal of troops and the police from the township, the lifting of the ban on committees representing students, and the introduction of "people's education", the establishment of rent the people could afford, proper electrification of the township, the release of all political prisoners, and the unbanning of all banned organisations. These demands combined the aspiration for political emancipation with the yearning for a better life.

Soon after the boycott was started there were signs that it was becoming effective. White businessmen and shopkeepers in nearby Sandton were the first to show their anxiety. They began probing the possibility of negotiating with the Alexandra inhabitants. As a matter of fact the boycott declared by the people of Alex was not an isolated case. Similar boycotts had been declared by the residents of another 12 townships in various parts of the country: near Pretoria, Krugersdorp, Port Elizabeth, and Nelspruit.

Among the first things to be undertaken by the people's local government bodies was the renaming of the streets in the township. Sellborne Street, one of the principal thoroughfares, became ANC Street. Squares, streets, and schools were named after Nelson Mandela, Govan Mbeki, Walter Sisulu, and Moses Mabhida. One street was named after Vincent Tshabalala, an ANC fighter who died in a shoot-out with the police in Alexandra. A community school, Bovet, was renamed after an ANC cadre, Solomon Mahlangu, who was hanged by the racists. Before the new names were adopted and the name-plates attached to houses they were discussed by the street committees. The new names appeared at the close of May despite the reinforced presence of police and troops.

It was inevitable that the actions of the new local government bodies would trigger a further brutalisation of police terror and repressions. On May 11, 1986 the township was surrounded by a solid ring of troops, while more than 1,600 policemen and troops carried out a combing operation. They made a house-to-house search, arresting hundreds of people. And all this in spite of the formal repeal of the state of emergency, when shooting and fires had ceased, when life in Alexandra was gradually returning to normal thanks to the efforts of the people's local self-government bodies.

The unrest generated in Alexandra by the police terror spilled over into other areas time and again. Factories, shops, and cars were set on fire in the adjoining "white" areas. And yet, despite the savage repressions by white racists the democratic organisations of the movement of resistance to the apartheid regime firmly abided by the principles of humanism and racial tolerance. It was, after all, their main objective to create a united, democratic, and non-racial South Africa. This is what determines their tactics and strategy, and hence the absence of surprise or objections on the part of the township's inhabitants when the Action Committee called upon the white residents of Johannesburg to spend May 18 visiting the graves of the persons killed in Alexandra and meeting with their mothers, fathers, and widows. At a meeting of whites organised by the Johannesburg Democratic Action Committee a representative of the Alexandra Action Committee declared that although the activists in the township were constantly exposed to danger they would guarantee the safety of the whites responding to the call.

On Sunday, May 18, 1986 "the most extraordinary political demonstration" took place in Alexandra.[36] Thousands of blacks filled the streets in order to meet and welcome white residents of Johannesburg. Some 300 came to the township to lay flowers on the graves of murdered Africans and thereby show their solidarity with the struggle of the black inhabitants of Johannesburg. The police futilely tried to stop them with threats of arrest.

One of those who came to the cemetery in Alexandra was Nadine Gordimer, a world famous South African authoress. The flower laying ceremony was dramatically brief, for the police announced that Minister Louis le Grange had banned this "gathering of a mob" and given them ten minutes to leave the cemetery. To make the point the police fired a tear-gas canister. Whites and blacks ran to save themselves from the gas. As they ran blacks shook hands with whites, thanking them for their solidarity and moral support.

May Day Centenary and the Foreboding
Month of June

No sooner had the April violence in Alexandra simmered down than preparations began for an upcoming anniversary. This was May Day, a public holiday of the workers of the world. The working class movement of South Africa had marked many May Days, when the workers demonstrated their unity and international solidarity. But this was to be a special occasion—the workers were planning to mark the centenary of May Day.

Back in 1895 the Johannesburg Council of Trade Unions passed a decision to mark May Day annually as a day of workers' solidarity. In 1904 some 2,000 workers marched with red banners to an international solidarity rally in Johannesburg's Market Square. In 1917 May Day was marked in response to a call from the International Socialist League, the precursor of the South African Communist Party. It was the first time a May Day rally was addressed by a black—Horatio Mbele, a Transvaal activist of the ANC. This was the first May Day in South Africa when workers acted from a non-racist position, and it was what disturbed the government most of all. With the aid of troops the police broke up the rally.

May Day of 1931 was made a notable event by the fact that at the call of the non-racial African May Day Committee 3,000 blacks marched in a single column with 1,500 white workers. Carrying red banners they marched from Market Square past the Native Affairs Department and Police Headquarters to the Corner House, the headquarters of the mine-owners. Once again the police swung their batons, attacking blacks and whites. In the 1940s May Day demonstrations were conducted by the Council of Non-European Trade Unions with the slogans: "We Want Bread" and "Work for Wages".

Then there was May 1, 1950. On that day mass rallies protesting the Suppression of Communism Bill and demanding higher wages and better working conditions were held throughout the country despite the ban imposed by the government. More than 80 per cent of the workers staged a strike on that day in the Reef industrial area in the Transvaal. Police and troops were moved in against the workers.

In Alexandra and Sophiatown they opened fire, killing 19 persons and wounding 30. A 6,000-strong demonstration took place in Cape Town, and 10,000 workers marched in Durban. The May Day events of 1950 gave a powerful impetus to the resistance to the apartheid regime in the 1950s, when the Freedom Charter was adopted. The orgy of mass police terror in subsequent years and the bans imposed on the black trade unions denied the workers the possibility of marking their festival. After a long interval they were only able to do so in 1982 and 1983. And now the centenary of the day of workers' solidarity was approaching.

The Congress of South African Trade Unions, which had 650,000 members, undertook to organise the upcoming actions of the South African working class. Shortly before May Day it made the following demands on behalf of the workers:

— the right to organise all workers in democratic unions;
— the right to work;
— May Day to be declared a public holiday;
— a 40-hour working week on a living wage with social security;
— the right of students to form democratic SRCs (students' representative councils);
— equal pensions for all on a monthly basis;
— the right to free political activity and the unbanning of all banned organisations, the release of political prisoners and the dropping of all treason charges;
— the right to free movement and decent housing at rents which workers can afford, as well as an immediate end to influx control and pass laws.

These were thus both economic and political demands. The interests of students were taken into account and this further reinforced the unity of action that was taking shape between the working class and this active contingent of the resistance movement. The fact that these demands were indeed consistent with the vital interests of the working people was clearly shown by the response to them among the workers, students, and other oppressed sections of the South African people. One response was the general political strike to support them and commemorate the centenary of May Day.

On May 1, 1986, up to 2.5 million people, i.e., 80 per cent of black workers, stayed away from work. More than a million went on strike on that day in just the Transvaal, despite the threat of police repressions, sacking, eviction from the city, and other punishments by the apartheid regime. On that day practically no blacks were to be seen in the "white" cities of the Transvaal, factories and mines stopped, 210,000 miners stayed away, and offices and shops were empty of staff. Practically all Indian shopkeepers did not open their businesses. A similar situation prevailed in other parts of the country. All workers stayed away in the Port Elizabeth industrial area.

The workers, who marked their holiday with a general strike, were joined not only by students but also, and for the first time, by teachers. The chairman of the 54,000-strong African Teachers' Association of South Africa declared: "We've decided to throw our full weight behind the call for a complete workers' stay-away on May 1."

While in "white" Johannesburg, where blacks were usually predominant in the street scene, virtually none were to be seen on May 1, Soweto teemed with people on that day. By midday some 20,000 assembled in the Orlando stadium for the May Day celebrations. It was a genuine workers' holiday of joy. People sang freedom songs, danced, chanted slogans, heard speeches from, among others, COSATU president Elijah Barayi, NUM Secretary General Cyril Ramaphosa, and Soweto Civic Association organiser Amos Masondo.

Around the stadium the scene was entirely different. Hundreds of policemen and troops filled the approaches to the stadium and all the streets in its vicinity. They were reinforced by three Casspirs, six Buffaloes, vans, and three huge police buses nicknamed "Mellow Yellow". On this occasion the police and troops confined themselves to a show of strength without venturing to hinder the public festival. Many police cars patrolled the other streets in Soweto and there, too, they confined themselves to the role of observers.

The trains of Johannesburg ran empty on that day, while PUTCO buses made no appearance on their routes: all the drivers were on strike. Such was the situation in Soweto, roughly the same was to be observed in other black ghetto-townships, while in the "white" cities the streets were deserted.

"A nation-wide stay-away left factories deserted, with much of the country's workforce flocking to May Day rallies, called to mark the 100th anniversary of international labour day," a Johannesburg newspaper wrote.[37] "It was the largest national general strike in South Africa history, placing the issue of May Day as a public holiday firmly on the political agenda."[38] A view stated by *Sunday Times* in an editorial addressed to whites on the significance of the 1986 May Day events merits attention: "May Day 1986 will inevitably be branded by some as a workers' revolt against oppression and by others as an organised conspiracy to subvert the state. Either way, its implications cannot be ignored. No white South African, obliged on Thursday to make his own tea, load a truck or man a cash register, could have escaped a self-evident conclusion: the people of this country are inextricably bound together by history, the economy, and the pursuit of power."[39] This is yet another acknowledgement of that apartheid, which divides the South African people, setting one section against the other, is both senseless and vicious.

Massive political demonstrations held on the centenary of May Day were a major success of the South African working-class and liberation movements.

Shortly before these demonstrations the black population, notably the working class of the Transvaal, had blocked the elaborate festivities planned for another centenary, that of the "Golden City" of Johannesburg. These were launched by the city's white authorities together with Big Business and the government. The preparations were put into the hands of the Johannesburg Centenary Festival Association specially set up for the occasion. It was hoped to involve large numbers of blacks, who comprised at the time at least two-thirds of the city's population. But the blacks not only refused to participate; they disrupted the festivities.

Practically all African public and trade union organisations—the ANC, the COSATU, tens of others, including even the Soweto Chamber of Commerce that unites African businessmen and shopkeepers—proclaimed a boycott of the preparations under the slogan: "100 years of exploitation.

We have nothing to celebrate."

The attitude of advanced democratic forces towards this issue was stated by the ANC president Oliver Tambo: "We can no longer accept the situation in which we exist in the urban townships as suppliers of labour to the white areas with no access to the wealth that we create and which goes to enrich and improve the white areas of our towns and cities. In this regard, we should take the occasion of the centenary of the city of Johannesburg ... as one for the most determined offensive to ensure that the political situation changes in this prime example of the iniquity of the system of colonial and racist rule. White South Africa feels it has every right to celebrate this centenary. We, on the other hand, confined in black ghettoes on the periphery of the city, have nothing to celebrate." He said that the people's power and democratic administration being established in the black townships should spread to Johannesburg and to all municipal areas where blacks live and which they had built with their own hands.[40]

The widespread and well-organised boycott disrupted most of the "Golden City" centenary festivities. This was publicly acknowledged by the chairman of the Festival Association himself.

There were many anniversaries in South Africa in 1986. Hardly had one been marked than another drew near. Preparations were under way in the whole of South Africa to mark June 16, the tenth anniversary of Bloody Wednesday, when the police fired at an orderly demonstration of schoolchildren in Soweto and sparked the revolt of 1976. Each of the opposing sides, however, planned the preparations in their own way.

Oliver Tambo said that the 10th anniversary of the Soweto massacre and uprising should be seen as a beginning of a mass popular offensive directed at the destruction of the apartheid system.

Most of the trade unions decided to mark June 16, Soweto Day, with a nation-wide strike. Moreover, it was decided that on June 15 and 16 memorial church services would be held for the victims of the Soweto uprising. The National Education Crisis Committee planned to make this day a public holiday and called for a stay-away from schools. All these initiatives got the backing of the

United Democratic Front.

Among whites there were people prepared to express solidarity with the Soweto inhabitants on June 16. Apartheid had broken off all normal contacts between blacks and whites, and for that reason new ways of expressing this solidarity had to be found. It was announced that "A Garland of Flowers for Soweto" campaign would be conducted on June 16: all that people had to do was to paste a yellow paper daisy on the windshield of their cars.

The apartheid camp likewise made its preparations for June 16. The keynote was set by retired Police Brigadier Theuns Swanepoel, known as "The Beast": this was the man who ordered the police to shoot down the peaceful demonstration of Soweto schoolchildren in 1976. In recalling the events of that year he expressed his regret—not for the murder of Hector Peterson and other children in Soweto—but for the fact that the police had not shown proper determination, in other words, that they had not killed enough. "I personally could not give a damn if it would be necessary to shoot 100 or 10,000, but if you must restore law and order at the cost of 10,000 lives, do so."[41] These were not accidental revelations by a bestial butcher. Swanepoel's public statement, the newspaper Sowetan noted, "echoed sentiments expressed privately by senior police officers who feel security forces have sufficient fire power to put the lid on unrest but are unable to use it because of what they see as government restraint".[42]

It is open to doubt whether the racist government in Pretoria hamstrung the police in suppressing the actions of the country's black majority. In the period from September 1984 to the close of May 1986 the number of people shot and killed was 1,782. As many as 213 were killed in one month, May. A police report said that in 1985 nearly 2,000 persons were wounded and more than 21,000 arrested. (It is indicative that the security forces suffered only seven fatalities.)

However, it seems that not only the retired butcher Swanepoel but also the government of South Africa saw this as not enough. On June 12, 1986, four days before the anniversary of the Soweto revolt, a state of emergency was proclaimed throughout the country, while somewhat later the Minister of Law and Order Louis le Grange declared that apartheid's problems could be solved if "they shoot enough blacks".[43] This statement is evidence that Swanepoel's recommendations were adopted by the government.

The state of emergency gave the police and the security forces unlimited repressive powers for forestalling the actions planned for June 16. As soon as the state of emergency was proclaimed the police arrested hundreds of trade union functionaries and many leaders and activists of the UDF and of the organisations affiliated to it. Workers, students, journalists, and priests—in fact all whom the regime saw as dangerous—were taken into custody. All rallies and strikes were banned, the censorship was hardened, and the townships were put out of bounds to reporters. The least violations of the state of emergency rulings were punished by imprisonment for a term of up to 10 years. Concurrently, two new repressive laws were rushed through Parliament. One gave the Minister of Law and Order the authority to proclaim any area an "unrest area" and thereby enable the police to exercise state of emergency powers. The other permitted detainees to be held without a charge for 180 instead of the usual 14 days. Thus, even with the state of emergency formally lifted, the police could be given unlimited repressive powers by orders from their minister.

The 10th anniversary of the Soweto revolt was commemorated in a situation of rampant police repressions. On Soweto Day almost all of the country's big industrial areas were paralysed by a stay-away. Nearly 1.5 million people stayed away from work in the Pretoria-Witwatersrand-Vereeniging, Port Elizabeth-Uitenhage, and Cape Town areas. Countrywide, including remote areas in all the four provinces, up to 3 million people stayed away on that day, despite the state of emergency.

On June 16, ignoring the state of emergency, Sowetans filled the Orlando stadium, exactly where the schoolchildren had wanted to go but had been dispersed and shot ten years before. Although armoured carriers with armed troops stood in the streets around the stadium and although police and army units patrolled all streets, the rally in memory of the Soweto victims took place. Of course, the police dispersed, beat, and arrested demonstrators, but this no longer surprised anybody. The virtual military occupation had

272

become part of lifestyle in that black township.

Brutality reached shocking proportions in the township of Naledi, the "Far West" as Sowetans call it. There the security forces opened fire on a column of demonstrators, killing several of them and wounding scores. The scene in Soweto was horrifying: police and troops were to be seen everywhere, armoured carriers raced along the streets, there were wreathing clouds of tear gas, and the people themselves gave first aid to the wounded and the beaten. Regardless of all this the 10th anniversary of the Soweto uprising was commemorated.

At this time not only rallies and meetings were banned, restrictions were imposed on funerals of police victims: they could be buried only one at a time, and the number of mourners was limited to 200. A striking contrast to all this was the rally in the Jabulani Amphitheatre at the close of June. Not only were the people not dispersed, they were protected, and the principal speaker came in a helicopter. Guarded by South African police and his own police from the Bantustan of KwaZulu, Gatsha Buthelezi addressed Zulu migrants brought to the amphitheatre from Soweto hostels and from KwaZulu. He was the only person permitted to speak in Soweto under the state of emergency regime. The reason for this was that he said what the government in Pretoria wanted to hear: he vindicated his collaboration with the Botha government, denounced the anti-apartheid struggle, and argued in favour of the notorious reforms launched to perpetuate white minority rule.

Buthelezi was valued for his efforts to pit Zulus against all other blacks, split the united front against apartheid, and champion tribalism. Playing on the chauvinism of Gatsha Buthelezi and his entourage, the government, as it had done ten years before, incited the Zulus in Soweto against the other blacks, who had risen to fight their oppressors. Noting the implications of Buthelezi's speech in the amphitheatre, the ANC General Secretary Alfred Nzo said: "Gatsha Buthelezi has demonstrated very clearly that his role is counter-revolutionary. It is well known that he has given himself the task of assisting the apartheid regime in his futile effort to destroy the democratic movement."[44]

The people of Soweto commemorated the 10th anniversary of the 1976 events not only in a state of emergency situation. Discontent with the living conditions in Soweto had been mounting steadily. This came to a head on June 1 when most of the Sowetans declared they would no longer pay the rent for their matchbox houses. The reason for this boycott was a very simple one: the low wages made the continuously rising rents unaffordable for the majority of Sowetans.

The rent boycott decision was preceded by meetings of the street committees at which the plight of the people was discussed. The Soweto Civic Association then worded the people's demands. As well as lower rents they raised the question of the withdrawal of troops from the townships and the resignation of all collaborationist township councillors. By this time analogous demands had been articulated by the inhabitants of many other townships throughout the country.

The authorities responded by ordering the forcible eviction of non-payers of rent. This was the most terrible punishment for urban blacks. Even from prison one could return home and go on living. But the loss of a home signified the loss of everything. Hence the determined resistance to this official order.

The situation in Soweto deteriorated drastically at the close of August 1986. In the evening of the 26th, workers of the township of Jabavu returning from work found that their families together with all their earthly possessions had been put out into the street. When angry people gathered together to consider what to do next they were attacked by the police, first, as usual, with tear gas and then bullets. Stones and petrol bombs were hurled in reply. The streets were barricaded. The violent clashes with the police continued into the morning of the next day. The unrest spread to other Soweto townships. But the opposing forces were unequal, of course. More than 20 people were killed and over 200 wounded.

The conflicts and clashes over rent now erupted into a real war, with killed and wounded. The apartheid regime takes the most brutal measures up to firearms, even if people are only protesting against rent increases. This is not surprising. Discontent inevitably linked any individual official measure to the entire apartheid system and developed into an action against this system. The Pretoria regime

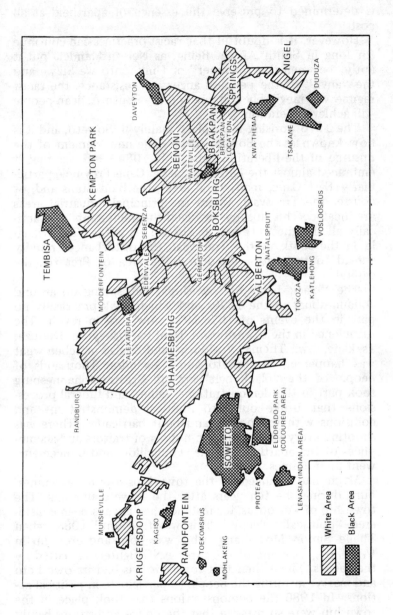

White Area
Black Area

TEMBISA
KEMPTON PARK
DAVEYTON
BENONI
SPRINGS
NIGEL
DUDUZA
BRAKPAN
BRAKPAN LOCATION
WATTVILLE
KWA-THEMA
TSAKANE
BOKSBURG
SEBENZA
MODDERFONTEIN
EDENVALE
GERMISTON
ALBERTON
NATALSPRUIT
VOSLOOSRUS
TOKOZA
KATLEHONG
ALEXANDRA
RANDBURG
JOHANNESBURG
MUNSIEVILLE
KRUGERSDORP
KAGISO
SOWETO
ELDORADO PARK
(COLOURED AREA)
RANDFONTEIN
TOEKOMSRUS
PROTEA
LENASIA (INDIAN AREA)
MOHLAKENG

is determined to preserve the essence of apartheid at all costs.

However, it is doubtful that racist practices can continue for long in South Africa. Being, as Nelson Mandela put it aptly, between the "hammer" of Umkhonto we Sizwe and the "anvil" of the people's anger and resistance, the racist regime will inevitably collapse and the South African people will achieve liberation.

The 1976 uprising took place mainly in Soweto, and it is now known as the Soweto revolt. The new element of the upsurge of the liberation struggle in 1984-1986 was that it embraced almost the entire country: Cape Province, particularly East Cape, many rural areas, the Bantustans and, of course, the Transvaal, where the principal industrial areas are located. This upsurge involved the inhabitants of practically all the ghetto-townships. Beginning in the Vaal Triangle in the south of the Transvaal, the disturbances rapidly spread to the entire Rand and the area of Pretoria, the capital.

The "black belt" of townships that sprang up around Johannesburg in the 1970s and which took practically no part in the events of 1976-1977 now rose in revolt. The turbulence in the townships of Tembisa, Daveyton, Duduza, Tsakane, Kwa Thema, Vosloorus, and Kagiso matched what was happening in Soweto and Alexandra. Thousands of people of the "black belt" around Greater Johannesburg took part in the demonstrations, rallies, and funeral processions that broke out into political demonstrations and collisions with the police, and built barricades. There was shooting everywhere, and the houses of traitors and accomplices of the apartheid regime—councillors and policemen— went up in flames.

Much had changed in the townships around Johannesburg during the ten years after the Soweto uprising. The township of Vosloorus, for instance, had always been considered "politically sleepy". This was true until 1983, when Thelle Simon Mogoerane, who was born and grew up in Vosloorus, was one of the three ANC fighters executed by the racists. Since then this township has had its own hero and martyr inspiring the people to participate in political actions. In 1986 the demonstrations that took place in the township were so massive that the police and troops barely managed to contain them with recourse to violence and retain their position. Reporting how in July 1985 the people of the township of Duduza drove out all the police and councillors and virtually turned the township into a liberated area, the South African newspaper *Weekly Mail* wrote: "The era of subservience in Duduza had come to an end, forever."[4] [5]

The involvement of growing numbers of oppressed people raised the struggle to a higher level, making it countrywide. To offset this development the apartheid regime brought in more police and troops and resorted to new, more sinister tactics. In addition to the huge machine of military and police repression, used for the suppression of the insurgent people, the Pretoria government began to have more frequent recourse to reactionary elements among the black population. Groups of "vigilantes" appeared in the townships. They operated murderously during the above-described unrest in Alexandra and in the township of Crossroads near Cape Town. They committed outrages in other townships and cities.

It will be recalled that in 1976 the police had provoked Zulu migrants in Mzimhlope to attack insurgent Sowetans. This provocation quickly lost steam. But now the preparations were more thorough. More often than not groups of "vigilantes" were formed of black policemen and even members of the community councils. In some cases these groups consisted of the most backward and conservative elements in the black township communities. For instance, the Makgotla groups that operated in the townships in 1976-1977 were reincarnated as "vigilantes". The same socio-politically backward elements, the same people who had not gone through the arduous process of cultural-psychological urbanisation and strove to adapt to life under apartheid and white minority rule, were once again in the camp of the enemies of the South African people.

Inkatha, headed by Gatsha Buthelezi, played an unseemly role in the events of 1984-1987. This narrow chauvinist Zulu organisation did not confine itself to divisive activities to erode the united front of resistance to the apartheid regime. Many Inkhata groups in the cities and villages of Natal Province and the KwaZulu Bantustan terrorised activists of the United Democratic Front and progressive trade unions and youth organisations.

The powerful tide of the liberation struggle that rose in 1984 and reached its highest pitch in the year of the 10th anniversary of the Soweto revolt brought with it qualitatively new, constructive phenomena. The resistance movement increasingly revealed a tendency to form an alternative, people's power at the level of local self-government bodies in the townships. The formation of street committees, people's courts, self-defence units, and other elements of people's self-government to replace the puppet community councils rejected by the people was a very significant development. "The establishment of people's power in these areas, however rudimentary and precarious," ANC President Oliver Tambo noted, "is of great significance for the further advancement of our struggle."[46]

The first steps were taken to switch from the destructive tactic expressed in the slogan "making apartheid unworkable and the country ungovernable" to the constructive policy of setting up an alternative system of government, at the level of local self-government in the townships as a start. This laid the beginning for the formation and establishment of a people's democratic power in South Africa. The message of the ANC National Executive Committee on the occasion of the ANC's 74th anniversary stated: "We are the alternative power. As such, we pursue goals and share aspirations that are diametrically opposed to those of the oppressive white minority regime and must ensure that our will, as that alternative power, prevails."[47]

That the will of the embattled people is prevailing was seen, in particular, in the virtual legalisation of the African National Congress, which was banned by the apartheid regime in 1960. Percy Qoboza, a leading South African analyst, offers this comment: "The ANC is a fact of life—and no amount of government hysteria can wish it away. The government has religiously worked for over 20 years to crush the organisation and its influence in our communities—with total non-success... the ANC has not only survived but as scientific research shows it is still growing in leaps and bounds."[48]

That the people regard the ANC as a legal organisation is eloquently proved by the circumstance that ANC flags are displayed everywhere, at every rally and demonstration, and this has to be accepted by the authorities. The people have themselves unbanned the organisation representing and championing their interests without waiting for the Parliament, in which they have no representatives, to pass the relevant decision.

The Second National Consultative Conference of the ANC was a landmark event in the history of the South African liberation movement. Held in Zambia on June 16-22, 1985, it passed decisions on stepping up the ideological and armed struggles and on opening the ANC at all levels to all South Africans, including whites. The Conference's Call to the People of South Africa said: "The Black giant is rising to his feet, tall and strong. He is breaking the chains that have bound him for centuries. He is marching on in confidence and with strength to a new social order. He is determined to liberate not only himself but also the whites themselves, whose lives have been corrupted by the apartheid system... Forward, our people, in a single mighty current. The struggle is yet hard. There will be many more sacrifices. There is no easy road to freedom. But we are on the advance... The ANC is with you, your instrument, your weapon of unity, your spearhead of liberation."[49] The resolutions passed by the Conference reflected the new situation in the South African resistance movement and at the same time facilitated further intensification of the struggle against the apartheid regime.

Umkhonto we Sizwe Fighters

Books and songs will be written about the people carrying on an armed struggle in Soweto, about the Umkhonto we Sizwe fighters, about the ANC patriots working in secrecy, about the South African Communists. Meanwhile we learn about them only when they speak of themselves in their last statement in a court or only after their death.

One of them was Mosima Sexwale. He was one of 12 patriots sentenced by a racist court in Pretoria in March 1978. The following is what he told the court:

"I was born in Soweto on 5th March, 1953, the third child in a family of six children. During most of my childhood the sole breadwinner in our family was my father.

He had fought for his country and for his ideals during World World II, and when the peace returned he was employed as a clerk in the 'Non-European' Section of the Johannesburg General Hospital. He has continued in this position up to this day.

"My mother was willing and able to work and indeed needed to work in order to supplement my father's meagre income. However, she had been born in Pietersburg and had come to live in the 'prescribed area' of Johannesburg only after she had married my father. As a result, she was not able to obtain the required permission from the authorities to work in Johannesburg, and for about 15 years she was unable to take up employment.

"At about the time when I joined my two elder brothers at high school, my uncle passed away and my father had to take over his family responsibility. This meant another six children in the family, and a doubling of the family's financial problems. At about this time my mother finally received permission to work in Johannesburg, and this relieved the desperate situation to some extent.

"I do not intend to suggest by what I have said that I had a childhood which was deprived in relation to those with whom I grew up. On the contrary, I found that my childhood friends were in much the same sort of situation as I was. We all lived in poverty and we were all subjected to the humiliations which the whites imposed upon the blacks. We lived in the same typical 'matchbox' houses; we were continually aware that there was not enough money available to meet our needs for food, clothing and education. In fact, there was one respect in which, in comparison with my friends, I was privileged: my parents laid great store by education and made considerable sacrifices so that their children could receive a proper schooling.

"Looking back, I now see that it was during my primary school years that the bare facts concerning the realities of South African society and its discrepancies began to unfold before me. I remember clearly having to go to school without breakfast because my family could not afford it. The meal of the day was in the evening, and that meal was usually all I had to eat until the next evening. I remember the humiliation to which my parents were subjected by whites in shops and in other places where we encountered them and I remember the poverty. I remember, too, a period in the early 1960s when there was a great deal of political tension, and we often used to encounter armed police in Soweto. We saw slogans painted on walls—I remember particularly vividly a slogan reading 'Release Nelson Mandela and Others' painted on the walls of a building I passed each day on my way to school.

"All these things had their influence on my young mind, and by the time I went to Orlando West High School I was already beginning to question the injustice of the society in which we lived. I became an active participant in the South African Students' Organisation (SASO) and its subsequent high school equivalent, the South African Students' Movement (SASM).

"Like other members, I attended discussions, participated in meetings and cultural activities, read books with others, and investigated, examined, and discussed the situation in South Africa. We passed resolutions, issued statements, and took decisions about peaceful action for improving the position of the black man in South Africa.

"I rapidly appreciated, however, that our efforts were small and ineffective and had no influence on government policy. I realised that it was only political organisations which could hope to play a part in changing the situation.

"There were many former members of the African National Congress living in the townships. I talked to former members, read whatever literature I could lay my hands on, and generally informed myself about its ideals and activities. The ideals appealed to me as authentic, rational, and highly democratic. I learnt, too, of the history of the ANC...

"While I was a student in Swaziland I met exiled members of the ANC and my views were confirmed. And so it was that I decided to join the ANC...

"I was, and am, essentially a peaceful person—but I felt myself driven to this position, feeling that to counter the violence meted out against us we were forced to defend ourselves: there was no option.

"It is true that I was trained in the use of weapons and explosives. The basis of my training was in sabotage, which was to be aimed at institutions and not people.

"It has been suggested that our aim was to annihilate the

281

white people of this country. Nothing could be further from the truth.

"The ANC—in association with the alliance it has formed with people from all walks of life and representing all sections of the population—is a national liberation movement committed to the liberation of all the people of South Africa, black and white, from racial fear, hatred and oppression. The Freedom Charter, the fundamental policy document of the ANC, puts forward the ideal of a democratic South Africa, for all its people. We want to be active participants in shaping the face and course of direction in South Africa."[50]

That was what Mosima Sexwale said in his last statement to the court. He was sentenced to a prison term of 18 years.

Take another example, a Sowetan whose life was cut short when he was only a little over 20. His name was Petros Linda Jobane, but he was better known by his underground alias Gordon Dikebu. In the history of the liberation struggle he is known as the Lion of Chiawelo.

This name was given to him by people who saw him fight the enemies. Early one morning in the township of Chiawelo a large force of police stormed a house in which Gordon was hiding. He fought to his last bullet and then blew himself up with a hand grenade so as not to fall into the hands of the police. Eyewitnesses said that "he fought like a lion". This young South African Communist, Gordon Dikebu, thus became the "Lion of Chiawelo", and he was soon spoken of by the whole of Soweto.

He was born in Soweto and was brought up by his mother, a washer-woman. His father died whilst he was very young. The family lived in poverty. His mother could only afford to keep him in school until Standard Five. After that Gordon worked to help his mother keep the family going.

After the Soweto uprising was suppressed Gordon left his country to return as a fighter of Umkhonto we Sizwe. Harsh experience and his commitment to the struggle led him to the ranks of the South African Communist Party.[51]

Motso Mokgabudi was killed in Matola, a Maputu suburb, in January 1981, when South African commandos attacked a house occupied by ANC members. He was 29. He, too, had an alias, Obadi. His relatives live in Orlando and could be targets of police reprisals if his real name were known.

His mother, a matron in a hospital, worked hard to give him a good education. He managed to gain admission to Turfloop University, where he studied law. Learning came easily to him, and he took an especially keen interest in political problems. He dropped out as a result of student unrest, and upon returning to Soweto turned his capable hands to many things, from teaching to installing TV sets in white houses.

Obadi epitomised the Soweto generation that went to the barricades in 1976. He was energetic, intelligent, confident that the cause was just, and brave. Like his fellows, he sought answers to questions posed by life, looked for the path ahead, and was maturing and transforming as an individual. Outwardly, too, he was no different from all the other young people of Soweto. Intellectually he had bounded way ahead but carried with him the challenging stance and optimism of youth. He studied, argued, and fought.

His comrades-in-arms remember that when he was admitted to the Communist Party he radiated with joy and pride. He once said that if he died he would like to be known that he was a Communist.[52]

[1] Unless otherwise specified, this refers to Greater Soweto here and to the end of the book.

[2] *Weekly News Briefings*, London, No. 18, 1982, p. 15.

[3] Ibid., No. 12, 1985, p. 13.

[4] Ibid., No. 12, 1986, p. 18.

[5] Ibid., No. 17, 1983, p. 16.

[6] *A Survey of Race Relations in South Africa (Annual)*, Johannesburg, 1984, pp. 258-260.

[7] *The Star*, Johannesburg, November 23, 1983.

[8] *Weekly News Briefings*, London, No. 23, 1983.

[9] Ibid., No. 22, 1983, p. 1.

[10] Ibid., No. 26, 1983, p. 3.

[11] *The African Communist*, London, No. 100, 1985, p. 11.

[12] *Weekly News Briefings*, London, No. 45, 1984, p. 1.

[13] Ibid., No. 46, 1984, p. 1.

[14] *The Star*, Johannesburg, December 11, 1984.

[15] *Weekly News Briefings*, London, No. 46, 1984, p. 5.

[16] Ibid., No. 5, 1985, p. 6; No. 18, 1985, p. 1.

[17] *Sechaba*, London, August 1985, p. 5.

[18] *Weekly News Briefings*, London, No. 7, 1985, p. 11.

[19] Ibid., No. 20, 1985, p. 2.
[20] Ibid., No. 25, 1985, p. 5.
[21] Ibid., No. 34, 1985, p. 6.
[22] Ibid., No. 40, 1985, p. 16.
[23] Ibid., No. 44, 1985, p. 10.
[24] Ibid., No. 42, 1985, p. 1.
[25] Ibid., No. 47, 1985, p. 3.
[26] Ibid., No. 44, 1985, p. 10.
[27] Ibid., p. 11.
[28] Ibid., p. 5.
[29] *The Star*, Johannesburg, May 19, 1985.
[30] *Weekly News Briefings*, London, No. 8, 1986, p. 5.
[31] *Observer*, London, February 23, 1986.
[32] *Weekly News Briefings*, London, No. 10, 1986, pp. 6, 10.
[33] Ibid., p. 10.
[34] Ibid.
[35] Ibid., No. 12, 1986, p. 6.
[36] *Guardian*, London, June 25, 1986.
[37] *Weekly News Briefings*, London, No. 18, 1986, p. 17.
[38] Ibid., p. 16.
[39] Ibid., No. 19, 1986, p. 18.
[40] *Sechaba*, London, March 1986, p. 10.
[41] *Weekly News Briefings*, London, No. 24, 1986, p. 11.
[42] Ibid.
[43] *Mayibuye*, Lusaka, August 23, 1986.
[44] *Weekly News Briefings*, London, No. 28, 1986, p. 1.
[45] Ibid., No. 29, 1985, pp. 2-3.
[46] *Sechaba*, London, March 1986, p. 10.
[47] Ibid., p. 9.
[48] *Weekly News Briefings*, London, No. 5, 1986, p. 1.
[49] *Sechaba*, London, August 1985, p. 8.
[50] Ibid., March 1979, pp. 23-26.
[51] *The African Communist*, London, No. 87, 1981, pp. 43-44.
[52] Ibid., pp. 45-47.

CONCLUSION

The history of the black townships is a history of the resistance of urban Africans to racial discrimination and oppression, a history of their struggle for national liberation and social emancipation.

The scattered black townships that sprang up around Johannesburg in the 1940s and 1950s were potentially a growing threat to white racist minority rule. South Africa's rulers believed they would eliminate this threat by demolishing these townships and, in their stead, setting up Soweto as a huge ghetto for workforce under constant and rigid control. But Soweto shook off this control. The 1976 revolt and the events of subsequent years—general stay-aways, mass protest campaigns, and the actions of Umkhonto we Sizwe fighting units—indicated that Soweto had become a centre of the resistance to the apartheid regime. Not only did the Sowetans not accept the lot prepared for them by the racist government but, by their actions, they laid the beginning for a new and much more effective stage of the liberation struggle in South Africa.

Nor were the government's plans for dismantling the ring of black townships around "white" Johannesburg tenable. Although some townships were destroyed in the 1950s, innumerable new townships appeared. Today Soweto is part of the new "black" ring built in the 1980s around Greater Johannesburg. The same socio-political processes are developing in the new townships as in Soweto; the same struggle against the apartheid regime is unfolding in them as in Soweto.

The restoration of the ring of black townships is due to the operation of the socio-economic laws that proved to be stronger than apartheid's legal norms and the intentions of the racist government.

The inhabitants of the new and old townships have identical reasons for grievances that evolve into anger and open struggle against the practices prevailing in South Africa: the onerous economic conditions, political deprivation, impingement of civil rights, and constant racial discrimination, in other words, everything brought by white minority rule based on capitalism and apartheid.

The South African government has been powerless in its efforts to control the urbanisation of blacks, much less the social aspects of this process. Cultural-psychological urbanisation created the ground for the conscious participation of the inhabitants of Soweto and other black townships in the 1976 uprising and in the continuing resistance of South Africa's black population. The eradication of tribalism and adoption of modern values have increased the socio-political potential of urban Africans and fostered a more active participation in the struggle against apartheid.

The Soweto uprising showed that its most militant participants were persons who were most keenly aware of their status as oppressed people. The level of cultural-psychological urbanisation was the factor that largely influenced the attitude of the various strata and groups of the Soweto population to the 1976 uprising and, generally, to the resistance to apartheid.

In the course of decades of cultural-psychological urbanisation in Soweto traditional values were supplanted by modern values, while individual elements of traditionalism underwent a modification under the impact of modern factors in the new African urban culture. These processes developed despite apartheid and the retribalisation policy pursued by the Pretoria regime. Meanwhile, traditionalism and its most essential element, tribalism, survived in the new urban culture as a residue or in a transformed form. Thus, elements of traditionalism still play some role in the life of the black urban population.

Residual and transformed traditionalism and tribalism had practically no direct part in the tense, critical situation that took shape in Soweto during the uprising. Nor did anything come of the efforts of the police to use tribalistic instruments such as the Makgotla and Inkatha organisations against the insurgents. The calculations on kindling inter-ethnical strife among the Africans in Soweto likewise

proved to be hollow.

The inter-ethnic distinctions and survivals of tribalism dividing Sowetans to this or that extent fade into the background in the face of the common threat posed by the racist regime, which is a powerful and ruthless opponent. While retribalisation factors are visible in a relatively tranquil situation, these factors cease to function in the life of the Soweto urban community in times of crisis, when resistance to apartheid grows. The struggle against the common enemy reinforces the integrational tendencies among urban blacks.

Johannesburg is a complex social organisation that stemmed from the combined development of colonialism (domestic colonialism in this case) and modern European civilisation and culture. Urban blacks are an inalienable part of this social organisation just as the white inhabitants are, and have brought their own culture. Concurrently with the formation of a new black urban culture, two different cultures—traditional African and modern European—are coming into contact. In the specific conditions prevailing in South Africa the proponents of these cultures hold diametrically opposite statuses in society: dominant and subordinate. The Africans are eager to assimilate European culture, and this is a positive phenomenon. But they cannot accept it in its entirety as it is associated for them with the domination of the white minority. This accounts for their dual attitude to European culture: acceptance and rejection. Hence the growth of the tendency to return to traditional values, to rejuvenate and preserve traditional African culture. This is seen most visibly in social psychology and, to a lesser extent, in material culture and the relations of production.

The attitude to European culture and civilisation, whose proponents were colonialists and oppressors (this being the case in South Africa to this day), changes with the abolition of colonialist rule. In noting that "when a great social revolution shall have mastered the results of the bourgeois epoch, the market of the world and the modern powers of production, and subjected them to the common control of the most advanced peoples, then only will human progress cease to resemble that hideous, pagan idol, who would not drink the nectar but from the skulls of the slain,"[1] Karl Marx had in mind a total and irreversible change of the image given to modern civilisation by capitalism and bourgeois society. In the case of present-day realities in South Africa this idol is, above all, apartheid and racist oppression. The eradication of these evils will clear the way not only for the political liberation, social emancipation and progress of the oppressed majority but also for a beneficial and mutually enriching relationship between African and European cultures, for a more comprehensive acceptance of modern civilisation. This will be a step towards society's full flowering that will come with the "great social revolution".

The author felt it would be expedient to back up his conclusions with statistics. These are to be found in the addenda. Most of the research of various aspects of the life of urban Africans, including questions related to social psychology, has so far not been conducted by the Africans themselves. Without belittling the merits of such research, much of which is quite objective, it must be noted that its authors are understandably limited in their possibilities for penetrating the in-depth sentiments and feelings of the people inhabiting the ghetto-townships.

And yet, despite the difficulties encountered in studying the social and political problems of the African urban population of South Africa, some conclusions can be drawn about the development trends and growth of the liberation movement in that country.

The liberation struggle, of which the African working class movement is an essential component, is developing primarily in the ghetto-townships located in the principal industrial areas. Johannesburg and the townships ringing it, notably Soweto, are the central theatre of this struggle. This, not the pseudo-independent Bantustans, is where the future of South Africa will be decided. The largest, and still growing, concentration of the African proletariat is in Johannesburg. With the sophistication of their cultural-psychological urbanisation and the growth of their political consciousness, the people of Soweto are becoming active participants in the struggle. In mass actions such as the 1976 uprising, the general political stay-aways, and the turbulent events of 1984-1987 they acquired experience of revolutionary struggle. The ANC and the South African Communist Party are rapidly winning particularly great prestige precisely in Soweto. All of the government's attempts to control the social and political processes in the ghetto-townships by, among other things, bantustanisation are coming to naught. The urban blacks in Soweto and other similar townships are thus the main, strike force of the liberation movement in South Africa.

The South African people's resistance to and struggle against white racist minority rule are proceeding under the slogan of "Power to the People" ("Amandla ngawethu") entirely in keeping with the basic principle of all of South Africa's progressive and democratic forces, who have proclaimed that South Africa belongs to all those who live in it, black and white. Fidelity to this principle is the earnest of the liberation movement's successful development in South Africa.

[1] Karl Marx, Frederick Engels, *Collected Works*, Vol. 12, p. 222.

ADDENDA

I

Sowetans Speak of Themselves

A clerk. He is thirty now, born in Soweto, of parents born in Transkei.

"I am a clerk in a factory that supplies hardware to builders, but I am registered as just a labourer.

"There is a white man supervising me. There's a big gap between his salary and mine. He's getting about seven hundred rand a month, I'm getting two hundred.

"I would like to do something else, something better, if I could, but I don't think I will ever get a chance, because I only got that job through a friend of a friend who just pushed me in there, and I know that I must work there my whole life. I can't get a job anywhere else. About three or four times when I try for a job the security police phone to say, 'That man is no good.' They want me where I am so they can keep an eye on me.

"My wife is a teacher in Transkei. I get home to see her only on holidays, maybe once or twice a year. I am still trying to get permission for her to stay here with me. But even if she gets a Transkei passport to travel here she has no right to live in Johannesburg because she is a citizen of the homelands. So I will never be able to have her living here, permanently, with me. They are trying to force me out, to go to Transkei. But I'm not prepared to do this. There are jobs there, maybe, but there's no money there. At one time if there had been a job in Transkei worth taking I would have taken it. But not now that it's a so-called independent state. I wouldn't take a job there now on principle. I feel very bitter that most of the people who were born in Transkei can't get jobs in the cities of South Africa. They can't benefit from what little rights workers do have in the cities; they can only work here under a contract. They can work for thirty years in a factory here and they

290

are still on a contract. They get no pension, and when they eventually leave, they leave with nothing.

"The only time I get to talk to the white people where I work is when they tell me to do something, nothing else. They never ask me about my life. I never get a chance to talk with white people outside of the job. I might be interested to talk to them but they are not interested to talk to me—the black man is there just to work, that's all.

"I send some of my money to Transkei, but after paying for my car there isn't much left over. I cannot save. I need the money to eat, pay the rent, buy clothes. There's nothing left over.

"I feel safe among the people of Soweto. I feel sorry rather than afraid for the criminals of the township. They are dissatisfied with their lives, with the government, but have no direction to follow. I make my own protest—I refuse to carry the passbook ... so long as the white man doesn't have to carry a passbook. I tell the police that when they stop me. So they take me to the police station. Sometimes they release me, sometimes they take me to court. Then I tell them I won't pay the fine, I'd rather go to jail than pay their fine. So I go to jail for thirty-one days. Then I've been held in security detention. I've been in plenty of police stations and prisons. I was never charged with anything. But I still refuse to carry my passbook. I know the security police here very well by now. They watch me and I watch them. I don't really know what the police are after.

"I am not a member of any of the local political organisations. But as individual my attitude has no effect on the government, of course. Nothing will change until we act together. But we will act together, as one people. It's only a matter of time before we get organised. We talk about this every day. Here in the township and at work. We talk in our own language and the whites don't understand what we say."[1]

A migrant worker. The last thing he does is to check that he has his passbook in his jacket.

"I was once picked up without my pass," he recalls, "and held in jail overnight before they put me on a train back to Rustenburg," a city neighbouring on Bophuthatswana, his homeland in the western Transvaal. "When I got to Rustenburg, I walked across to the other side of the railway line and got on another train going back to Johannesburg. I only missed two days of work.

"When I first came to Johannesburg, in about 1968, I was working part-time. I found a man who got me some papers—I paid him some money and didn't ask any questions. I registered for temporary employment because I could not be registered permanently. But even then I couldn't get accommodation in Soweto because I belonged to Bophuthatswana. I did not know the formula for staying legally in Johannesburg. I didn't know what steps to take. So I told my boss the whole thing, and he told a bit of a lie, saying I was a domestic servant staying at his place. That was the only way I could get permission to stay in the city. According to my passbook I was a domestic servant, but I worked in my boss's company as a salesman.

"My contract as a migrant worker is for twelve months, and every year I have to return to Rustenburg and renew the contract for another year. At present I'm registered as a clerk. I work for an export company. I have been doing this for almost ten years.

"I am happy with this company because I feel that they are giving me an opportunity to slowly learn more.

"I live at Dube men's hostel, in the centre of Soweto, not far from the railway station. The hostel is like a barracks for soldiers. It's not a nice place for anyone to stay at. I stay there because it's cheap and I want to save money. There is no plaster on the walls and the floors are rough concrete. More than seven hundred people are crammed into it. We have only cold showers, and no canteen or cooking facility. You cook your own food on a primus-stove. A lot of my friends say, 'How can you stay in that terrible place?' But it suits me. I don't spend too much, and I am saving a little money.

"We are not allowed to have women in the hostel. The police raid it frequently and arrest any women they find there. The men are lonely, a long way from home, and they have to have women—there's not much anyone can do about it. I'm lucky because I can get a bus sometimes at weekends to see my wife in Rustenburg.

"If I don't go home over the weekends, I watch soccer matches in the township. And if there is no soccer, I go to bioscopes (the movies). On Sunday I go to church in Soweto—the Lutheran church.

"The men who live in Dube come from all over the place. They are different nations—Shangaans, Zulus, Tswanas, Pedis—and they seem to get on reasonably well with each other. Only the Zulus are funny; they keep their group separate from the others.

"I get 300 rand a month. Five years ago I was earning half that much. The worst thing is being away from your family for such a long time. But there is nothing you can do. We just have to accept these conditions. If I stay in Rustenburg, I am not able to earn enough to make a living... I feel that if at some stage we are allowed to live where we want to live, I would bring my family and stay in Johannesburg. I would still be happy to be a Bophuthatswana citizen provided that my wife and family could stay with me. But now they are trying to tighten the law."[2]

A union leader. His father, a black South African, was a migrant labourer.

"When I went to Johannesburg, I was not yet circumcised. I was still a boy. My father died in an explosion at a dynamite factory shortly after I was born. I had worked in Umtata, selling used mealie (maize) sacks to miners, who used them to make jackets. And I have worked underground in the Transvaal mines, driving a hauling engine. It lasted about six weeks, until I ran away and came to Egoli (golden city, Johannesburg) to look for a better job. The first thing I did here was to register at the Labour Bureau. My reference book number was 426515266. I worked as a newsboy and then as a clerk in the Johannesburg City Council... In my time off I learned how to drive at the Easy Driving School. It was then that I went home to Transkei for my tribal circumcision. It was only then that I became a man.

"When I came back I started to look for a better job. The National Cold Storage Company took me on part-time as a driver. All the full-time drivers were whites, and we were allowed to do the job only if a white driver was not available. During that period I studied my matric at Union College by correspondence. I wanted to earn more money, so I applied for a city council bus-driving job. The council had decided that black drivers could drive 'black' buses, but we were not paid the same rate as the white drivers. We were paid twelve rand a week. I understood there was a union, but we were not allowed to join it. So we went on without a union. Still, we were trying to investigate how a union works when I became involved in SACTU—the South African Congress of Trade Unions.

"I resigned from the city council and started to work as a long-distance truck driver ... driving for a week and arriving back in Johannesburg with a sore back and aching kidneys. We were getting twenty-five rand to drive from Johannesburg to Cape Town—a thousand miles. There were no allowances for staying on the road, there was nowhere to stay—we slept underneath our trucks.

"Today I am heading this Black Municipality Workers Union with the experience I got from those earlier days...

"When we said we were going to form our own union, they tried to tell us not to... Of course, we are still struggling. Our organisers are not officially allowed to enter the Johannesburg compounds where our members live. But the men who work at the compound gates are sympathetic to us and they do not bar us from entering. We think we have about 12,500 members. But we're not sure because they don't all carry our cards. Some of them cannot carry cards because they might lose their jobs...

"In July 1980 some 10,000 black municipal workers went on strike for a minimum wage of sixty rand a week and recognition of the new union... What our union needs is recognition.

"Right now, no one would employ me. They wouldn't employ a person who asks as much as I'm asking."[3]

A student. She was fifteen when the Orlando march began in June of 1976....

"We were at a good school, a good high school. We liked our teachers and we studied hard. But when the word went out, we knew we had to join the rest.

"I used to say to my mother and father: 'Do you know what discrimination means? Do you know what it does to people? It kills them very slowly.' They would tell me to hush, and look at me as though I was saying something that was very bad, very evil. 'You are getting a good education,' they would say. 'Why do you want to destroy what we have done for you?' I could not give them an answer.

"My parents were worried and afraid. They didn't want me to go with the crowds, because they said they didn't want me to die. They tried to stop me, but each time I slipped out. I would climb the fence at the back of our house.

"The schools were closed in 1976 after the June riots. They opened in 1977 but closed again after more riots. I was involved in the crowds at that time. I got the tear gas many times. Even now my chest bothers me from it. Some of my friends were hurt and some died. One of my girl-friends was killed. There is a boy who lives next door to us now who was blinded. He stays at home, and there is no one to teach him.

"Altogether I missed about a year of school. The schools were opened again in 1978, but it was a struggle to get in and we waited for weeks to get registered.

"I was sad that I did not qualify for the university. I only got a senior school-leaving certificate. To be able to apply for the university, I'd have to write these subjects again. But I can't because I don't have the money. Even if I had my matric, I couldn't get into the university without a scholarship. It would cost two thousand or three thousand rand—too much. I have applied for training in nursing at a hospital, near Krugersdorp.

"My father was an electrician, but now he is sick and not working. One of my brothers is in jail. We don't know why he is there. All they will tell us is that he was not taken by the security police. We haven't been able to find out anything.

"We pay for the rent with what my mother earns. My mother is working but only at temporary jobs, earning four rand a day. She does washing, ironing, cleaning houses. Then she has to take the train. That is sixty cents a day. When you take that off how much is left? Sometimes she has to borrow from other people to make it through the month, and when she gets the money she repays them. We do not know where we will get the money if they put up our rent to thirty-five rand. If we don't get the money the house will be locked against us and we will be put outside. Then we will have to sleep outside. They are doing it with other people.

"Sometimes I go into Johannesburg to see the big city. I look around and I think that things there are for the people who earn more or who are high. And if you come to Soweto you can see that this is low and not very well developed. They say it is being developed and that is why they are increasing the rent, and yet I cannot see it. We have no electricity in our house. We have cold water from a tap outside the house. When we studied at school we stayed at the school at night because it had electricity. Otherwise we studied by candlelight at home. I enjoyed school. I liked it. But now it's all finished. I can't go anymore. I am sad about that."[4]

A township teacher. For twenty years she had lived in Soweto. She is married to a leather cutter and has four children.

"We are luckier than most of the families here in Soweto. We bought our home twenty years ago; we got a loan from the Johannesburg City Council, and now it is all paid off. The housing situation here is difficult. Ten or more people live in the same four-room house. We are ten-one-A'ers, according to the government. This means that we can legally move from city to city as long as we can find jobs and a place to live. But this is difficult. Housing is almost impossible to find, so we can't really go anywhere.

"People get frustrated, so the crime rate is high. Plenty of problems revolve around crime. After dusk, it is not safe to send my daughters to the shops. And if your husband goes out, you are not at ease until you have seen him again; anything can happen. I hear there are sometimes three murders a day.

"Together my husband and I make about 780 rand a month. That is considered a good income for Soweto. But we don't have a savings account. The family has never had a vacation together. It's not that we don't want to, but we cannot afford it... During the week I teach at a primary school... I started the school eighteen years ago.

"Besides teaching, I have the church. I attend Mass on Sundays at Saint Margaret's, and then sometimes I go to the Anglican church services with one of my friends.

"And we belong to a neighbourhood bereavement club. When someone in the neighbourhood dies, each family in the club gives money to cover the funeral costs. It's a sort of burial policy.

"I am not very active in the struggle. I've never had a chance to attend meetings. Except for what I casually read in the papers, I don't think I have enough information.

"I am not used to discussing politics. We grew up at a time when fear was ruling us, and it's difficult to break out of it. Informers are one big thing that makes people keep quiet. You don't know who is who and the next thing you know, there is a knock on the door at night and you are interrogated. During the riots I didn't join any of the black parents' organisations. They were under surveillance all the time.

"I was extremely worried. Police were just picking up most of these youngsters. We working parents were the most unhappy because the children didn't tell us. The day they went to storm John Vorster (the central police station in Johannesburg), we woke up to find them gone. Other things happened too. See that (she points to a small hole in the wall); that was one of what the police call 'stray' bullets. You know, those stray ones that kill people."[5]

[1] *South Africa: Time Running Out. The Report of the Study Commission on US Policy Toward Southern Africa*, University of California Press, Berkeley and Los Angeles, 1981, pp. 255-258.

[2] Ibid., pp. 1-5.

[3] Ibid., pp. 378-381.

[4] Ibid., pp. 381-383.

[5] Ibid., pp. 19-22.

II

Tables

Table 1

Population of South Africa (1970)*

	Total	%	Of which			
			Urban	%	Rural	%
Total	21 794 328**	100.0	10 410 293	47.8	11 384 035	52.2
Africans	15 339 975	70.4	5 069 776	33.1	10 270 199	66.9
Whites (of European origin)	3 773 282	17.3	3 274 158	86.6	499 124	13.2
Coloureds (mixed race)	2 050 699	9.4	1 519 738	74.1	530 961	25.9
Asians	630 372	2.9	546 621	86.7	83 751	13.3

* Source: *Population Census 1970. Report No. 02-05-10. Geographical Distribution of Population*, Department of Statistics, Pretoria, March 1976, p. 2.
** In 1984 the population numbered 32 642 730 of which there were 24 103 458 Africans, 4 818 679 whites, 2 830 301 coloureds, and 890 292 Asians. *A Survey of Race Relations in South Africa, 1984*, Johannesburg, 1985, p. 185.

Table 2

Ethnic Composition of the African Population (1970)*

	Total	Urban population		
		Number	% of ethnic group	% of total urban population
Total	15 339 975	5 069 776	33.1	—
Zulu	4 085 100	1 259 276	30.8	24.8
Xhosa	3 988 404	1 219 041	30.5	24.0
Tswana	1 704 202	659 160	38.7	13.0
Pedi	1 634 134	385 460	23.6	7.6
Seshoeshoe (Sotho)	1 387 613	593 203	42.8	11.7
Shangaan	664 523	159 454	24.0	3.2
Swazi	483 072	166 976	34.6	3.3
Venda	364 789	65 570	18.1	1.3
Ndebele	417 993	125 974	30.1	2.4
Others	95 102	39 865	42.4	0.8
Foreign Bantu	516 043	395 797	76.7	7.9

* Source: *Population Census 1970. Report No. 02-05-10*, pp. 2-3.

Table 3

Growth of Urban Black Population*
('000)

	Total African Population	Urban African Population	Growth Index (1904—100)	Urbanisation Level %	White Population (for comparison)
1904	3 490	353	100	10.1	588
1911	4 019	508	144	10.8	658
1921	4 698	587	166	12.5	848
1936	6 597	1 142	324	17.3	1 307
1946	7 832	1 689	478	21.6	1 719
1951	8 560	2 329	660	27.2	2 071
1960	10 928	3 471	983	31.8	2 582
1970	15 340	5 070	1 436	33.1	3 274

* Source: *South African Statistics 1976*, Department of Statistics, Pretoria, 1976, p. 1, 8.

Table 4

Sex and Age Composition of the Black Urban Population
in White Cities (1970)*
('000)

Age Group	Males	Females	Age Group	Males	Females
Under 1	48.10	49.44	30—34	243.44	142.10
1—4	175.42	178.22	35—39	207.30	126.72
5—9	225.68	232.60	40—44	167.96	101.40
10—14	206.98	223.98	45—49	132.62	78.38
15—19	229.86	193.32	50—54	95.50	61.18
20—24	334.00	187.10	55—64	94.12	71.04
25—29	295.42	166.36	65—74	35.62	35.46
			75+	11.92	18.98

* Source: *Population Census 1970. Report No. 02-02-02. Sample
Tabulation, Bantu Age, Occupation, Industry, School Standard,
Birthplace,* Department of Statistics, Pretoria, March 1973, pp. 3-4.

300

Table 5

African Population by Occupations (1970)*

| | Countrywide | In White Cities | |
		Total	% of gainfully employed population
Total economically active	5 605 140	2 282 760	
Professionals	93 300	39 400	1.7
Administrative	3 400	720	0.03
Clerical workers	96 280	74 620	3. 3
Sales workers	110 880	76 000	3.4
Service workers	1 011 940 (716 700 women)	667 680 (444 040 women)	29.3
Farm workers	2 051 600	84 580	3.6
Production and transport workers	1 688 840	1 202 440	52.7
Not classified	548 900	137 320	6.0

* Source: *Population Census 1970. Report No. 02-02-02*, pp. 13, 15.

Table 6

Per Capita Annual Income*
(rand)

	Income of an African	Income of a White
1954	55	—
1956	66	755
1958	66	—
1960	78.5	—
1961	—	885
1964	—	1100
1966	85	—
1968	82	1400
1970	84	1600
1973	120	2350
1974	135	—
1976	—	3400
1977	190	—

* Source: J.C. Laurence, *Race, Propaganda and South Africa*, Victor Gollanz, London, 1979, pp. 110, 113.

Table 7

Literacy Rate of the African Population (1970)*

	Number of literate persons**	%***	Number of persons with a high school education	%
South Africa as a whole	3 421 460	26.6	39,800	0.3
White cities	1 668 980	37.1	207 000	0.5
White rural areas	345 700	11.3	1 320	0.04
Bantustans	1 406 780	23.9	17 760	0.03

* Source: *Population Census 1970. Report No. 02-02-02*, pp. 1-12.
** As defined by Ellen Hellmann (*Soweto, Johannesburg's African City*, p. 16), literate or "functionally literate" persons are those who have had four years of schooling, including two years of preparatory schooling.
*** The proportion of literate persons is calculated on the basis of the numerical strength of the African population in the relevant areas minus the number of children of pre-school age (up to age 5).

Table 8

Population of the Witwatersrand*

	Whites	Blacks
1904	111 100	119 500
1960	775 400	1 322 100
1970**	986 000	1 649 900

* Sources: *The South African Journal of Economics*, Johannesburg, No. 1, 1975, p. 39; *Bulletin of Statistics*, Pretoria, No. 1, 1974, pp. 1-2; *Population Census 1970. Report No. 02-05-10*, pp. 30-38.
** Moreover, in the Witwatersrand in 1970 there were 117 000 coloureds and 53 500 Indians (*South African Statistics 1976*, Department of Statistics, Pretoria, 1976, pp. 1, 23). In the cities there were 985 947 whites and 1 636 805 blacks.

Table 9

African Population in the Industrial Areas
of the Transvaal*
('000)

	1946	1951	1960	1970	1980	1985 (esti- mates)
Johannesburg (including Soweto)	385	491	645	814	929	1 132
West Rand (Krugersdorp, Randfontein, Westonaria, Roodepoort, Carlton- ville)	126	141	197	242	273	328
East Rand (Kempton Park, Tembisa, Germiston, Alberton, Natalspruit, Boksburg, Benoni)	164	208	281	418	520	721
Pretoria (including Garan- kuwa, Mabopane, Ver- woerdburg)	105	123	204	304	375	513
Vereeniging	38	73	100	145	175	234
Total	818	1 036	1 427	1 923	2 272	2 928

* Source: *South Africa's Urban Blacks: Problems and Challenges.* Ed. by G. Marais and R. von der Kooy, University of South Africa, Pretoria, 1978, p. 24.

Table 10

Ethnic Composition of the Black Urban Population
of the Province of the Transvaal and
Johannesburg (1970)*

	Province of the Transvaal	Johannesburg
Zulu	551 720	241 840
Tswana	428 420	144 640
Pedi	314 000	77 880
Seshoeshoe (Sotho)	306 240	98 060
Xhosa	293 260	80 700
Swazi	153 460	27 720
Shangaan	132 020	50 200
Venda	60 420	31 640
Ndebele and others	128 060	18 300
Foreign Bantu	280 840	29 520
Total	2 648 440	800 500

* Source: *Population Census 1970. Report No. 02-02-02*, pp. 36-175.

Table 11

Population of Johannesburg*
('000)

	Whites	Africans
1904	83.4	59.8
1911	120.0	103.0
1936	257.6	229.1
1951	365.7	491.8
1960	413.2	650.9
1970	501.0	810.0

* Sources: *Bulletin of Statistics*, Pretoria, No. 1, 1974, pp. 1, 2; *The South African Journal of Economics*, Johannesburg, No. 1, 1975, p. 39; *African Affairs*, London, April 1969, p. 107.

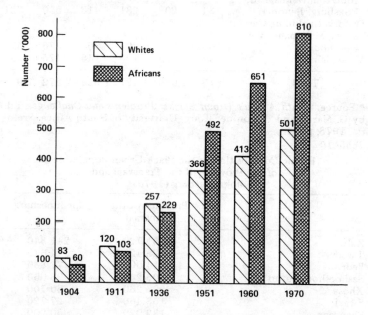

Table 12

Occupation of Earners—Blacks*

(%)

	Johannesburg		Pretoria	
	1970	1975	1970	1975
Skilled labour	6.5	7.8	3.3	4.1
Semi-skilled labour	28.7	21.9	19.8	20.1
Unskilled labour	34.6	43.9	52.5	52.9
Professionals	3.7	3.8	3.9	6.5
Administrative and clerical	6.3	7.1	2.6	6.7
Proprietors and managers	2.2	2.5	1.7	3.3
Other	18.2	13.0	16.3	6.4

* Source: *South Africa's Urban Blacks: Problems and Challenges*, p. 263.

Table 13

Wages Paid to Africans in Johannesburg*

Monthly Wage, Rand	Persons Receiving Indicated Wage, %	
	1965	1969
Up to 26.00	4.0	0.8
26.01 — 34.67	40.4	8.2
34.68 — 43.33	41.6	51.9
43.34 — 52.00	7.9	21.6
52.01 — 63.00	4.5	11.2
63.01 +	1.6	6.3

* Source: Ellen Hellmann, *op. cit.*, p. 30.

Table 14

Education Level of Breadwinners of Black Families*
(%)

	Johannesburg		Pretoria	
	1970	1975	1970	1975
No education	19.7	16.8	23.4	18.4
Up to 6 classes	75.6	58.9	62.2	58.4
7 or 8 classes	3.3	16.0	7.4	14.4
9 classes and over	1.4	8.7	6.9	8.6

*Source: *South Africa's Urban Blacks: Problems and Challenges*, p. 265.

Table 15

Ethnic Composition of Soweto's Population (1970)*

	Number	%
Zulu	198 303	33.0
Tswana	110 065	18.3
Seshoeshoe (Sotho)	82 443	13.6
Xhosa	56 784	9.4
Pedi	48 772	8.0
Shangaan	38 179	6.3
Venda	23 430	4.0
Swazi	21 686	3.9
Ndebele and others	9 485	1.4
Foreign Bantu	12 883	2.1
Total	602 017	100.0

* Source: *Population Census 1970. Report No. 02-05-10*, pp. 32-33.

Table 16

Family Average Monthly Income in Soweto*

Occupation of household head	Surveyed households %	Average number of earners	Average income, rand
Professionals	1.8	1.7	92.35
Proprietors or managers	4.8	1.8	74.56
Administrative and clerical	3.9	1.9	82.44
Skilled labour	1.1	1.7	87.40
Semi-skilled labour	22.2	1.6	70.21
Unskilled labour	56.8	1.8	53.58
Pensioners	1.9	2.0	36.79
Housewives	2.5	1.6	44.10
Unemployed	3.4	1.4	39.06
Unemployable	1.6	1.8	50.79

* The above figures are based on a selective survey of 1 409 families conducted by the Johannesburg City Council in 1962 (Ellen Hellmann, *op. cit.*, p. 31).

Table 17

Minimum Expenditure (Poverty Datum Line)
of a Family of Five in Soweto*

	Essential monthly living costs, rand	Source
1962	45.86	Ellen Hellmann, *op. cit.*, p. 8.
1966	55.57	*A Survey of Race Relations in South Africa (Annual)*, Johannesburg, 1967, p. 209.
1967	53.32	*The African Communist*, London, No. 34, 1968, p. 63.
1969	59.70	Ellen Hellmann, *op. cit.*, p. 8.
1970	65.64	Ibid.
1972	82.19	*The African Communist*, London, No. 55, 1973, p. 10.
1973	91.14	Ibid.
1974	95.37	*Rand Daily Mail*, Johannesburg, February 5, 1974.
1975	108.66	*A Survey of Race Relations in South Africa (Annual)*, Johannesburg, 1976, p. 161.
1976	132.90	*To the Point*, Johannesburg, No. 25, 1977, p. 8.
1977	158.43	*Financial Mail*, Johannesburg, January 20, 1978.
1978	178.22	*Post*, Johannesburg, July 19, 1979.
1979	192.73	Ibid.

* Computed by the Johannesburg Chamber of Commerce.

INDEX

A. Organisations

B. Selected Individuals

A

Adam, H. — 66, 156

B

Baraji, E. — 268
Bernstein, H. — 31
Biko, S. — 145, 254
Boesak, A. — 114, 244
Boshoff, C. — 218
Botha, P. W. — 116, 249, 251, 259
Breytenbach, B. — 141
Brickhill, J. — 21, 22
Brooks, A. — 21, 22
Bunting, B. — 98, 155
Buthelezi, G. M. — 97, 131, 132, 180, 238, 239, 245, 273, 276
Buthelezi, M. — 172
Buti, S. — 53, 55, 259, 260, 262

C

Chikane, F. — 241, 243, 261

D

De Ridder, J. — 95, 99, 118, 145
Dube, J. — 274

E

Engels, F. — 11

F

Fischer, B. — 253
Forman, L. — 43
Fugard, A. — 136

H

Harmel, M. — 135
Hellmann, E. — 18, 19, 27, 77, 95
Herskovits, M. — 15
Huddleston, T. — 37, 40, 48, 60, 66, 113

Hunter, M. — 96, 121, 145

J

Jobane, P. (Dikebu G.) — 281

K

Kane-Berman, J. — 20
Kavanagh, R. — 143
Kente, G. — 139
Khanyile, V. — 241
Khasago, A. — 241
Khumalo, B. — 244
Khuzwayo, E. — 203
Koornhof, P. — 223
Kotane, M. — 98, 125
Kruger, J. — 129, 160-62, 169, 177, 181
Kunene, E. — 240, 248
Kuper, L. — 16

L

Lambert, R. — 217
Le Grange, L. — 209, 246, 265, 271
Lenin, V. I. — 10, 94, 204, 232
Lephanya, P. — 241
Lolwane, D. — 203
Longmore, L. — 84, 118, 121

M

Mabasa, L. — 23
Mabhida, M. — 264
Mafutsanyana, E. — 125
Mahlangu S. — 144, 229
Makeba, M. — 136, 137
Makhaya, T. — 126, 177
Mandela, N. — 78, 125, 202, 211, 229, 231, 232, 239, 247, 254, 259, 264, 275
Mandela, W. — 177, 190
Manthata, S. — 128
Maponya, R. — 74, 197, 198
Marks, J. B. — 138
Masondo, A. — 241, 268

REQUEST TO READERS

Progress Publishers would be glad to have your opinion of this book, its translation and design and any suggestions you may have for future publications.

Please send all your comments to 17, Zubovsky Boulevard, Moscow, USSR.